A GUIDE TO
PHRASAL VERBS

THOMSON™

A GUIDE TO
PHRASAL VERBS

THOMSON
™

A Guide to Phrasal Verbs

Editors
Kay Cullen, Penny Hands, Una McGovern and John Wright

Published by arrangement with Chambers Harrap Publishers Ltd.

Publisher/Global ELT: *Christopher Wenger*
Executive Marketing Manager, Global ELT/ESL: *Amy Mabley*

Printed in Croatia by Zrinski d.d
1 2 3 4 5 6 7 8 9 10   06 05 04 03 02 01

Heinle, Thomson and the Thomson logo are trademarks used herein under license.

For more information contact Heinle, 25 Thomson Place, Boston, MA 02210 USA,
or you can visit our Internet site at http://www.heinle.com

A CIP catalogue record for this book is available from the British Library.

13 digit ISBN: 978 1 84480 526 6
10 digit ISBN: 1 84480 526 3

Typeset by Chambers Harrap Publishers Ltd

Contributors

Publishing Manager
Elaine Higgleton

Editors
Kay Cullen
Penny Hands
Una McGovern
John Wright

Contents

Introduction

A phrasal verb is a short two-word (or sometimes three-word) phrase made up of a verb, such as **get**, **give**, **make** and **see**, and an adverb (an adverbial particle) or a preposition, such as **in**, **off**, **out** and **up**. Because a phrasal verb is a form of idiom it has a meaning which 'is different from the sum of its parts'. In other words, knowing what the verb and adverb or preposition mean will not necessarily help you understand the combination when they are used together as a phrasal verb. For example, you may know the meaning of the verb **polish**, but may not know that the combination 'to **polish off**' means to finish something quickly and easily. Similarly, you may know the meaning of the verb **chew**, but may not know that when you **chew** someone **out** you strongly criticize them.

This guide is designed to help anyone who wants to know about phrasal verbs, including not only what they mean but also how to use them. The most commonly used phrasal verbs in British and American English are represented here, clearly labelled.

Each phrasal verb has its own entry with a full-sentence definition, which allows phrasal verbs to be shown in their correct grammatical context. Information is also given on which register or level of language the phrasal verb belongs to. Synonyms or near-synonyms are shown at the end of definitions, as are cross-references to other phrasal verbs if they are useful for comparison. You will also find examples of how phrasal verbs are actually used, all based on corpus material. Learners may find phrasal verbs difficult to use because they are not sure where to put the adverbial particle. Several different positions may be possible, or there may just be one fixed position. Both full-sentence definitions and examples show where the adverbial particle can go.

This guide also includes a section of Language Study panels on the adverbial particles used to form phrasal verbs. These give the broad range of meanings that each particle has, and show which of the particles are used by native speakers to form new phrasal verbs. These panels will help you to develop your knowledge of how phrasal verbs are formed and how they function in English. They also contain additional phrasal verbs to those found in the dictionary.

Pronunciation guide

Key to the phonetic symbols used in this book

CONSONANTS

p	/piː/	pea
t	/tiː/	tea
k	/kiː/	key
b	/biː/	bee
d	/daɪ/	dye
g	/gaɪ/	guy
m	/miː/	me
n	/njuː/	new
ŋ	/sɒŋ/	song
θ	/θɪn/	thin
ð	/ðɛn/	then
f	/fan/	fan
v	/van/	van
s	/siː/	sea
z	/zuːm/	zoom
ʃ	/ʃiː/	she
ʒ	/beɪʒ/	beige
tʃ	/iːtʃ/	each
dʒ	/ɛdʒ/	edge
h	/hat/	hat
l	/leɪ/	lay
r	/reɪ/	ray
j	/jɛs/	yes
w	/weɪ/	way

VOWELS

Short vowels

ɪ	/bɪd/	bid
ɛ	/bɛd/	bed
a	/bad/	bad
ʌ	/bʌd/	bud
ɒ	/pɒt/	pot
ʊ	/pʊt/	put
ə	/əˈbaʊt/	about

Long vowels

iː	/biːd/	bead
ɑː	/hɑːm/	harm
ɔː	/ɔːl/	all
uː	/buːt/	boot
ɜː	/bɜːd/	bird

Diphthongs

eɪ	/beɪ/	bay
aɪ	/baɪ/	buy
ɔɪ	/bɔɪ/	boy
aʊ	/haʊ/	how
oʊ	/goʊ/	go
ɪə	/bɪə(r)/	beer
ɛə	/bɛə(r)/	bare
ʊə	/pʊə(r)/	poor

Notes
(1) The stress mark (ˈ) is placed before the stressed syllable (*eg* **announce** /əˈnaʊns/).
(2) The symbol (r) is used to represent *r* when it comes at the end of a word, to indicate that it is pronounced when followed by a vowel (as in the phrase *tower above* /taʊə(r) əˈbʌv/).

Organization of entries

Definitions are numbered and written as whole sentences, showing the phrasal verb being used in a natural and grammatically correct way, and showing where the adverbial particle goes. No abbreviations except *AmE, BrE,* and *eg* (meaning 'for example') are used in the guide.

act /akt/: **acts, acting, acted**

○ **act on** *or* **act upon**

1 You **act on** or **act upon** advice or suggestions when you do what is advised or suggested: *An experienced nurse can act on her own initiative.* □ *In a constitutional monarchy, the Queen acts on the advice of her Prime Minister.* [*same as* **follow**] 2 Something such as a drug, or an influence present in your surroundings, **acts on** you when it has an effect on you: *Caffeine is a stimulant which acts on the nervous system.*

Verb parts – the third person singular, the present participle, past tense and part participle are shown for all verbs.

agree /ə'griː/: **agrees, agreeing, agreed**

○ **agree with** (*informal*)

Something, usually food, doesn't **agree with** you when it makes you feel ill: *These small, smoky rooms don't agree with his health.*

Pronunciation is given for the headword verb and irregular parts as necessary.

Register labels: phrasal verbs, synonyms and antonyms are labelled for register (for example *informal* or *formal*) where necessary.

announce /ə'naʊns/: **announces, announcing, announced**

○ **announce for** (*AmE*)

You **announce for** a political office when you say that you are going to be a candidate for that office: *It was not a surprise when Governer Bush announced for President.*

Phrasal verbs are labelled to show whether they are common in British English (*BrE*) or American English (*AmE*).

○ **back out**

You **back out** when you decide not to do something you had previously agreed or promised to do: *If they back out of the contract at this stage, we'll be finished.* [*same as* **pull out**]

Synonyms and antonyms are given at the end of the definitions, where appropriate.

cook /kʊk/: **cooks, cooking, cooked**

○ **cook out** (*AmE*)

You **cook out** when you cook and eat food outdoors, especially a barbecue for several people: *We tried to cook out, but the rain ended that.*

▶ *noun* **cookout: cookouts:** *The celebrations ended with a cookout in the park.*

Derivatives: nouns and adjectives formed from phrasal verbs are given after the phrasal verb.

hold /hoʊld/: **holds, holding, held** /hɛld/

○ **hold against**

You **hold** something **against** someone when you deal with them harshly or unfairly because you disapprove of or dislike something about them: *Her father says, 'So, you married an Englishman. We won't hold it against you.'* ▫ *Perhaps their lack of computer competence will be held against them.* [compare **count against**]

Cross references: references are made to other phrasal verbs if they are useful for comparison.

level /ˈlɛvəl/: **levels, levelling** (*AmE* **leveling**), **levelled** (*AmE* **leveled**)

○ **level off** *or* **level out**

1 You **level off** a surface when you make it smooth or level: *Once the concrete begins to set you can level it off with a square edge, or a plasterer's float, for a really smooth finish.* **2** Something that is rising or falling in number, amount, degree or extent **levels off** or **levels out** when it stops rising or falling and remains steady or level: *Student intake had reached over 25,000 before it began to level off.* ▫ *The road climbed steeply and then levelled out.* **3** An aircraft **levels off** or **levels out** when it begins to fly horizontally after flying up or down: *We levelled out at 35,000 feet.*

American spellings are shown in brackets.

Examples supported by the British National Corpus show the range of ways a phrasal verb can be used, and show where the adverbial particle can go.

wake /weɪk/: **wakes, waking, woke** /woʊk/, **woken** /ˈwoʊkən/

Note that in American English **waked** is often used as the past tense and past participle of **wake**.

Grammatical notes follow the headword verb.

The Dictionary

A a

ace /eɪs/: **aces, acing, aced**

○ **ace out** (*AmE*)

You **ace out** a test when you answer all of the questions correctly or when you receive a grade 'A': *Henry hardly ever studied, but he aced out his English exam.*

act /akt/: **acts, acting, acted**

○ **act on** *or* **act upon**

1 You **act on** or **act upon** advice or suggestions when you do what is advised or suggested: *An experienced nurse can act on her own initiative.* □ *In a constitutional monarchy, the Queen acts on the advice of her Prime Minister.* [*same as* **follow**] **2** Something such as a drug, or an influence present in your surroundings, **acts on** you when it has an effect on you: *Caffeine is a stimulant which acts on the nervous system.*

○ **act up** (*informal*)

1 Something such as a machine **is acting up** when it's not working properly: *The speakers seem alright, but the tape-deck's acting up again.* **2** Someone, especially a child, **is acting up** when they are behaving badly or uncooperatively, and causing trouble: *She couldn't trust him not to act up when something upset him.*

add /ad/: **adds, adding, added**

○ **add on**

You **add** something **on** when you include it or attach it as an extra: *Add on £2.50 for postage and packing.* □ *You have space enough at the back of the house to add a conservatory on later, if you decide to.*

○ **add up**

1 You **add up** numbers or amounts when you calculate their total: *You haven't added the figures up correctly.*

□ *You'll save 30p a week, and it all adds up.* **2** You say that figures or numbers don't **add up** if their total has been wrongly calculated. **3** (*informal*) Things **add up** if they make sense: *I can't think why she left so suddenly; it doesn't add up.*

agree /əˈɡriː/: **agrees, agreeing, agreed**

○ **agree with** (*informal*)

Something, usually food, doesn't **agree with** you when it makes you feel ill: *These small, smoky rooms don't agree with his health.*

aim /eɪm/: **aims, aiming, aimed**

○ **aim for**

1 You **aim for** something when you have it as a target, and you direct a weapon or other object towards it: *He was aiming for Swinton on the right wing, but the pass was intercepted.* **2** You also **aim for** something when you plan or intend to achieve it: *The Deutsche Bank is aiming for 30 branches in the former East Berlin by the end of the year.*

announce /əˈnaʊns/: **announces, announcing, announced**

○ **announce for** (*AmE*)

You **announce for** a political office when you say that you are going to be a candidate for that office: *It was not a surprise when Governer Bush announced for President.*

answer /ˈɑːnsə(r)/: **answers, answering, answered**

○ **answer back**

Someone, especially a child, **answers** you **back**, or **answers back**, when they reply rudely: *She won't give him the job; he's answered back once too often.* [*same as* **talk back**]

○ **answer up** (*AmE*)

You **answer up** when you reply to a question: *I was the first person to answer up when the teacher asked what Mark Twain's real name was.*

argue /ˈɑːɡjuː/: **argues, arguing, argued**

○ **argue down** (*AmE*)

You **argue** someone **down** when you win an argument with them: *Carl insisted that a Ford is better than a Chevrolet, but I argued him down.*

ask /ɑːsk/: **asks, asking, asked**

○ **ask after**

You **ask after** someone when you ask for news about them: *I saw Phil in town yesterday; he was asking after you.* □ *He remembered to ask after my mother's health.*

○ **ask for**

1 You **ask for** something when you say you would like someone to give it to you: *You could ask for an increase on your overdraft limit.* □ *Don't be afraid to ask for help if there's anything you don't understand.* [*same as* **request** (*formal*)]
2 You **ask for** someone when you say you want to speak to them: *A Mr Davies phoned this morning asking for you personally.* **3** You say someone **is asking for** it, or **asking for** trouble, if the way they are behaving is certain to get them into trouble or difficulties: *It was asking for it to drive after drinking four whiskies.* □ *Walking through an area like that after dark is really asking for trouble.*

○ **ask in**

You **ask** someone **in** when you invite them to come into your house or another place you are in, or to go in with you: *We stood on the doorstep chatting, and all the time I was waiting for her to ask me in for a drink.*

○ **ask out**

You **ask** someone **out** when you invite them to go somewhere with you socially, *eg* to the cinema or to a restaurant: *I didn't know what to say: I'd never been asked out by a woman before.* □ *I think I might ask her out to dinner.*

back /bak/: **backs, backing, backed**

○ **back down**

You **back down** when you stop demanding, insisting on, or fighting for some-

thing: *The unions refused to back down over pay and conditions.* □ *If we back down on a single issue, they'll sense weakness and walk all over us.* [*same as* **give in**]

○ **back out**

You **back out** when you decide not to do something you had previously agreed or promised to do: *If they back out of the contract at this stage, we'll be finished.* [*same as* **pull out**]

○ **back up**

1 You **back** someone **up** when you support or help them: *They had, of course, sworn to back up the President no matter how shady or underhand his dealings with foreign powers were.* □ *Backed up by a network of loyal, if undisciplined, militiamen he had ruled the country with an iron fist.* **2** You **back** someone **up** when you confirm that they are telling the truth; you **back up** a statement when you provide evidence to prove that it's true: *No-one would back up her story.* □ *Send photos of the damage and builders' estimates for repairs, to back up your claim.* **3** To **back up** information stored on a computer is to make a copy of it, *eg* on a floppy disk.

ball /bɔːl/: **balls, balling, balled**

○ **ball up** (*AmE; informal*)

You **ball up** when you are confused; you **ball** something **up** when you create a confusion: *Whenever I get an important assignment, I seem to ball it up.*

▶ *noun* **ballup: ballups:** *Murry's presentation to the board was a real ballup.*

▶ *adjective* **balled up:** *Tom is so balled up, he thinks it's Friday.*

bang /baŋ/: **bangs, banging, banged**

○ **bang up** (*AmE*)

You **bang up** something, or it becomes **banged up**, when it becomes damaged, usually in an accident: *I can't tell Dad I banged up his car door.* □ *The removal company banged up my computer.*

barrel /ˈbarəl/: **barrels, barrelling (barreling** *AmE***), barrelled (bareled** *AmE***)**

○ **barrel along** *or* **barrel away** *or* **barrel down** (*AmE; informal*)

Someone or something **barrels along**, or **barrels away**, or **barrels down**, when they travel very fast: *Those kids always bar-*

rel along the path on their bikes. ❑ *The teenagers barrelled away in their cars when the police appeared.* ❑ *Fred came barrelling down the road in his new truck.*

bat /bat/: bats, batting, batted

○ **bat out** (*AmE*; *informal*)

You **bat out** something, or **bat** it **out** when you create it quickly: *The director had him bat out a new script over the weekend.* ❑ *She batted another verse out while we were there.*

beat /biːt/: beats, beating, beat, beaten

○ **beat up**

Someone **beats** you **up** when they punch, kick or hit you violently and repeatedly: *He claimed he'd been beaten up by the police.* ❑ *He'd want to beat up anyone who harmed his children in any way.* [*same as* **assault**]

belly /'bɛli/: bellies, bellying, bellied

○ **belly up to** (*AmE*; *informal*)

You **belly up to** something when you move or stand very close to it: *Jake bellied up to the bar and ordered two beers.* ❑ *The stranger strode across the room and bellied up to the bar.*

belt /bɛlt/: belts, belting, belted

○ **belt down** (*AmE*; *informal*)

You **belt down** a drink, or you **belt** it **down**, when you swallow it quickly: *He was a man who could belt down beers all night.* ❑ *She belted most of a bottle of wine down before dinner had even begun.*

bid /bɪd/: bids, bidding, bid, bidden

○ **bid in** (*AmE*)

You **bid in** at an auction when you bid the highest amount of money to keep your own items: *After his bankruptcy, Governor Connelly was able to recover much of his property by bidding in at his Texas auction.*

blab /blab/: blabs, blabbing, blabbed

○ **blab off** *or* **blab off about** (*AmE*)

You **blab off**, or **blab off about** something, when you talk too much: *Who wants to go to the council meeting just to hear Fred blab off.* ❑ *Everytime I see Linda, she blabs off about her kids.*

black /blak/: blacks, blacking, blacked

○ **black out**

1 A place or building **is blacked out** when all the lights are switched off and it is made completely dark, or windows and other openings are covered so that lights on inside the building cannot be seen from the outside: *Wardens patrolled the streets to make sure every house had been properly blacked out.* **2** Someone **blacks out** when they lose consciousness for a short time: *I must have blacked out: the next thing I remember is two men pulling me from the car.* [*same as* **pass out**, **faint**] **3** To **black out** a television or radio programme is to prevent it from being broadcast: *Orders from Beijing were to black out all scheduled news bulletins.*

bleep /bliːp/: bleeps, bleeping, bleeped

○ **bleep off** (*AmE*; *informal*)

Telling someone to **bleep off** is an offensive way of telling them to go away: *I'm tired of your complaints, so why don't you just bleep off!*

blow /bloʊ/: blows, blowing, blew /bluː/, blown

○ **blow out** (*AmE*; *informal*)

A sports team **blows** an opponent **out** when it defeats them badly: *I thought Pittsburgh was a good team, but we blew them out.*

▶ *noun* **blowout**: **blowouts**: *Those tickets cost a lot, but the game was a blowout.*

○ **blow over**

1 Something such as an argument **blows over** when it ends and people forget about it: *It only took a few days for the scandal to blow over.* [*same as* **subside**; *compare* **die down**] **2** A storm **blows over** when it ends: *We huddled together in the cellar and waited for the hurricane to blow over.* [*same as* **subside**; *compare* **die down**]

○ **blow up**

1 People **blow** something **up** when they destroy it with a bomb or other exploding weapon; something that **blows up** is destroyed in this way: *It seems that the terrorist planting the device had accidentally triggered it, blowing himself up.* ❑ *If flames had reached the fuel store, the whole place would certainly have* *blown up.* [*same as* **explode**] **2** You **blow up** something such as a tyre or a balloon when you fill it with air or gas. [*same as* **inflate**] **3** To **blow up** a photograph is to make a bigger copy of it: *The detail will be much clearer if we blow it up.* [*same as* **enlarge**] **4** You **blow** something **up** when you make it seem more impressive, important or serious than it really is: *Once the newspapers got their hands on the story, it was blown up out of all proportion.* [*same as* **exaggerate**] **5** A storm **blows up** when it begins: *The horses get nervous when there's a storm blowing up.* **6** Something such as trouble or an argument **blows up** when it begins suddenly: *A heated row blew up between the director and the team manager only hours before the big match.* **7** (*informal*) Someone **blows up** when they suddenly start shouting or behaving very angrily: *Peter blew up at one of the students for not handing her work in on time.*

bog /bɒg/: bogged

○ **bog down**
You **are bogged down** by something when you give so much attention to it, or become so involved in it, that you fail to make proper progress or any progress at all: *We must be careful not to get bogged down in trifling detail.* ▫ *I thought we were becoming a little bogged down, so I tried to move the discussion on a bit.*

boil /bɔɪl/: boils, boiling, boiled

○ **boil down to**
People sometimes say that a complicated situation **boils down to** one particular thing when they are pointing out that that thing is its basic or most important aspect: *As with all committee decisions, it all boils down to money.* ▫ *What it boils down to is a fundamental difference in religious approach.*

bomb /bɒm/: bombs, bombing, bombed

○ **bomb out** (*AmE*; *informal*)
You **bomb out** when you completely fail, especially in front of an audience: *The band was okay, but the comedian bombed out.*

book /bʊk/: books, booking, booked

○ **book in** *or* **book into** (*BrE*)
You **book in** when you announce your arrival at a place, usually a hotel; you **book** someone **in** when you arrange for them to stay in a place such as a hotel: *When we booked in, we were asked to leave our passports.* ▫ *They decided to book into the first guesthouse they saw, to save time.* ▫ *Eddie had booked the group in to play four nights at the famous 'Lollipop Club'.* ▫ *She returned from her wanderings and booked herself straight into a London clinic for a couple of weeks.* [*compare* **check in**]

○ **book up**
1 (*BrE*) You **book up** for something when you arrange to have it or take part in it at some time in the future: *Am I too late to book up for the Paris trip?* ▫ *Last year's holiday was a last-minute thing, but this year we decided to get booked up nice and early.* **2** Something you want to take part in or attend **is booked up** when there are no seats or tickets left: *I'm afraid the three o'clock flight is all booked up.* ▫ *The hotels along the front were all booked up solid the whole summer.*

bottle /'bɒtəl/: bottles, bottling, bottled

○ **bottle up**
You **bottle up** a strong emotion you frequently feel when you don't allow yourself to express it: *You have to appreciate that she's been bottling this up for some time.* ▫ *She kept her anger bottled up inside her for years.* [*same as* **keep back, suppress**; *opposite* **let go, reveal**]

bounce /baʊns/: bounces, bouncing, bounced

○ **bounce back**
You **bounce back** after a failure or disappointment when you soon become cheerful, hopeful or enthusiastic again: *I think you have to question how likely it is that British manufacturing can bounce back from such a sustained onslaught.* [*compare* **pick up**]

bowl /bəʊl/: bowls, bowling, bowled

○ **bowl over**
You **are bowled over** by something or someone when you are immediately

surprised or shocked by how impressive they are: *The friendliness of the Greeks just bowled me over.* [*same as* **take aback, overwhelm, stagger**]

branch /brɑ:ntʃ/: **branches, branching, branched**

○ **branch out**

You **branch out** when you do something new or different, perhaps something rather exciting or a little uncertain or dangerous: *Several aeronautics companies branched out into the manufacture of weapons.* ▫ *I can't imagine Gerry branching out on his own.*

break /breɪk/: **breaks, breaking, broke** /brəʊk/, **broken** /ˈbrəʊkən/

○ **break down**

1 A vehicle or machine **breaks down** when it stops working properly and needs to be repaired: *The policy covers you if you break down outside a five-mile radius of your home.* ▫ *We won't be able to afford the repair bill the next time the tumble-drier breaks down.* [*same as* **pack up** (*informal*)] **2** Things such as relationships, partnerships and discussions **break down** when they come to an end, because of a disagreement: *When marriages break down, we have to put the interests of the children first.* [*same as* **fail, collapse**] **3** Someone **breaks down** when they completely lose control of their emotions and begin to cry, or perhaps laugh, uncontrollably: *We have often seen relatives of victims break down in front of the cameras.* [*same as* **collapse**] **4** Someone also **breaks down** when they suffer for a longer period from a serious illness of the nerves which makes them unable to deal with everyday life: *He simply broke down under the pressure.* [*same as* **crack up**] **5** To **break down** a door is to hit it so hard that parts of it break and it falls to the ground: *Two police officers with sledgehammers came to break the door down.* **6** You **break** something **down** when you consider the separate parts that form it: *The national statistic can be broken down into four geographical sub-groups.* ▫ *Overall outgoings break down into household expenses, childcare, and the cost of running a car.* **7** A substance **breaks down** when chemical processes cause it to separate into the simpler substances that formed it: *Vegetable-based plastics readily break down when buried in soil.* ▫ *The body's own acids break down the food in your stomach.* ▫ *They've developed a drug that treats the poison by breaking it down.*

○ **break in**

1 Someone **breaks in** when they enter a building by force or dishonestly, usually intending to steal things inside: *They appear to have broken in through a rear window.* **2** You **break in** when you interrupt a conversation between other people: *I'm sorry to break in, but I think you're both wrong.* ▫ *'Isn't this all a bit irrelevant?', Sonia broke in.* [*same as* **cut in, butt in**] **3 a** You **break** something that is new or untested **in** when you use or wear it for a while until you are sure that is working properly or is comfortable: *He wore the boots around the house for a few days to break them in.* **b** You **break** someone **in** when you make them familiar with a new job or situation: *It was Hanlon's responsibility to break in the new boys from the college.*

○ **break out**

1 A prisoner **breaks out** of prison when they escape: *If three of us managed to break out, what would happen to the other two when the break-out was discovered?* **2** Violent, noisy and disturbing situations **break out** when they begin, often suddenly or unexpectedly: *Complete chaos broke out when the relief supplies arrived.* ▫ *They had had secret talks as late as the week before war broke out.* **3** You use **break out** to refer to the sudden spread of things such as sweat or spots on your skin: *Within seconds she was breaking out in a cold sweat.* ▫ *An angry red rash had broken out all over his body.* **4** You also use **break out** to talk about setting yourself free from something that prevents you from doing what you would like to do: *The only route to happiness seemed to lie in breaking out of this mind-numbing routine.* ▫ *Most kids want to leave the island and break out on their own.*

○ **break up**

1 You **break** something **up** when you divide it into pieces or separate parts; something **breaks up** when it becomes separated into pieces: *He spent the first hour breaking up logs for firewood.* □ *If they got any closer, the boat would certainly break up on the rocks.* **2** To **break up** a gathering of people is to bring it to an end: *Neighbours called the police, who broke the party up.* □ *Then Mark, in a display of drink-inspired bravado, stepped in to break the fighting up.* □ *The meeting broke up at around eleven, and some of us went to the pub for a last drink.* **3** People **break up** when their relationship or partnership comes to an end: *How did you feel once you knew your parents were breaking up?* □ *If you go through with such an unwise marriage, you will only succeed in breaking up the family.* □ *We would be sad to see such a long-standing organization break up over such a trivial affair.* [*same as* **split up**] **4** (*BrE*; *informal*) A school **breaks up**, or the pupils in it **break up**, when the school term ends and the holidays begin: *My daughter doesn't break up until next week.* **5** (*AmE*) Someone **breaks up** when they are very upset: *She broke up just before her mother's funeral.* **6** (*AmE*) You **break** someone **up** or they **break up**, when they cannot stop laughing: *My joke about the duck really broke Angela up.* □ *Dad simply broke up when he saw Mum's new hair style.*

bring /brɪŋ/: **brings, bringing, brought** /brɔːt/

○ **bring about**
You **bring** something **about** when you cause it to happen: *They're hoping this next round of talks will bring about a settlement of the pay dispute.* □ *This is a very strange attitude; I don't know what's brought it about.* [*same as* **produce**]

○ **bring off** (*informal*)
You **bring** something difficult **off** when you manage to do it: *It's a difficult dive but she should be able to bring it off.* [*compare* **pull off**]

○ **bring out**
1 A company that **brings out** a new product makes it available for people to buy; a publisher **brings out** a new book when they publish it: *The BBC decided to bring out a gardening book to accompany the television series.* □ *'You've brought a new album out, of songs collected on your journey round Ireland.'* **2** People often use **bring out** to refer to the way something is made more obvious or noticeable: *The reading of a talented and sensitive actor brings out the subtleties of Shakespeare's texts.* □ *These tasks are designed to bring out the natural competitiveness in children.* □ *Football always brings out the worst in him.* [*same as* **reveal**] **3** To **bring** someone **out** is to help them to become less nervous about meeting or talking to other people: *I think membership of the uniformed organizations goes some way to bringing out the shy child.*

○ **bring up**
1 You **bring up** a child when you care for them and educate them: *She was brought up by her aunt.* □ *I'd like to think I brought my sons up to be kind and thoughtful.* □ *Their children were brought up rather strictly.* [*same as* **raise, rear**] **2** You **bring** a subject **up** when you mention it: *It does nobody any good to bring up painful episodes from the past.* [*same as* **raise**; *compare* **come up**] **3** You **bring up** food when your stomach throws it out through your mouth: *At least one of the babies will bring a feed up at some point in the day.* [*same as* **throw up** (*informal*), **vomit**]

brown /braʊn/: **browns, browning, browned**

○ **brown out** (*AmE*)
Something **browns out** when its electricity supply becomes weak and light is reduced: *The lights browned out just before the hurricane hit.*
▶ *noun* **brownout: brownouts**: *New York City suffered its second brownout in a month.*

brush /brʌʃ/: **brushes, brushing, brushed**

○ **brush up** *or* **brush up on**
You **brush up** something, or **brush up on** it, when you refresh or improve your knowledge of it: *I'll need to brush up my Shakespeare before the course starts.* □ *You could do with brushing up on your*

French vocabulary.

buddy /ˈbʌdi/: **buddies**, **buddying**, **buddied**

○ **buddy up** (*AmE*; *informal*)

You **buddy up** to someone when you become very friendly towards them, usually to gain some advantage: *Why are you buddying up to me? Do you need a loan?*

bug /bʌg/: **bugs**, **bugging**, **bugged**

○ **bug off** (*AmE*; *informal*)

1 You **bug off** when you leave, often under pressure: *When Sue begins talking about religion, it's time to bug off.* **2** When someone tells you to **bug off**, they are saying in a rude way that you should leave them alone: *Can't you see I'm working? Just bug off for a while.*

○ **bug out** (*AmE*; *informal*)

You **bug out** when you leave quickly: *Let's bug out before Dad finds the broken window.*

build /bɪld/: **builds**, **building**, **built**

○ **build up**

1 Something **builds up** when it gradually increases in size, strength or amount; you **build** something **up** when you make it increase gradually in size, strength or amount: *Traffic is building up on the approach to the Newbridge roundabout.* ◻ *Money is urgently needed to help build up supplies of basic foodstuffs and medicines.* ◻ *We're looking for ways to build his confidence up a bit.* ◻ *From humble beginnings in Rochdale, they have built the company up into what is now a multinational concern.* **2** You **build** someone or something **up** if you make them seem more impressive than they really are: *As a live performer, she was not all that she had been built up to be.* ◻ *By the end of the discussion, Frank had been built up into everyone's vision of the ideal man.* **3** To **build** someone **up** is to make them stronger and healthier, usually by giving them more to eat: *Doctors are insisting that he builds himself up a bit before they'll release him.* ◻ *Like mothers everywhere, Heather's seemed to think I needed building up.* **4** An area that **is built up** has many buildings in it: *The farms are no longer there, and the woodland has been built up long since.*

bump /bʌmp/: **bumps**, **bumping**, **bumped**

○ **bump into**

1 You **bump into** a person or thing when you accidentally knock or hit them, sometimes damaging or hurting them as a result: *I can't see how bumping into a table could produce a bruise like that.* ◻ *Another car bumped into me from behind.* [*same as* **run into**, **bang into**] **2** (*informal*) You **bump into** someone if you meet them by chance: *You're bound to bump into him sooner or later.* [*same as* **run into**]

burn /bɜːn/: **burns**, **burning**, **burned** *or* **burnt**

Burned and **burnt** can both be used as the past tense and past participle of **burn**.

○ **burn down**

A building **burns down**, or **is burned down**, when it is destroyed by fire: *Most of the medieval abbeys were burned down in the sixteenth century.* ◻ *They were scared to leave the kids alone, in case they burned the place down.*

○ **burn out**

1 A fire **burns out**, or **burns** itself **out**, when all the burning material is finally destroyed and the fire stops burning: *A few revellers stayed on until the bonfire had burnt out.* ◻ *The forest fire has been contained and will now be left to burn itself out.* **2** Electrical wires and pieces of electrical equipment **burn out** when they become damaged or destroyed by being used too much, or by having too much electric current passed through them: *The motor has burned out and will have to be replaced.* **3** (*informal*) You **burn** yourself **out** when you use up all your energy and become thoroughly exhausted: *Juantarina had nothing left for the last two laps: he'd burnt himself out in the first half of the race.*

butter /ˈbʌtə(r)/: **butters**, **buttering**, **buttered**

○ **butter up** (*informal*)

Someone **butters** you **up** when they flatter or praise you as a way of persuading you to do something: *She thinks the money'll be no problem if she butters up her parents a bit.* ◻ *He tried to butter me up by telling me I was looking very nice* *tonight.*

call /kɔːl/: **calls, calling, called**

○ **call by** (*BrE*)

You **call by** when you visit a place for a short time on your way to somewhere else: *I'll call by on my way to work and pick up the books from you.* [*compare* **call in, call round**]

○ **call in** (*BrE*)

1 a You **call in** to see someone *eg* at their home, at hospital, or at their place of work when you pay them a short visit there: *The district nurse will be calling in again tomorrow to see that you're all right.* **b** You **call in** at a place when you go there, usually when you are on your way to somewhere else: *Would you call in at the butcher's on your way home and pick up my order?* [*compare* **call by, call round**] **2** You **call** someone **in** when you ask them to come to give you help or advice: *If you don't stop that racket I'm going to call in the cops!* ▫ *Granny doesn't look too good; do you think we should call the doctor in?* ▫ *He had called in a firm of local builders to carry out the essential repairs.* **3** A lender **calls in** a loan when they demand that it is paid immediately and in full, especially if the borrower has broken the terms of the loan agreement in some way: *When the bank heard of the firm's financial difficulties it called in its overdraft.*

○ **call off**

1 When an event that has already been scheduled or planned **is called off** it is cancelled: *Harry said he didn't see why the match should be called off just because there was snow forecast.* ▫ *Seven meetings have been called off in the last few days.* **2** A search or investigation **is called off** when it is stopped or halted: *The search for the missing climber had to*

be called off when it got too dark. **3** You **call off** *eg* your dog when you order it to stop attacking someone: *I yelled to the man to call off his dog.*

○ **call out** (*AmE*)

In baseball, a batter is **called out** when the umpire decides and indicates that he is out: *Sosa thought he was safe at first base, but he was called out.*

○ **call round** (*BrE*)

You **call round** to a place, usually somewhere that is not a very great distance away, when you go there to pay a short visit: *I'll call round at your flat sometime after work.* [*compare* **call by, call in**]

○ **call up**

1 You **call** someone **up** when you telephone them: *Barry called me up last night to ask me if I would like to go to the game with him.* [*same as* **phone up, ring up**] **2** When someone **is called up** they are officially ordered to join the armed forces of their country: *He was called up in 1941 and was wounded during the Normandy landings.* ▫ *a reservist called up in the course of the Gulf conflict.* [*same as* **draft**] **3** (*BrE*) The person in charge of organizing a particular team or activity **calls** someone **up** when they select that person to be part of the team or take part in that activity: *The selectors have called up several younger and less experienced players for the Test against Australia.* **4** (*AmE*) A major league baseball team **calls up** a player, or they are **called up**, when they are brought up from a minor league team owned by the major one: *St Louis called up three players from their Memphis club.* **5** You **call up** information from a computer when you obtain it by instructing the computer to search for it in its memory: *Would you call up the latest sales figures and give me a printout before this morning's meeting.* **6** Something **calls up** something from the past, or an idea, when it causes you to think of it: *We were finding ways of starting to write in our own voice: through calling up early memories, waking up the senses, and developing an ear for the rhythms of speech.* ▫ *It really was what I'd dreamed about, a sort of crystal ball in which I could call up everything I* had ever known. [*same as* **bring back**, **evoke** (*formal*)]

calm /kɑːm/: **calms, calming, calmed**

○ **calm down**

You **calm** someone **down** when you do something that helps them to stop feeling anxious, upset or angry; you **calm down** when you stop feeling anxious, upset or angry: *She'd become quite hysterical; the doctor had to give her a sedative to calm her down.* □ *For goodness sake, calm down! It's only a spider.*

cancel /'kansəl/: **cancels, cancelling** (*AmE* **canceling**), **cancelled** (*AmE* **canceled**)

○ **cancel out**

1 When one thing **is cancelled out** by another, or when two things **cancel** each other **out**, each thing has the opposite effect of the other so that, when they occur together, no effect is produced: *Make sure the charges on your policy don't cancel out the tax savings.* □ *the increase in output in one market cancelling out the fall in output in the other.* [*same as* **neutralize** (*formal*), **nullify** (*formal*)] **2** (*AmE*) If you **cancel out** of an event you planned to attend, you do not attend it: *I hurt my ankle just before the golf tournament, and had to cancel out.*

carry /'karɪ/: **carries, carrying, carried**

○ **carry out**

You **carry out** something such as a task, duty, procedure or order when you do it, complete it or put it into operation or practice: *How to find the money necessary to carry out the charity's work has always been a worry.* □ *The union leaders had refused to carry out a ballot prior to calling a strike.* [*same as* **perform, undertake, execute, fulfil**]

catch /katʃ/: **catches, catching, caught** /kɔːt/

○ **catch on** (*informal*)

1 Something **catches on** when it becomes popular: *Baseball has never quite caught on in England; cricket is much more popular.* **2** You **catch on** when you begin to understand what is happening or being said; you **catch on** to something when you become aware

that it is happening: *He's a smart kid; it doesn't take him long to catch on.* □ *It was some time before the police caught on to the fact that large quantities of drugs were being smuggled in through remote villages on the West Coast.*

○ **catch out** (*BrE*)

You **catch** someone **out** when you trick them into making a mistake, especially one that shows that they have been lying or have done something wrong: *Be careful when you are giving evidence; the defence lawyer will do everything he can to catch you out.*

○ **catch up**

1 You **catch up** with someone moving ahead of you when you manage to reach them by moving faster: *Slow down and let the others catch up.* □ *You'll have to run faster if you want to catch him up.* **2** You **catch up**, or **catch up** with someone, when you reach the same standard or level as they are at: *She's fallen behind a little because she's been off school for so long, but if she works hard she'll soon catch up.* □ *We're so far behind the rest of Europe, I fear we'll never catch up.*

check /tʃɛk/: **checks, checking, checked**

○ **check in**

1 You **check in** at an airport before you board a flight when you show your ticket so that the airline knows that you have arrived; the airline staff **check** you **in** when they examine your ticket before you get on a flight: *I'll just check in and then we can go and have a drink.* **2** You **check in** at a hotel, or you **check into** a hotel, when you arrive, sign your name in the register and collect the key for your room: *We arrived at 2 am and were checked in by the night porter.* □ *The first thing we did when we arrived in New York was check into the Waldorf Astoria.* [*opposite* **check out**]

○ **check out**

1 You **check out** of a hotel when you pay your bill and leave: *We'll have a room available after lunch when the couple in number 10 have checked out.* [*opposite* **check in**] **2** (*informal*) You **check** something **out** when you find out about it: *All I have to do now is check out the times of direct flights to Paris.*

❑ *We've had a report of a disturbance in Cambridge Street and I've sent two constables along to check it out.* [*compare* **check up**] **3** (*informal*) You **check** someone **out** when you find out all that you can about them, usually without them knowing that you are doing so: *I don't know if he's who he says he is; we'll have to have him checked out.* [*compare* **check up**] **4** (*AmE*; *informal*) If you **check out**, you die.

○ **check up**
1 You **check up** to see if something is true or accurate when you make enquiries about it with a reliable source: *If you want to check up that their flight will be arriving on time, just phone the airport enquiry desk.* ❑ *I wasn't sure if I had taken his number down properly so I checked it up in the telephone directory.* [*compare* **check out**] **2** You **check up** on someone or something when you find out if they are all right or are behaving or working as they should be: *Sometimes my parents drop in unexpectedly just to check up on me.*

cheer /tʃɪə(r)/: **cheers, cheering, cheered**
○ **cheer up**
Someone or something **cheers** you **up** when they make you feel happier and more hopeful; you **cheer up** when you begin to feel happier and more hopeful: *I thought you were looking a bit down so I brought you a little present to cheer you up.* ❑ *Oh, do cheer up! You've nothing to be depressed about.*

chew /tʃuː/: **chews, chewing, chewed**
○ **chew out** (*AmE*)
You **chew** someone **out** when you strongly criticize them: *When Frank lost the cheque, his boss chewed him out for an hour.*

chicken /'tʃɪkɪn/: **chickens, chickening, chickened**
○ **chicken out** (*informal*)
You **chicken out** when you don't do something risky or dangerous because you have lost the courage to do it: *Henry was going to do a parachute jump but he chickened out at the last minute.* ❑ *I'm prepared to bet that he'll chicken out of the fight when he finds out who his opponent is.*

chill /tʃɪl/: **chills, chilling, chilled**
○ **chill out** (*informal*)
People say they **are chilling out** when they are relaxing, either physically or mentally, after a period of very energetic activity or mental stress: *Sit down, have a beer, and chill out, man.*

choke /tʃəʊk/: **chokes, choking, choked**
○ **choke up** (*AmE*)
You **choke up**, especially in sports, when you fail because you are under pressure and too nervous: *Every time the game depends on Riggs, he chokes up.*

chow /tʃaʊ/: **chows, chowing, chowed**
○ **chow down** (*AmE*; *informal*)
You **chow down** when you eat a meal: *As soon as the tents were up, the soldiers chowed down.*

clean /kliːn/: **cleans, cleaning, cleaned**
○ **clean out**
1 You **clean out** something such as a cupboard or room when you empty it completely, get rid of the things you don't need, and clean it thoroughly: *Dad's cleaning out the garage and getting rid of all that old junk he's been hanging on to for years.* **2** (*informal*) If someone or something **cleans** you **out** they take all the money you have: *I can't afford to go out for a meal; today's trip to the garden centre cleaned me out completely.*

○ **clean up**
1 You **clean** something **up** when you make it clean again: *How did you manage to get chocolate all over your face? We'll have to clean you up before your mum comes to collect you.* **2** You **clean up** a mess when you get rid of it: *Get a damp cloth and clean up the blackcurrant juice you've spilt on the table.* **3** You **clean up** after someone when you clean a place that they have made dirty: *It's not fair to expect your mother to clean up after you all the time.* **4** (*informal*) Someone **cleans up** a place or organization when they take action to get rid of vice or crime there: *We would undoubtably require that the authorities be seen to have cleaned up their act.* ❑ *With all these accusations of 'sleaze'*

it's time someone did something to clean up the government's image.

clear /ˈklɪə(r)/: **clears**, **clearing**, **cleared**

○ **clear off**

1 (*informal*) Someone **clears off** when they go or run away; if you say **'clear off!'** to someone you are telling them rudely to go away: *Here come the coppers; we'd better clear off quick!* ◻ *Clear off! This is private land.* **2** You **clear off** a debt when you pay it all back: *We've decided to use the money we won on the lottery to clear off our mortgage.*

○ **clear out**

1 You **clear out** something such as a room or cupboard when you take everything out of it, throw away the things that you don't want to make more space, and tidy the things you want to keep: *Will you help me clear out this cupboard?* **2** You **clear out** when you leave a place quickly; you tell someone to **clear out** when you want them to leave immediately: *Her husband threatened to clear out that night if she didn't stop nagging him.* ◻ *The landlord has told us to clear out of the flat if we can't pay the rent we owe before the end of the week.*

○ **clear up**

1 You **clear up**, or **clear** a place **up**, when you make it tidy and put things away in their proper places: *I won't let you do any baking unless you promise to clear up afterwards.* ◻ *It's 4.30, and everyone is clearing up before going home.* **2** You **clear up** after someone when you tidy a place that they have made untidy: *You'd better put all these things away; I'm not going to clear up after you anymore.* **3** You **clear up** a mystery, misunderstanding or problem when you solve it or settle it satisfactorily; the police **clear up** a crime or crimes when they find out who the criminal or criminals are and arrest them: *I'd like to clear up a few minor points before I sign the contract.* ◻ *With the new powers the police have become more successful at clearing up crime.* **4** The weather **clears up** when it becomes fine again: *It's been raining all day even though the forecast said it would clear up in the afternoon.* **5** An illness or condi-

tion **clears up** when it gets better: *Has the rash cleared up yet?* ◻ *The joint and skin problems should be transient and will clear up in due course.*

clock /klɒk/: **clocks**, **clocking**, **clocked**

○ **clock up** (*BrE*; *informal*)

You **clock up** a particular speed, distance, score or total when you reach or achieve it: *Jerry's really been clocking up the miles* [= driving long distances] *in the last few weeks; he's had to drive from Manchester to London every day.* ◻ *He reached the final with apparent ease, clocking up some of the highest winning scores in the history of the tournament.* [*same as* **register**, **record**]

close /kləʊz/: **closes**, **closing**, **closed**

○ **close down**

1 A factory or business **closes down,** or it **is closed down**, when it stops operating permanently: *The steel mill is closing down with the loss of 5000 jobs.* **2** (*BrE*) A radio or television station **closes down** when it stops broadcasting for a time, especially during the night: *'We're closing down now until 6 o'clock tomorrow morning. I've just got time to wish all our listeners a peaceful night. Goodnight.'*

○ **close up**

1 You **close up** a building or business premises when you close the doors and windows and lock them so that no-one can get in: *The librarian told us to choose our books quickly because she was just about to close up for the night.* ◻ *The house was closed up and everyone had gone.* **2** You **close** something **up**, or it **closes up**, when you close it, or it closes, completely: *the specially adapted leaf closes up trapping the unfortunate fly inside* ◻ *Father closed up the huge family Bible.* **3** People **close up**, or things **are closed up**, when they move, or are moved, closer together so that there are no spaces between them: *The sergeant-major gave the order to close up ranks.* ◻ *She looked for an escape gap, but the crowd had shifted again and closed up.*

coast /kəʊst/: **coasts**, **coasting**, **coasted**

○ **coast along**

1 You **coast along** in a car or on a bicycle when you continue to move forwards after switching off the engine or stopping pedalling. **2** You **coast along** *eg* in your work when you do it without making much of an effort: *Henry doesn't try all that hard; he seems to prefer to coast along.*

coffee /'kɒfi/: **coffees, coffeeing, coffeed**

○ **coffee up** (*AmE; informal*)
You **coffee up** when you drink a lot of coffee: *Samuel always had to coffee up before he began his farm duties.*

come /kʌm/: **comes, coming, came** /keɪm/
Come is both the present tense and the past participle.

○ **come about**
When you ask how something **came about** you are asking how it happened: *How did it come about that the patient was given the wrong dose of the drug?* □ *The situation came about through a misunderstanding.* [*same as* **happen, occur, come to pass** (*formal*)]

○ **come across**
1 You **come across** something when you discover or encounter it without looking for it or expecting it: *Digging in the garden, he came across a piece of broken pottery that looked as if it might be Roman.* □ *Did you happen to come across my old school tie when you were tidying out the wardrobe?* □ *No matter how experienced you are you're bound to occasionally come across problems that you had never anticipated.* [*same as* **run across, run into**] **2 a** Someone or something **comes across** in a particular way if that is the impression they make on people: *His speech came across well.* □ *Some of the dancing was way below standard but the ballet still came across as one of Macmillan's most monumental pieces.* [*same as* **come over**] **b** Someone **comes across** as a particular type of person when that is how they appear to others: *She comes across as someone who is kind and caring.* **3** (*informal*) Someone **comes across** with *eg* money or information when they hand it over, especially reluctantly and after a delay: *He grumbled a bit but eventually he came*

across with the cash. [*same as* **come up with** (*informal*), **produce**]

○ **come along**
1 Something such as an opportunity **comes along** when it occurs or arrives: *I don't think I'll take that job; I'll wait until something better comes along.* [*same as* **crop up, turn up**] **2** When you ask how someone or something **is coming along** you want to know about their progress; someone or something **is coming along** when they are making good or satisfactory progress: *How's our young trainee coming along?* □ *'How's my father today, doctor?' 'He seems to be coming along fine; he might even be able to go home tomorrow.'* [*same as* **come on**] **3** You say **'come along'** to someone when you want them to hurry up, or do something that they do not want to do: *Come along now, ladies and gentlemen; it's closing time.* □ *Come along, eat up your vegetables like a good boy.*

○ **come around** *see* **come round.**

○ **come away**
1 You **come away** when you leave the place where you are to go elsewhere, or when you move away from something: *He asked me to come away with him for the weekend.* □ *Come away from the water; you might fall in.* **2** Something **comes away** when it separates, often very easily, from the thing it has been attached to: *Plaster had come away from the walls from ceiling to floor.*

○ **come back**
1 You **come back** when you return to a place, often after being away for some time: *All these young men going off to war not knowing if they will ever come back.* **2** Something **comes back** to you when you remember it: *'Oh, what was his name?' Don't worry, it'll come back to you.'* □ *Yes, this was where it happened; it's all coming back to me now.* **3** Something **is coming back** when it is becoming fashionable again, after being out of fashion for a time: *I see those horrible platform shoes are coming back again.*

○ **come by**
1 Someone **comes by** when they move towards you and pass you: *She sat on the wall and watched as the parade came*

by. [compare **go by**] **2** Someone **comes by** when they come to the place where you are to pay you a short visit: *Kirsty came by this morning to show me photographs of her latest work.* **3** You **come by** something when you get or obtain it, often by good luck or chance: *We were lucky to get it; these old farmhouses are hard to come by.* ▫ *Are you able to tell me how you came by all that money?* [*same as* **acquire**, **get hold of**]

○ **come down**
1 Something **comes down** when it moves, drops, falls or collapses downwards: *Some of the plaster on the ceiling has come down.* ▫ *They stood in a miserable huddle while the rain came down in buckets.* [= it was raining very heavily] ▫ *They have climbed out on to the prison roof and are refusing to come down.* **2** Levels or amounts **come down** when they decrease, are reduced, or get lower: *We are pleased to be able to announce that the unemployment rate has come down for the third month running.* [*opposite* **go up**] **3** In a dispute or argument, you **come down** on one side or the other when you decide finally which side you will support: *Unmistakably, though, he has come down on the side of the demonstrators and against the East German leader.*

○ **come down with**
You **come down with** an infectious illness when you catch it: *I suspect Will's coming down with flu.*

○ **come from**
1 a You **come from** a particular place or country when that is where you were born and brought up: *I know you've lived here for a long time but where did you come from originally?* ▫ *He's so weird I'm beginning to think he comes from another planet!* **b** You **come from** a particular family or class of people when you are descended from them; you **come from** a particular background when you were brought up in that way or you have experienced that type of life: *'I'm still as fit as I was twenty years ago. That's because I come from good peasant stock,' he said, with a smile.* ▫ *He doesn't come from a musical background.* [= his parents didn't sing or

play a musical instrument] ▫ *Both men came from humble backgrounds.* **2** One thing **comes from** another when that other thing is its source or origin: *Where's this water coming from?* ▫ *I don't know where that story came from.* ▫ *He could hear the murmur of voices coming from the pigsties.* ▫ *Milk comes from cows and goats.* ▫ *The word used is 'chronos', from which comes our word 'chronology'.* **3** (*informal*) If you say you know where someone **is coming from**, you mean that you understand their intentions or motives: *Now I think I understand where he's coming from; he wants someone to look after him.*

○ **come in**
1 Someone **comes in** when they enter a place: *Hullo, it's nice to see you; do come in.* ▫ *'Come in,' called a lady's voice.* ▫ *Jack and Alison came in, followed by Marcus and Ludens.* ▫ *Caroline didn't even knock; she just came straight in.* **2** Something such as news **comes in** when you receive it: *The president's wife was in bed when news of the assassination attempt came in.* ▫ *Soon after the group was set up referrals were regularly coming in.* ▫ *There's a report coming in of a serious crash on the M5.* **3** Someone **comes in** when they become involved or are included in a scheme, or have a role in it: *It's a family matter, so I don't quite see where someone who is a complete stranger comes in.* **4** You have money **coming in** when you have an income: *With my husband out of work and me only working part-time we don't have much coming in.* **5 a** Something **comes in** when it becomes fashionable: *The so-called 'New Look' came in when rationing was ended after World War II.* [*opposite* **go out**] **b** Something new **comes in** when it comes into force, is introduced, or becomes available: *All new buses will have to be fitted with seat-belts when the law comes in in October.* ▫ *When telephone banking came in customers didn't have to visit their branch so often, so fewer staff were needed.* **c** A political party **comes in** when it wins an election and forms a government: *When the Tories came in, unemployment stood at over a million.*

[*same as* **get in**] **6** You **come in** *eg* first, second or last when that is the position you finish in in a race or competition: *Sebastian Coe won the race, with the other British runners coming in third and sixth.* **7** The tide **comes in** when the level of the sea rises to a higher point on the shore. [*opposite* **go out**]

○ **come in for**

You **come in for** praise, blame or criticism when you are the subject of blame, praise or criticism: *The Labour leader came in for a bit of a battering in the Tory press.*

○ **come in on**

Someone **comes in on** a plan or scheme when they join it or make some contribution to it: *I know a couple of blokes who'll be willing to come in on the venture if they think they'll make a bit of money by it.*

○ **come into**

1 You **come into** money when you inherit it: *He's come into a fortune.* **2** You say that someone '**comes into** their own' when they have the opportunity, in particular circumstances, to display their talents, especially after a long period when their talents weren't recognized or known about: *Out on the hills, the four-wheel drive comes into its own.* **3** Something **comes into** a situation if it is one of the factors or issues involved in it: *Vanity doesn't come into it; I just want to look my best.*

○ **come off**

1 You **come off** a horse, a bicycle or a motorbike when you fall off it: *He hit a patch of oil on the road and came off his bike.* **2** A piece or part of something **comes off** when it becomes separated, or can be separated, from the main part: *The handle's come off the bathroom door.* □ *'The top of this jar won't come off.' 'Let me try. Look, it comes off quite easily.'* **3** A mark or stain **comes off** when it is removed or can be removed: *I hope to goodness this chocolate stain comes off.* **4** A scheme **comes off** if it is successful: *Our plans for early retirement didn't quite come off as we had hoped.* **5** (*informal*) An event **comes off** when it takes place: *There's a five-a-side football tournament coming off next Sa-*

turday. Would you like to go along as a substitute? **6** (*informal*) You **come off** well or badly when you end in a good or bad position after an event: *It was a hard fight for Bruno, but he came off the better of the two.* **7** You **come off** a drug when you stop using it: *He had a very bad time when he was coming off heroin.* □ *Carol's doctor told her she'd to come off the Pill because she has high blood pressure.*

○ **come on**

1 When you ask how something **is coming on** you want to know about its progress; you say that something **is coming on** when it is progressing or growing well: *How's the science project coming on?* □ *'These carrots and beans are growing well.' 'Yes, they're coming on.'* [*same as* **come along**] **2** You say '**come on!**' to someone as a way of encouraging them to hurry up, or to do something, or to be more reasonable: *Come on, you two, we're going to be late!* □ *Oh, come on, Bill! Things aren't that bad.* **3** (*BrE*) Something **comes on** when it begins: *We had just set up our picnic when the rain came on.* **4** A light **comes on** when it lights up or is switched on: *Someone must be in; I saw a light come on in one of the bedrooms.* **5** You have *eg* a cold **coming on** when it is starting: *Whenever I feel a migraine coming on I lie down in a darkened room.* **6** An actor **comes on** when he or she makes their entrance on stage; a player in a sporting team **comes on** when they join their team on the field while a match is being played: *You don't come on again until the last act.* □ *The fans roared their approval when Barnes came on in the second half.* **7** A film, play, television or radio programme **comes on** when it is shown, performed or broadcast: *When's the next series coming on?* □ *There's a new production of 'Fidelio' coming on at the Theatre   Royal.* **8** (*AmE*; *informal*) If you **come on** in a certain way, you make an impression in that way: *The new office manager is coming on too strong.*

○ **come on to** (*informal*)

If you **come on to** someone, you make sexual advances to them: *Beth stopped* *seeing Tom because he always was coming on to her.*

○ **come out**

1 When the sun and moon **come out** they appear in the sky. **2** A fact or the truth **comes out** when it becomes known publicly: *What came out of the statistical analysis was how infrequently people actually use these idioms.* ❑ *The truth came out when she finally admitted that she was the one who had done it.* [*same as* **emerge**] **3** Marks or stains **come out** when they disappear or are removed as a result of washing or some other cleaning process: *I put my jacket into the dry cleaner's hoping that the wine stain would come out.* **4** Colour or dye **comes out** of a fabric if it fades, or is removed, *eg* as a result of washing: *This is a rinse, not a dye; it comes out of your hair in a couple of weeks.* **5** You **come out** in favour of something when you openly declare your support for it: *We were astonished when a life-long pacifist appeared to come out in favour of re-armament.* **6** You **come out** on top when you beat your opponent or opponents: *It looks as if it will be an American golfer who comes out on top.* **7** (*BrE*) Workers **come out**, or **come out** on strike, when they stop working and leave their workplace because of an industrial dispute: *Do you really expect the miners to come out again after last time?* **8** The way something **comes out** is its final result or consequence: *It'll all come out okay in the end, you'll see.* **9** A photograph **comes out** when it is processed successfully and its subject can be clearly seen: *The photograph has come out well.* **10** A new product **comes out** when it becomes available to the public; a book or magazine **comes out** when it is published: *The new model comes out in August.* ❑ *She's got another book of poetry coming out in the autumn.* **11** Flowers or buds **come out** when they appear on a plant: *It's guaranteed to rain as soon as the flowers on the cranesbill come out.*

○ **come over**

1 Something such as a violent emotion **comes over** you when it suddenly affects you: *I'm so sorry for losing my temper; I don't know what came over me.* **2** (*BrE*; *informal*) You **come over** faint or dizzy when you suddenly feel as if you are going to faint. **3** Someone or something **comes over** in a certain way if they make that impression on people: *She came over as very intelligent and enthusiastic at the interview.* [*same as* **come across**]

○ **come round**

1 Someone **comes round** or **around** to an idea when they change their mind and accept it: *I knew she would eventually come round to our way of thinking.* **2** A particular season or event **comes round** or **around** when it occurs at its regular time: *I can hardly believe it's nearly Christmas time again; it seems to come round more and more quickly as I get older.* ❑ *We'll do some decorating when spring comes around.* **3** Someone who is unconscious **comes round** or **around** when they regain consciousness: *I saw his eyelids flicker; I think he's coming round.* [*same as* **come to**]

○ **come to**

1 Someone who is unconscious **comes to** when they regain consciousness: *When he came to he found himself in a hospital bed.* [*same as* **come round**] **2** A bill **comes to** a certain amount when that is the amount arrived at when all the items on it are added together: *Surely you've made a mistake; what we've eaten can't possibly come to £65!* **3** You **come to** something that you have to deal with when you reach it after dealing with a series of others before that thing: *'What about the new computer equipment?' 'I was just coming to that.'* **4** You can also use **come to** to talk about how successful someone or something becomes, or how they turn out in the end: *We'd great plans for expanding the business, but they didn't come to anything.* ❑ *Accepting charity! Surely we haven't come to this?*

○ **come under**

1 Something **comes under** a heading if it is in the section or category that has that heading: *Mystery novels come under 'crime fiction'.* ❑ *Would you say dic-*

tionaries come under 'General Reference' or 'Language'? **2** Something **comes under** a certain body or authority if that body or authority controls it or has responsibility for it: *Public transport comes under the regional rather than the district council.*

○ **come up**

1 Something **is coming up** when it is about to happen or appear: *Coming up after the break, Robert de Niro in his very first television interview.* **2** Something **comes up** when it happens suddenly and unexpectedly: *I'm afraid something's come up and I won't be able to go after all.* **3** A message **comes up** on a computer screen when it appears there: *An error message came up when I tried to load the file.* **4** Something **comes up** in a conversation or discussion when it is mentioned; a question on a particular topic **comes up** in an examination paper when it is included in the paper: *The question of the trade deficit is bound to come up in today's Cabinet meeting.* ❑ *I hope you've done some revision on the life cycles of the butterfly and the frog; one of them always comes up in the biology paper.*

○ **come up with**

You **come up with** an idea when you think of it; you **come up** with a suggestion when you make it: *Who was it that came up with the bright idea to have a barbecue in March?*

cook /kʊk/: **cooks, cooking, cooked**

○ **cook out** (*AmE*)

You **cook out** when you cook and eat food outdoors, especially a barbecue for several people: *We tried to cook out, but the rain ended that.*

▶ *noun* **cookout: cookouts:** *The celebrations ended with a cookout in the park.*

○ **cook up** (*informal*)

1 You **cook up** an excuse when you invent it: *When he was late for school, he cooked up this incredible story about the wheels falling off the bus.* **2** You **cook up** something such as a plan or scheme when you form or create it: *Most of the theories may seem outlandish curiosities, cooked up by teachers of literature who need to seem professional, or powerful.*

cool /kuːl/: **cools, cooling, cooled**

○ **cool down**

Someone **cools down** when they become calm after being angry: *Wait until he's cooled down a bit before you broach the subject again.*

○ **cool off**

You **cool off** when you become less warm, or less angry or excited: *The sun's too hot; I'm going for a swim to cool off.* ❑ *He lost his temper with one of the other kids so we put him in a room by himself to cool off.*

cosy (*AmE* **cozy**) /'kəuzi/: **cosies** (*AmE* **cozies**), **cosying** (*AmE* **cozying**), **cosied**

○ **cozy up to** (*AmE*)

1 You **cozy up to** someone when you lie against them in a comfortable way, as for affection or warmth: *Mum always let us cozy up to her before bedtime.* **2** You **cozy up to** someone when you try hard to win their approval or gain something from them: *If you want that rise, you had better cozy up to the boss.*

cotton /'kɒtən/: **cottons, cottoning, cottoned**

○ **cotton to** (*AmE*; *informal*)

You **cotton to** someone or something when you begin to like them: *I didn't cotton to him at first, but he's okay.*

count /kaunt/: **counts, counting, counted**

○ **count against**

Something such as your age or lack of experience **counts against** you if you are rejected or penalized by others because of it: *You're certainly well enough qualified, but your lack of practical experience may count against you.*

○ **count for**

When you say that something **counts for** nothing or doesn't **count for** anything, you mean that it has no value or importance: *She said her parents liked him tremendously and surely that must count for something in this day and age!*

○ **count on**

1 You can **count on** someone when you can rely on them: *I'm counting on Nancy being there to help.* ❑ *The Times could be counted upon for lengthy discussions of* *cricket and Rugby Union.* **2** You **count on** something when you are so sure that it will happen or be the case that you take account of it in your plans: *'I'm sure your father will lend us the money.' 'I wouldn't count on it if I were you.'* ❑ *We should count on taking at least three days to get there.*

cover /'kʌvə(r)/: **covers, covering, covered**
○ **cover up**
1 You **cover** something **up** when you put something over it to protect or hide it: *She lay down on the sofa and covered herself up with a rug.* ❑ *Make sure the delicate new growth is covered up at night to avoid frost damage.* ❑ *You're nearly naked! For goodness sake, cover yourself up.* **2** You **cover up** something dishonest or embarrassing when you try to hide it and prevent people from finding out about it: *She likes to cover up the truth like she covers up a naked light.* ❑ *Try as they might, they can't cover up the fact that he is a painter of no technical mastery, no intuitive feeling for pictorial space.* [*same as* **hush up**] **3** You **cover up** for someone else who has done something wrong when you try to prevent other people from finding them out: *Cameron covered up for Gillies without thinking it out.*

crack /krak/: **cracks, cracking, cracked**
○ **crack down**
The authorities **crack down** on something when they take firm action to prevent or control it: *The Department of Social Security is cracking down on benefit fraud.*
○ **crack up**
1 Someone **cracks up** when they have a nervous breakdown: *I don't seem to be able to handle stress anymore; I think I'm cracking up.* **2** (*informal*) Someone **cracks up** when they lose control of their emotions and become extremely upset or angry: *Your father'll crack up when he sees the mess you've made!*

crank /kraŋk/: **cranks, cranking, cranked**
○ **crank out** (*AmE*)
You **crank** something **out**, or you **crank** it **out**, when you produce something

quickly, usually in great quantity and often without much thought: *The senator could crank out a speech for any occasion.* ❑ *India is famous for cranking out films.*

crop /krɒp/: **crops, cropping, cropped**
○ **crop up**
Something **crops up** when it occurs or appears, especially unexpectedly: *One or two problems have cropped up since our last meeting.* ❑ *We won't be able to come to your anniversary party; something's cropped up.* [*same as* **come up**]

cross /krɒs/: **crosses, crossing, crossed**
○ **cross off**
You **cross** a word or name **off** a list when you draw a line through it to indicate that it is no longer on the list: *If he doesn't apologise for what he did, I'll be crossing him off my Christmas card list.*

cut /kʌt/: **cuts, cutting, cut**
○ **cut back**
1 You **cut back**, or **cut back** spending, when you spend less money: *We've had to cut back a great deal since my husband lost his job. There are no expensive holidays now and we can't afford a new car.* **2** A plant, tree or shrub **is cut back** when most or all of its branches or stems are cut off: *You can cut it right back to the old wood without damaging it.*
○ **cut down**
1 You **cut** a tree **down** when you cut or saw through its trunk so that it falls to the ground. [*same as* **fell**] **2** You **cut** something **down** when you reduce it in amount: *We'll have to find ways of cutting down our expenses.* ❑ *You'll have to cut down your beer-drinking if you want to lose weight.* ❑ *If we cut the text down we should be able to fit it into 400 pages.*
○ **cut out for** (*informal*)
You **are cut out for** a particular job or activity when you are suited to it: *She found after a couple of months that she wasn't really cut out for life in the country.*
○ **cut up**
1 You **cut** something **up** when you divide it into pieces by cutting: *Thinking she was still at home with the children she absentmindedly cut her husband's meat up for him.* **2** (*informal*) You **are cut up about** something if you

are upset about it: *She was very cut up about failing her driving test.*

dam /dam/: **dams, damming, dammed**

○ **dam up**

1 To **dam up** a river or stream is to build a dam across it, or to block it in some other way, so that the water is held up: *Only a trickle of dirty water ran in the bed of the stream below the point where it had been dammed up by rubbish.* **2** When someone **dams up** strong feelings they make a great effort not to show them, often doing so for a long time and putting themselves under a great deal of mental strain as a result: *She broke down at last, all the grief and frustration that had been dammed up for so long pouring out in helpless sobs.* [*same as* **bottle up**]

dawn /dɔːn/: **dawns, dawning, dawned**

○ **dawn on** *or* **dawn upon**

A fact or the truth **dawns on** or **upon** someone when they suddenly or gradually realize or understand it: *Annabel was nowhere to be seen, and then it dawned on him that she had never intended to come.*

deal /diːl/: **deals, dealing, dealt** /dɛlt/

○ **deal with**

1 You **deal with** situations, problems, people or other matters when you attend to them or take whatever action is necessary or appropriate in the circumstances: *Leave it to me; I'll deal with it.* □ *He's not very good at dealing with crises.* □ *What are the police doing to deal with the ever-increasing problem of drugs in Britain's inner cities?* □ *Have you dealt with those invoices yet, Miss Arnold?* □ *You'll be dealing with the public in this job so you should have a* pleasant manner and a smart appearance. □ *It's proved to be a particularly difficult problem to deal with.* **2** A book, article, speech or film **deals with** a particular subject or topic when that is what it is about: *The last two sections of the novel dealt with her attempt to rediscover herself.* □ *Her books deal mainly with feminist issues.* **3** You **deal with** a particular shop or business organization when you use their services or do business with them: *We've always dealt with Brodies' in the past.*

die /daɪ/: **dies, dying, died**

○ **die away**

1 A sound **dies away** when it becomes fainter and stops, or can no longer be heard; a light or a feeling **dies away** when it becomes weaker and disappears: *The sounds of their singing and laughter died away as they disappeared into the distance.* □ *The look of almost insane happiness in his eyes died away to be replaced by a blank stare.* **2** The wind **dies away** when it blows with less and less strength and finally disappears: *As they approached the equator the light breeze that had carried them along died away and they were becalmed.*

○ **die down**

Something **dies down** when it decreases in level or intensity: *When the fever eventually dies down he is likely to feel very tired and weak for a while.* □ *By the time we get to Jerez hopefully most of the fuss will have died down.*

○ **die off**

People or other living things **die off** when they all die: *It's the time of year when wasps are beginning to die off.* □ *People who could have best helped him in his inquiries had died off one by one.*

○ **die out**

Something **dies out** when it gets rarer and rarer and finally disappears; families or races of people **die out** when there are none left alive: *The craft of thatching had died out locally.* □ *Families died out and were replaced with others over the course of the century.*

dish /dɪʃ/: **dishes, dishing, dished**

○ **dish out** (*informal*)

1 You **dish out** something when you give

some of it to each of a number of people, especially in generous amounts: *This government has been dishing out honours like so many sweets to all their supporters.* [*compare* **give out**, **share out**] **2** You **dish** something unpleasant **out** to others when you give it to them: *He doesn't like being criticised but he's quite happy to dish it out.* [= to criticize others]

divide /dɪˈvaɪd/: **divides**, **dividing**, **divided**

○ **divide up**

1 You **divide up** something, or you **divide** it **up**, when you share it out between or among a number of people: *The land is to be divided up between his three sons.* **2** You **divide** something **up** when you cut or separate it into a number of parts: *According to the terms of the will, the estate cannot be divided up and everything will go to the eldest son.*

do /duː/: **does** /dʌz/, **doing**, **did** /dɪd/, **done** /dʌn/

○ **do about**

You **do** something **about** some problem or difficulty when you deal with it, attend to it, or solve it: *Are you going to do something about this mess?* □ *Is something going to be done about the litter in the streets?* □ *It really is a terrible problem and I don't know what can be done about it.*

○ **do over** (*especially AmE*)

You **do** something **over** when you do it again, usually because you have done it wrong the first time: *He'll have to do it over.* [*same as* **redo**]

○ **do up**

1 You **do up** something such as a piece of clothing, or you **do** it **up**, when you fasten it: *He was seven before he learned how to do up his laces.* [*opposite* **undo**] **2** You **do up** something in a parcel or package when you wrap it and tie it with ribbon or string: *The present was done up in gold paper with a big pink bow.* **3** A girl or woman **does** her hair **up** in a particular style when she ties it up using such things as hairpins and ribbons: *She always does her little daughter's hair up in a ponytail.* **4** You **do up** a building when you repair or decorate it: *She buys old properties and does*

them up for letting. □ *We'll need at least ten thousand pounds to do up the kitchen and bathroom.* [*same as* **renovate**]

○ **do with**

1 a You talk about one thing having something **to do with** another when you are discussing how or if they are related or connected to each other: *I don't see what it's got to do with him; it's our business, not his.* □ *How can I interfere? It doesn't have anything to do with me.* **b** Something is **to do with** something else when it concerns or involves that other thing: *I'm not quite sure what his exact job is but I know it's something to do with the security services.* **2** In questions and statements, you talk about what someone **did with** something when you are wondering where it is or where they've put it: *I don't know what I did with yesterday's newspaper. I may have thrown it away.* □ *What have you done with my black pen?* **3** You ask what is to be **done with** someone or something when you are wondering what action should be taken concerning them: *He just won't do what he is told. I don't know what's to be done with him.* □ *'What shall we do with these empty wine bottles?' 'Put them in a box and take them to the bottle bank for recycling.'* **4** When people say they could **do with** something they mean that they need or want it: *We could do with some new curtains in this room.* □ *I could do with a nice cold beer.* **5** You talk about what someone **does with** themselves when you are asking about or discussing what they spend their time doing: *He doesn't know what to do with himself now that he's retired.* □ *What did you do with yourselves when you were cut off from civilization for all those months?*

○ **do without**

You **do without** something that you want or need, or that you would normally have, when you manage or survive though you don't or can't have it: *We can't afford to buy a car so we'll just have to do without until we've saved enough to buy one.* [*same as* **go without**, **forego** (*formal*)]

dope /doʊp/: dopes, doping, doped

○ **dope off** (*AmE*; *informal*)

1 You **dope off** when you fall asleep: *Andy always doped off in the office during the lunch hour.* **2** You **dope off** when you neglect your work or responsibilities: *We don't want anyone doping off during this project.*

double /'dʌbəl/: doubles, doubling, doubled

○ **double back**

1 You **double back** when you turn and go back the way you came: *We came to a set of locked gates and had to double back and find another route.* **2** Something **is doubled back** on itself when it is bent so that it is formed into two connected lengths that are close to and parallel with each other: *The bottom sheet was doubled back on itself so that the unfortunate victim usually tore it when trying to force his feet towards the bottom of the bed.*

doze /doʊz/: dozes, dozing, dozed

○ **doze off**

You **doze off** when you fall into a light sleep, often when you did not intend to: *I didn't hear you come in; I must have dozed off.* [*same as* **drop off**, **nod off**]

drag /dræg/: drags, dragging, dragged

○ **drag out**

1 You **drag** information **out** of someone who is unwilling to give it when you persuade them, with a great deal of difficulty, to tell you it: *Any information about his progress at school has to be dragged out of him.* **2** You **drag** something **out** when you make it go on for longer than is necessary or reasonable: *The government has a vested interest in dragging the inquiry out for as long as possible.* [*same as* **draw out**, **spin out**, **stretch out**, **prolong**]

○ **drag up**

When someone **drags up** some unpleasant event or story from the past that everyone had forgotten about they remind people unnecessarily about it: *Why do you go on dragging up the fact that he went bankrupt ten years ago?* [*same as* **bring up**, **dredge up**]

draw /drɔː/: draws, drawing, drew /druː/, drawn /drɔːn/

○ **draw back**

1 You **draw back** from something unpleasant or frightening when you move back to get away from it: *When he moved towards her she drew back with a look of terror.* **2** You **draw back** from something that involves you making a definite decision or commitment when you show that you are unwilling to proceed: *Faced with two such diametrically-opposed alternatives, in the end Klein drew back from agreeing to either one.*

○ **draw up**

1 A vehicle **draws up** somewhere when it comes to a stop there: *A huge black limousine drew up outside the hotel, the doors flew open, and several secret service men jumped out.* [*same as* **pull up**] **2** You **draw up** a plan, schedule or document when you prepare it and produce it in a written form, often so that it can be shown to someone for their approval: *The enlightened bureaucrats responsible for drawing up the legislation may not have achieved everything they were striving for.* ❑ *I'm going to get my lawyer to draw me up a new will.* [*same as* **draft**] **3** You **draw up** a chair when you pull it nearer to someone or something so that you can sit close to them. **4** You **draw** yourself **up**, or you **draw** yourself **up** to your full height, when you stand upright, as tall and straight as you can.

dream /driːm/: dreams, dreaming, dreamt /drɛmt/

○ **dream up**

Someone **dreams up** something such as a scheme or plan when they invent it in their mind: *I'd like to meet the person who dreamed up this ridiculous scheme so that I could tell them what I thought of it.*

dress /drɛs/: dresses, dressing, dressed

○ **dress up**

1 People **dress up** when they put on smart clothes: *Why are you getting all dressed up? It's only an informal lunch.* **2** People **dress up** when they put on fancy dress; you **dress up** as someone or something when you put on a special costume so that you look like that person or thing: *Every Christmas he dressed up as Santa Claus.* **3** You **dress** something **up** when you add things to it to make it more impressive or attractive; you **dress** something unpleasant **up** when you try to make it seem more acceptable: *This very basic dish can be dressed up with some homemade hollandaise sauce and seasonal vegetables.* ◻ *The plain fact is they are giving me the sack, however they try to dress it up.*

drive /draɪv/: **drives, driving, drove** /drəʊv/, **driven** /ˈdrɪvən/

○ **drive at**
When you want to know what someone **is driving at** you want to understand what it is they are trying to say because they haven't made it very clear: *Do you know what he was driving at when he said he suspected some people were being disloyal?*

drop /drɒp/: **drops, dropping, dropped**

○ **drop back**
You **drop back** when you begin to move more slowly than others so that they get ahead of you: *He seemed to pull a muscle and dropped back so that he was trailing the rest of the field.*

○ **drop off**
1 You **drop off** when you fall asleep: *He had already dropped off to sleep when she began peeling the clothes from his back.* [*same as* **nod off** (*informal*)] **2** An amount or rate **drops off** when it decreases: *The latest statistics show that sales in the high street dropped off in January though they were forecast to rise.* ◻ *As you approach Bude the crowds increase, but one or two miles from the main centre the numbers quickly drop off.* **3** You **drop** a passenger in your vehicle **off** when you stop to let them get out somewhere, and then continue your journey; you **drop** something you have been carrying with you **off** when you leave it somewhere and continue on your journey: *My husband dropped me off at the station.*

○ **drop out**
1 You **drop out** of a competition, or some planned activity, when you take no further part in it: *He had to drop out*

after the first round because he sprained his wrist. **2** Students **drop out** of school or university when they leave it without finishing their course of study: *Some students are having to drop out because of lack of money.*

drown /draʊn/: **drowns, drowning, drowned**

○ **drown out**
A noise **drowns out** other sounds or people's voices when it is so loud that they cannot be heard because of it: *He turned up the music to drown out the sound of next-door's dog barking.*

duke /djuːk/: **dukes, duking, duked**

○ **duke out** (*AmE*; *informal*)
Someone is **duked out** when they are made unconscious by being hit on the head: *The British boxer duked out the champion in the fifth round.* [*same as* **knockout**]

dumb /dʌm/: **dumbs, dumbing, dumbed**

○ **dumb down** (*informal*)
Something is **dumbed down** when it is made simpler, especially for people who can not understand the original thing: *Television has dumbed down many of its programmes in order to attract more viewers.*

dummy /ˈdʌmi/: **dummies, dumming, dummed**

○ **dummy up** (*AmE*; *informal*)
You **dummy up** when you refuse to talk: *I tried to make her confess, but all she did was dummy up.*

dust /dʌst/: **dusts, dusting, dusted**

○ **dust off** (*AmE*; *informal*)
1 You **dust** someone **off** when you give them a physical beating: *If a member of the mob criticized Capon, somebody would dust him off.* **2** In baseball, a pitcher **dusts** a batter **off** by throwing the ball close to his body: *Williams liked to keep the batters uneasy by dusting them off.*

E e

ease /iːz/: **eases, easing, eased**

○ **ease off**

Something **eases off** when it becomes less intense or severe: *The rain was beginning to ease off so we packed up the car.* ▫ *The tension between them had not eased off a jot.* [compare **die down**, **let up**]

○ **ease out** (*AmE*)

An employee is **eased out**, or an employer **eases** them **out**, when they are convinced, in a nice way, to leave the company: *A big redundancy payment helped ease out the two oldest editors.*

○ **ease up**

You **ease up** when you work less hard or use less effort or energy; a situation **eases up** when it becomes less busy or tiring: *When managers say ease up a little, it's time to listen.* ▫ *There's a crazy period for about four weeks, then things ease up again.* [same as **slow down**]

edge /ɛdʒ/: **edges, edging, edged**

○ **edge out** (*AmE*)

One competitor or team **edges out** an opponent when they defeat them by a small margin or just as the game ends: *It was a close golf match, with Williams edging out Black on the 18th hole.*

egg /ɛg/: **eggs, egging, egged**

○ **egg on**

Someone **eggs** you **on** when they encourage you to do something risky, foolish or wrong: *He was basically a good lad who'd been egged on by so-called friends.* [opposite **talk out of**, **hold back**, **put off**; compare **urge on**]

end /ɛnd/: **ends, ending, ended**

○ **end up**

You **end up** in a particular place or doing a particular thing when you find yourself in that place or doing that thing, especially when it was not your intention: *We took the first train that came in, and ended up in Florence.* ▫ *The car wouldn't start, so I ended up having to walk.* [same as **wind up** (informal, **finish up**, **land up** (informal)]

even /ˈiːvən/: **evens, evening, evened**

○ **even out**

Things **even out**, or **are evened out**, when they become, or are made, more level or equal: *The path climbed steeply and then evened out towards the house.* ▫ *A rationing system was introduced to even the grain supply out over the whole year.*

○ **even up**

Things **even up** or **are evened up** when they become, or are made, more equal: *That's two points to Ian and Neil, which evens the scores up a bit.*

face /feɪs/: **faces, facing, faced**

○ **face up to**

You **face up to** something difficult or unpleasant when you are brave and honest enough to accept it and deal with it: *We've got to face up to reality.* ▫ *She had to face up to the fact that she was too old to be offered parts as the romantic lead.* [same as **come to terms with**]

○ **face with**

1 You **face** the outer surface of something **with** a different material when you cover it with a layer of that material: *a brick building faced with stone.* **2** You **are faced with** something unpleasant when you are confronted with it and cannot avoid looking at it or dealing with it: *He was faced with such overwhelming opposition that he was forced to back down.*

fall /fɔːl/: **falls, falling, fell** /fɛl/, **fallen** /ˈfɔːlən/

○ **fall back**

1 You **fall back** when you retreat or move back, usually because someone is attacking you or moving towards you in a threatening way: *Our troops had to fall back in the face of a determined assault by the enemy.* ▫ *The rioters fell back as the mounted policemen advanced.* [*same as* **draw back, retreat, retire** (*formal*)] **2** You **fall back** when you move backwards away from someone or something that you find frightening or horrifying: *Auguste fell back in horror when he saw what was in the box.* [*same as* **draw back, recoil**]

○ **fall behind**

1 You **fall behind** when you progress more slowly than other people and they get ahead of you: *He's fallen behind the rest the class and needs extra tuition to catch up.* ▫ *We mustn't let Britain fall behind in technology.* [*same as* **lag behind**] **2** You **fall behind** with payments that ought to be made at regular intervals when you fail to pay one or more of them when they become due; you **fall behind with** *eg* work that ought to be completed by a certain time when you do not complete it on time: *They've fallen behind with their mortgage payments and may have to sell their house.* ▫ *He's always falling behind with his paperwork.*

○ **fall for**

1 You **fall for** someone when you fall in love with them: *She always seems to fall for the most unsuitable men.* **2** You **fall for** something such a lie when you are deceived by it or believe that it is true: *You didn't fall for that old story, did you?* ▫ *He told me he was an expert in antiques and, like a fool, I fell for it.*

○ **fall through**

A plan **falls through** when it fails or cannot be achieved: *My plans for a winter break have fallen through.*

fan /fan/: **fans, fanning, fanned**

○ **fan out**

People or things **fan out** when they move forwards and outwards from the same starting point: *The six planes began the manoeuvre by flying in parallel formation, fanning out as they passed over the airfield.* ▫ *The villagers fanned out across the moor looking in every nook and cranny for the missing child.*

feel /fiːl/: **feels, feeling, felt** /fɛlt/

○ **feel up to**

You **feel up to** something when you feel able to do it or cope with it: *'Let's go for a long walk.' No, I'm sorry, I just don't feel up to it at the moment.'* ▫ *'If you feel up to it,' Noreen said at breakfast, 'we'll take you down to the Arts Centre in the van.'*

fight /faɪt/: **fights, fighting, fought** /fɔːt/

○ **fight back**

1 You **fight back** against someone or something who has attacked you when you defend yourself and attack them in turn: *For a while we thought the cancer was going to kill him, but he seems to be fighting back now.* ▫ *If you don't fight back he'll just go on bullying you.* [*same as* **retaliate**; *opposite* **give way to, submit**] **2** You **fight back** the impulse or desire to do something when you make a great effort to control yourself and stop yourself doing it: *As the train drew out of the station, she stood on the platform fighting back her tears.*

figure /ˈfɪɡə(r)/ *or* /ˈfɪɡjə(r)/: **figures, figuring, figured**

○ **figure on** (*especially AmE; informal*)

1 You **figure on** doing something when that is what you intend to do: *I figure on finishing the book by the end of the year.* **2** You **figure on** something happening when you make plans that depend on it happening: *I hadn't figured on Luther turning up, so there wasn't enough room for us all in the van.*

○ **figure out** (*informal*)

1 You **figure** the cost of something **out** when you calculate it: *You'll have to figure out the compound interest to find the overall cost of the loan.* [*same as* **work out**] **2** You **figure out** something that you do not understand or do not know how to do, when you come to understand it or find out how to do it by thinking hard about it: *The engine came in so many bits it was impossible to figure out which went where.* ▫ *I can't figure out why she left home so suddenly.* [*same as* **work out**]

fill /fɪl/: **fills, filling, filled**

○ **fill in**

1 You **fill** a hole or gap **in** when you put in material to make it level with the surrounding surface, or you add something that will make it complete: *workmen filling in the holes in the road* ▫ *I had to fill in the gaps in the conversation by talking about the weather.* **2** (*BrE*) You **fill in** a form, or you **fill** it **in**, when you write information in the spaces as required: *Take this form and fill in your name and age at the top.* ▫ *Fill this application form in and return it to the club secretary.* [*same as* **fill out, fill up**] **3** You **fill in** for someone when you do their job temporarily while they are ill or absent from work: *I'm going into hospital; could you fill in for me for a few days?* [*same as* **stand in, deputize**] **4** (*BrE*) You **fill in** time when you do something to occupy or pass the time while waiting for something to happen: *We filled in the four hours between flights by taking a bus into town and exploring.* **5** You **fill** someone **in** on something when you inform them fully about it: *Could you fill me in on the latest developments?* ▫ *When you've been filled in on all the details we can have a meeting to discuss the project.*

○ **fill out**

1 You **fill out** a form when you write information in the spaces as required: *He was getting tired of filling out application forms.* [*same as* **fill in, fill up**] **2** A thin person **fills out** when they gain weight: *After a few weeks of the healthy sea air and good food, her cheeks had filled out and acquired a healthy colour.*

○ **fill up**

1 a You **fill up** a container when you put enough of something into it to make it full: *They filled up their water bottles at a little stream.* ▫ *He kept filling up our glasses and we got quite drunk.* **b** You **fill up** your motor vehicle when you fill its petrol tank with petrol: *I'm just going down to the garage to fill the car up.* **2** A place **fills up** with something when it becomes full of it: *The shop filled up with customers as soon as the doors opened.* ▫ *He peeped through the curtain and saw that the theatre*

was filling up nicely. **3** (*BrE*) You **fill up** a form when you write information in the spaces as required: *You have to fill up so many forms when you take your car abroad.* [*same as* **fill in, fill out**]

find /faɪnd/: **finds, finding, found** /faʊnd/

○ **find out**

1 You **find out** something you did not know, or you **find** it **out**, when you discover it or learn about it, by chance or through investigation: *I found out that she had left home three days earlier.* ▫ *Find something out about Columbus before tomorrow's lesson.* ▫ *Children enjoy finding out how things work.* **2** You **find** someone **out** when you discover that they have done something wrong or dishonest: *Though he had been very careful to cover his tracks, his wife found out that he was having an affair.* ▫ *Aren't you afraid of being found out?* ▫ *Be sure your sins will find you out.*

finish /ˈfɪnɪʃ/: **finishes, finishing, finished**

○ **finish off**

1 You **finish off** a task when you do everything that needs to be done to complete it: *I'm just finishing off this essay.* [*same as* **complete**] **2** You **finish off** food or drink when you eat or drink the last bit of it: *Finish off your pudding quickly.* **3** (*informal*) To **finish** someone **off** is to kill or destroy them, or defeat them completely: *A sudden thrust of the cavalry officer's sword finished him off.*

○ **finish up**

1 You **finish up** somewhere, or in some situation, if that is what happens to you in the end: *He'll finish up in jail.* ▫ *He started in the company as a tea boy and finished up as managing director.* [*same as* **end up**] **2** You **finish up** with something when that is what you are left with at the end of a period of time: *If you don't stop smoking you're going to finish up with lung cancer or heart disease.*

fink /fɪŋk/: **finks, finking, finked**

○ **fink on** (*AmE*; *informal*)

You **fink on** someone when you inform on them: *My brother was always finking on me to my parents.*

○ **fink out** (*AmE*; *informal*)
Someone who **finks out** of something, such as a project, withdraws from it: *We had the whole trip planned, and then Jim finked out.*

fish /fɪʃ/: **fishes, fishing, fished**
○ **fish out** (*informal*)
You **fish** something **out** when you pull it out of the place or container it is in: *He fell off the pier into the sea and we had to use a boathook to fish him out.* ◻ *He put his hand in his coat pocket and fished out a crumbled card with his name and address printed on it.* [*same as* **pull out**]

fit /fɪt/: **fits, fitting, fitted**
In American English, **fit** is sometimes used as the past tense and past participle.
○ **fit in** *or* **fit into**
1 You **fit** something **in** somewhere when you manage to find or make enough room or space for it; something **fits into** a space when the space is large enough for you to put it there: *I don't think we could fit all four chairs in the boot.* ◻ *There's a bit of room on the back seat; I'm sure a small person could fit in.* ◻ *Would the bookcase fit into that space under the window?* ◻ *Charlie could only just fit his swollen toes into the leather boots.* [*same as* **get in, get into, go in, go into**] **2** Someone who doesn't **fit in** is different from others in a particular group or society, and doesn't really belong to it; you might also say that such a person doesn't **fit into** the group or society: *Thomas was a loner who never really tried to fit in.* ◻ *She knew her mother would never fit into the world of the idle rich.* [*same as* **blend in, belong, conform**; *compare* **stand out, stick out**] **3** You **fit** someone or something **in**, or **fit** them **into** your schedule, when you find time to deal with them: *I won't have the time to fit in everything I want to do.* ◻ *Could we fit a meeting in some time this afternoon?* ◻ *I'll see if the doctor can fit you in tomorrow morning.* **4** You might use **fit in** or **fit into** when you're talking about someone's role, function or status, usually in relation to others: *I don't really see where the assistant manager fits in.* ◻ *Would this*

kind of letter fit into the category of 'customer complaints'?

fix /fɪks/: **fixes, fixing, fixed**
○ **fix over** (*AmE*)
You **fix** something **over** when you redo or redecorate it: *I really want to fix this room over.* ◻ *We saved for a year so we could fix over the living room.*
○ **fix up**
1 You **fix** something **up** when you make firm plans or arrangements for it to happen: *We've managed to fix up a two-week holiday at the end of September.* ◻ *I've fixed up for her to go and see Dr Graham.* ◻ *The secretary has the job of fixing up temporary accommodation for visitors.* ◻ *John's asked me to fix him up a three-o'clock meeting with the directors.* [*same as* **arrange**] **2** (*informal*) You **fix** someone **up** with something when you provide them with it: *I can easily fix you up with a bed for the night.* ◻ *She's offered to put me up in her flat, till I get myself fixed up.* ◻ *If you can fix yourself up with a pair of boots, there's a place for you in the team.* ◻ *It was Jed who got me fixed up with a new one.* **3** (*informal*) You **fix** something **up** when you make or build it quickly, using whatever materials are available: *They managed to fix up a rough shelter with sheets of plywood and some old tarpaulins.* ◻ *We've fixed her up a sandpit in the garden, from a couple of sawn-off tea-chests knocked together.* [*same as* **rig up** (*informal*), **knock up** (*informal*), **improvise**] **4** (*informal*) You **fix** something **up** when you carry out the repairs or improvements necessary to make it fit to use: *It wouldn't cost much to fix up the flat.* [*same as* **do up** (*informal*), **refurbish** (*formal*), **renovate** (*formal*)]

flip /flɪp/: **flips, flipping, flipped**
○ **flip out** (*AmE*; *informal*)
When somebody **flips out**, they lose control of their emotions, usually because they are angry or excited: *When he called me a nigger, I just flipped out.* ◻ *I flipped out when I won the race.*

flub /flʌb/: **flubs, flubbing, flubbed**
○ **flub up** (*AmE*; *informal*)
You **flub up**, or **flub** something **up**, when you do it badly, without skill or care-

lessly: *I always seem to flub up my chances.* □ *The colonel always flubs it up at presentations.*

► *noun* **flub-up: flub-ups:** *Let's not make a flub-up of this important job.*

follow /'fɒloʊ/: **follows, following, followed**

○ **follow up**
1 You **follow up** what little information you have when you try to find out more: *Information from members of the public has given us some fresh leads, and we're following them up at the moment.* □ *Before I assign my best journalist to the story, I have to be sure it's worth following up.* [*same as* **pursue**; *compare* **look into, check out**] **2** You **follow up** something you have done when you do something else that develops it further or adds to it: *The success of the original dictionary was followed up by a series of workbooks and other spin-offs.* □ *We're proud of our achievements in the league and we're hoping to follow them up with good performances in the cup competitions.*

fool /fuːl/: **fools, fooling, fooled**

○ **fool about** (*BrE*) *or* **fool around**
You **fool about** or **fool around** when you behave in a deliberately silly way, sometimes to amuse people: *The boys went down to the river to swim and fool about.* □ *There were one or two serious students, but most of them fooled around all day until it was time to go to the pub.*

freshen /'freʃən/: **freshens, freshening, freshened**

○ **freshen up**
You **freshen up** when you get washed and make yourself neat, perhaps by changing your clothes: *They'll probably want to freshen up before dinner.* □ *I'll take some time to freshen myself up a bit.*

frown /fraʊn/: **frowns, frowning, frowned**

○ **frown on** *or* **frown upon**
Something **is frowned on** or **frowned upon** if people disapprove of it: *Increasingly, smoking is frowned on in public buildings.* □ *The company makes a great show of frowning upon any hint of sexist behaviour.*

gas /gas/: **gases, gassing, gassed**

○ **gas up** (*AmE*)
You **gas** a vehicle **up** when you fill it full of petrol; a vehicle **is gassed up** when it is full of petrol: *We gassed the car up the evening before we left.* □ *The rental truck should have been gassed up when they returned it.*

get /gɛt/: **gets, getting, got** /gɒt/
In British English the past tense and past participle of **get** is **got**. In American English **gotten** is often used as the past participle.

○ **get about** *or* **get around** (*informal*)
1 You **get about** or **get around** if you move around or travel to different places: *'She was in Cardiff on Monday, Birmingham on Tuesday and Edinburgh on Wednesday.' 'Yes, she gets about, doesn't she.'* □ *He's lost the use of his legs and doesn't get about much any more.* **2** If you can **get about** or **get around** you are able to walk or move about: *He's broken his ankle but he can still get about on crutches.* **3** News or information **gets about** or **gets around** as more and more people are told about it: *Keep this information to yourself; I wouldn't want it to get about.*

○ **get across**
1 You **get across** an obstacle when you manage to cross it: *How are we going to get across the river when there's no bridge and we don't have a boat?* [*same as* **get over**] **2** You **get** an idea, feeling or message **across** when you succeed in making other people understand it: *It's up to us to get across the message that, once again, the government has got it wrong.* [*same as* **get over**, **communicate**]

○ **get along** (*informal*)

One person **gets along** with another, or two people **get along**, when they have a friendly relationship, or they live or work well together: *I'm so glad you brought Mary; we've been getting along like a house on fire.* [= very well] ▫ *Somehow I never seemed to be able to get along with my parents-in-law.* [*see also* **get on**]

○ **get around**

1 You **get around** or **get round** to doing something when you finally do it, especially after a difficulty or delay: *Steven eventually got round to painting the garden gate.* **2** News or information **gets around** or **gets round** when more and more people hear about it: *It's a mystery to me how these rumours get around.* [*see also* **get about**] **3 a** You **get around** or **get round** a problem or difficulty when you find a way of avoiding it rather than dealing with it directly: *We'll just have to face it; I can't see any way of getting around it.* **b** You **get around** or **get round** someone when you manage to persuade them to do something, or to allow you to do something: *Don't worry about Mum; I can easily get around her.*

○ **get at** (*informal*)

1 When you ask or wonder what someone **is getting at** you want them to explain more clearly what they are suggesting or what they mean: *Do you know what he was getting at when he said there was trouble on the horizon?* **2** You **get at** someone when you criticize or find fault with them: *Do you think he was getting at me when he said he thought the system could be improved? ▫ I'm fed up with that teacher; she's always getting at me.* [*same as* **pick on**]

○ **get away**

1 You **get away** when you escape: *The police managed to catch three of the robbers but the leader of the gang got away. ▫ fishermen standing in the pub talking about the one that got away.* [= the big fish that they say they caught but which managed to escape] **2** You **get away** when you are able to leave, especially having been prevented from doing so earlier: *I'll have to get away by 11 o'clock if I'm to catch the last train.*

3 You **get away** when you are able to go away from your home or work on a holiday: *We're hoping to get away for a couple of weeks in the summer.*

○ **get away with**

1 You **get away with** something when you escape taking that thing with you: *The robbers had got away with nearly £100,000 worth of diamonds.* **2 a** Someone who **gets away with** something illegal or dishonest manages to avoid being caught or punished for it: *He's apparently been getting away with tax fraud for years. ▫ I didn't do my emergency stop properly, but I got away with it and passed my driving test.* **b** You **get away with** something that others would normally find unacceptable when you manage to do it without being criticized or found out: *I sang the first verse twice, but no-one seems to have noticed so I think I got away with it.*

○ **get back**

1 You **get back** when you return to your home or the place where you started out from: *Our train was late and we didn't get back until after midnight. ▫ This has been rather a long lunch; we better be getting back to the office. ▫ He got back just in time to dress for dinner.* **2** You **get** someone or something **back** when you return them to the place that they came from, or you get them to come back to a place: *I don't think we'll be able to get his dislocated shoulder back into its socket without giving him an anaesthetic. ▫ Do you think we should get him back for a second interview?* **3** You tell someone to **get back** when you order them to move to a position further back or away from you: *'Get back! I've got a gun, and I'll use it if you come any closer!'* **4** You **get back** something that belongs to you when it is returned to you; you **get** something that you have lost **back** when it returns or is returned: *I lent him my Bon Jovi tapes months ago and I don't think I'm ever going to get them back. ▫ After looking so pale and ill for so long, she's now got her normal healthy glow back.* [*same as* **recover**, **regain**]

○ **get behind**

1 a You **get behind** with *eg* work when you do not keep up to date with it: *This delay was due to one or other of the works departments getting behind with the manufacture.* **b** You **get behind** *eg* with your rent or with loan repayments when you do not pay them at the times they are due: *Because the sums involved were so much larger, getting behind with mortgage payments became a much more serious debt trap than bills at retailers.* [*same as* **fall behind**] **2** You **get behind** someone when you give them your support and encouragement: *The supporters should get behind their team instead of continually criticizing them.*

○ **get down**
1 You **get down** from a high position, or from a position above the ground, when you move down to a lower position, or on to the ground; you **get down** on your knees when you kneel: *The cat's climbed to the top of the tree and can't get down again.* [*same as* **descend**] **2** You **get** something **down** when you record it by writing it on paper, especially quickly: *The professor talks so quickly those of us who can't do shorthand find it difficult to get everything down.* ▫ *As soon as things quietened down he'd get as much down on paper as possible.* **3** (*informal*) Something **gets** you **down** when it makes you sad or depressed: *His constant criticisms are beginning to get me down.* ▫ *It was the fourth time in two weeks she had slept late, and it was beginning to get her down.*

○ **get in**
1 A politician or political party **gets in** when they are elected to power: *Do you think the Tories will get in again at the next election?* **2** You **get** something **in** when you find the time or opportunity for it: *I'd like to get another hour's work in before dinner.* ▫ *It was difficult to get a comment in, everyone was talking so furiously.* **3** You **get** someone **in** to do work of some kind for you when you get them to come to your home or place of work to do it: *'Will you be putting the new bathroom in yourselves?' 'No, we're getting a local firm of plumbers in.'* **4** A train or bus **gets in** when it arrives at its destination: *The last train gets in at*

midnight.

○ **get off**
1 If someone tells you to **get off** something they are telling you to move off or away from it: *Get off my land immediately or I'll have you prosecuted.* ▫ *'Ouch! Get off! You're standing on my toe.'* ▫ *Get your dirty feet off my clean floor!* **2** You **get** something **off** when you remove it: *I'll never get this stain off the carpet.* ▫ *Isn't there some sort of special solution that gets graffitti off?* **3 a** You **get off** a bus, train or plane when you get out of it: *Stop the bus! I want to get off!* ▫ *Have my seat. I'm getting off at the next station.* [*same as* **alight**] **b** You **get off** a bicycle, motorbike or horse when you dismount from it: *He had to get off his bike and push it up the hill.* **4 a** You **get off** when you leave *eg* to go on a journey: *We've packed all our camping equipment and are hoping to get off as soon as it's light.* ▫ *Get yourself off to school now; it's nearly half past eight.* **b** You **get** a letter or message **off** when you send it by post, e-mail, fax or radio: *Can you make sure this letter gets off before the last post tonight?* **5** You **get off**, or someone **gets** you **off**, when you are given little or no punishment for something wrong, illegal or dishonest that you have done: *I'd say you got off rather lightly.* ▫ *The lawyers got him off with a small fine.*

○ **get on**
1 People **get on**, or one person **gets on** with another, when they have a friendly relationship and live or work together harmoniously: *I don't think my son and his wife have been getting on very well recently.* ▫ *She doesn't really get on with her parents.* [*same as* **get along**] **2** You **get on** when you make progress in your career: *It seems that, in order to get on, you have to socialize with the bosses.* [*same as* **get ahead**] **3** (*informal*) When you say that someone **is getting on**, you mean they are becoming old: *I don't think Dad will be able to come on a walking holiday with us; he's getting on a bit, you know.* **4** (*informal*) When you ask or wonder how someone **is getting on**, you want to know generally what they are doing, or what progress they are mak-

ing; someone **is getting on** well when they are making good progress: *'How's David getting on in his new job?' 'He seems to be getting on fine.'* **5** You **get on** a bus or train when you board it at the start of a journey: *Several people got on at the next stop.* ▫ *Hurry up and get on the bus.* [*same as* **board**; *opposite* **get off**, **alight**] **6** You **get** clothes **on** when you put them on or dress: *She was trying to get her new jeans on.*

○ **get on with**
1 You **get on with** someone when you have a good or friendly relationship with them: *She wants to leave home because she doesn't get on with her stepmother.* **2** You **get on with** something when you begin to do it, or you carry on doing it: *I had better get on with this work if I want to finish it today.* ▫ *Have you got enough work to be getting on with?*

○ **get out**
1 When you tell someone to **get out** you are telling them to leave: *Go on, get out; I don't want you here.* ▫ *Get out of my sight, you disgusting child!* **2** A secret **gets out** when it becomes known publicly: *If this gets out, we'll be in real trouble.* **3** Someone or something **gets out** of the place where they have been kept prisoner, or contained, when they escape or can leave and go outside: *When he eventually gets out, he'll find it pretty difficult to adjust to life outside prison.* ▫ *Someone left the gate open and the dog got out.* **4** You **get out** when you spend time outside your home: *She's a bit frail now and doesn't get out much any more.*

○ **get out of**
You **get out of** something, or **get out of** doing it, when you manage to avoid doing it: *I don't want to go to their stupid dinner party but how on earth am I going to get out of it?* [*same as* **avoid**]

○ **get over**
1 You **get over** an obstacle when you manage to move over it to the other side: *I don't think that little pony will get over that big jump.* **2** You **get over** something such as an illness, shock or disappointment when you recover from it: *She's never really got over the death of her husband.* **3** You **get over** a problem

or a difficulty when you deal with it successfully: *We'll be able to relax a little once we've got over the busy period in the summer.* **4** You **get** a message **over** when you make other people understand it: *a concerted effort by the Labour Party to get the message over to the electorate that they aren't the 'tax and spend' party any longer.* [*same as* **get across**, **communicate**]

○ **get round** *see* **get about**.

○ **get through**
1 You **get through** work or a task when you finish or complete it: *It'll take me hours to get through all these letters.* **2** You **get through** an amount or supply of something when you use all of it: *We seem to be getting through an awful lot of coffee.* **3 a** You **get through** to someone when you succeed in contacting them by telephone: *I tried ringing him at the cottage but I couldn't get through.* **b** You **get through** to someone, or **get** something **through** to them, when you make them understand or realize something: *I can't seem to get through to them how important this is.* ▫ *This is vitally important. Am I getting through to you?*

○ **get to**
1 You **get to** a place or stage when you reach it or arrive at it: *What's the best way to get to the British Museum from here?* ▫ *'Where did you get to before Mr Campbell went off sick?' 'We got to the part where Hamlet saw the ghost of his father in his mother's bedroom.'* ▫ *He felt he was getting to the point where he couldn't cope anymore.* **2** You wonder where someone **has got to** or (*AmE*) **has gotten to** when they haven't arrived at the time or place they were expected: *He should have been here ages ago. Have you any idea where he might have got to?* **3** (*informal*) Someone or something **gets to** you when they upset or annoy you: *You shouldn't let him get to you. He's like that to everyone.* [*compare* **get at**]

○ **get together**
People **get together** when they meet, especially informally: *We must get together soon and discuss the project.*

○ **get up**
1 You **get up** when you stand from a sit-

ting or lying position, or when you leave your bed after waking: *Everyone got up when she came in the room.* ❑ *Raymond found it hard to get up on winter mornings.* [*same as* **rise**] **2** You **get** someone **up** when you make them get out of bed, usually earlier than they had intended: *She got me up at six o'clock just to watch the sun rise.*

○ **get up to**
You talk about what someone **is getting up to** when you are referring to what they are doing, especially if you think it is likely to be something you will disapprove of: *I hate to think what he and his mates are getting up to in Greece.*

give /gɪv/: **gives, giving, gave** /geɪv/, **given** /'gɪvən/
○ **give away**
1 a You **give** something **away** when you give it to someone else, usually because you no longer want it: *Her mother gave most of her old baby clothes away.* **b** You **give** something **away** when you lose it carelessly: *The centre forward gave that ball away.* [= allowed a member of the opposing team to get the ball through his carelessness] **2** Someone **gives away** the prizes at a prizegiving ceremony when they present them to the people who have won them: *We've asked Mrs Andrews of the PTA to give away the prizes.* [*same as* **give out, present**] **3 a** You **give** information **away** when you allow it to become known to other people, especially when you should have kept it secret: *It seems he had been giving away all sorts of valuable trade secrets.* **b** You **give** someone **away** when you betray them: *I don't want him to find me; you won't give me away, will you?* **4** You **give away** personal thoughts or feelings without intending to when your appearance or behaviour makes it clear what they are: *I wondered what she was thinking; her expression gave very little away.* **5** At the beginning of a wedding ceremony, the bride's father **gives** her **away** when he takes her to the altar of the church and officially hands her to her future husband so that they can be married: *Her father's dead so her uncle will be giving her away.*
○ **give back**

You **give** something **back** when you return it to its owner; something **is given back** to someone when it is returned to them: *Give me back my ball.* ❑ *The unexpected win gave the team its confidence back.*
○ **give in**
1 You **give in** when you admit that you have been defeated, allow yourself to be defeated, or agree to stop opposing or resisting something and allow it: *Others give in, decide they are past the stage where beauty has any relevance, and concentrate on looking tidy and presentable.* ❑ *They just keep battling on and refuse to give in.* ❑ *'They say that unless they have the money we'll fall behind the Russians. So I give in.'* [*same as* **surrender**] **2** You **give** something that has to be returned **in** when you hand it back to the person responsible for dealing with it: *Has everyone given their homework in to the teacher?* [*same as* **hand in**]
○ **give off**
Something **gives off** heat, light or a smell when it produces it or sends it out: *Most light bulbs give off more heat than light.* ❑ *The chemical gave off acrid fumes, stinging their eyes.* ❑ *... contracting and giving out gravitational energy as heat and light.*
○ **give out**
1 You **give** things **out** when you give one to each of a number of people: *We stood in the High Street giving out leaflets.* ❑ *Most neighbourhood police place the emphasis upon community service and informal contact, giving out few parking tickets.* [*same as* **hand out, distribute**; *compare* **dish out, share out**] **2** News or information **is given out** when it is announced or made known to the public: *I shall let it be given out that she fell from her horse.* ❑ *It's been given out by the Prime Minister's office that he and the Irish Taoiseach are close to agreement.* **3** A person or thing **gives out** a noise or sound when they send it out or make it: *The old engine was giving out a strange rattling noise.* ❑ *He jumped up and gave out the most tremendous shout of triumph.* **4** A supply of something **gives out** when

it has been completely used up and there is none of it left: *Jane tried to climb Kilimanjaro, but her strength gave out about 2000 feet from the summit.* [*same as* **run out**] **5** (*informal*) Something **gives out** when it stops working, especially suddenly: *The strain was too much and his heart just gave out.* **6** In cricket, a batsman **is given out** when the umpire decides and indicates that he is out: *When England batted, Gooch was given out caught behind and it seemed to dispirit his team-mates.*

○ **give up**
1 You **give up** something, or **give up** doing something, when you decide not to do it any longer: *Giving up smoking together is much more likely to be successful than doing it alone.* □ *Why are you giving up your job?* □ *Yet it's easy to cut down on fat without giving up all your favourite foods.* **2** You **give up**, or **give up** something you have been trying to do, when you stop trying to do it or stop trying to hold on to it, and admit defeat: *When I saw it, I felt like giving up, curling up into a tiny ball to be forgotten by everyone.* □ *I've given up trying to talk sense to him.* □ *'Come on, have another guess.' 'No, I give up, I haven't a clue what it is.'* **3** You **give** someone **up** when you stop having a relationship with them: *But I have given her up, and in any case she has meant nothing to me for years.* □ *If you don't give that boy up your father and I will stop your allowance.* **4** You **give** someone **up** for dead when you believe that they are dead; you **give** someone or something **up** as lost when you believe that they will never be found or recovered: *We had all given her up* [= believed she would die] *when she made this miraculous recovery.* **5** You **give** yourself **up** when you surrender yourself to someone in authority and become their prisoner: *The thieves were cornered by police and forced to give themselves up.* **6** You **give** something you have **up** to someone else when you allow them to have or take it: *They weren't prepared to entertain anything that entailed France giving up military sovereignty.* □ *They went round the town calling on the people to give up*

their dead. [*same as* **hand over**, **surrender**]

go /gəʊ/: **goes**, **going**, **went** /wɛnt/, **gone** /gɒn/
The usual past participle of **go** is **gone**, but **been** is also sometimes used.

○ **go about**
1 To **go about** is to move from place to place, often, but not necessarily, with a particular purpose: *William Kunster went about the world protesting against the trial on the grounds that it was political.* □ *We don't go about in cars, not in London.* **2** You **go about** something in a particular way when you deal with it or handle it in that way: *I couldn't think how to go about breaking the news to her.* □ *This seems an odd way to go about things.* **3** You **go about** doing something, often something other people disapprove of, when you do it often: *They both go about with permanent scowls.* □ *She'd gone about in awe of these adults.* □ *There's no need for him to go about insulting people like that.* [*same as* **go around**, **go round**] **4** (*especially BrE*) You say that something **is going about** when more and more people are talking about it, know about it, or are being affected by it: *There's a rumour going about that his wife's left him.* □ *Isn't there a bad cold going about?* [*same as* **go around**, **go round**]

○ **go about with** (*BrE*)
You **go about with** someone when you are friendly with them and you do things together: *He used to go about with one of the lads from the village, but I haven't seen them together for a while.*

○ **go after**
1 You **go after** someone or something when you follow them, trying to catch up with them: *Don't let her leave like that; go after her and tell her you're sorry for what you said.* **2** You **go after** a job when you try to get it: *He went after several jobs but didn't succeed in getting any of them.*

○ **go ahead**
1 You **go ahead** of someone when you move forward so that they are in a position behind you or following you: *He*

went ahead of us to see if he could find a way across the river. □ *Sheffield went ahead after 30 minutes when Gage knocked the ball past Allen.* **2** Something **goes ahead** when it takes place as planned: *Do you think their marriage will go ahead now that she's found out about his criminal record?* □ *Both events will go ahead amid tightened security.* □ *I assume that this can go ahead immediately.* **3** You **go ahead** with something when you do it as intended; if someone tells you to **go ahead** they mean that you should begin something, or they give you permission to do what you have said you want to do: *'Paul is going to tell us about his hobbies. Go ahead, Paul.'* □ *'Can I look through your record collection?' 'Yes, go ahead.'* □ *It was against the advice of most of his staff that he went ahead with it.* □ *The referendum, approved by Cabinet last night, will go ahead with all speed.*

○ **go along**
1 You **go along**, or you **go along** somewhere, when you travel or go there: *I fixed things up with Donald and went along to explain the plan.* □ *Just go along the corridor and it's the first on your left.* □ *'Are you going to the party?' 'I think I'll go along for half an hour or so.'* **2** You do something as you **go along** if you do it while you are continuing with some more general activity: *I couldn't speak any French when I came to France. I just learnt it as I was going along.* □ *Selected applicants begin to serve as trainees on the boats, literally learning the ropes as they go along.*

○ **go along with**
You **go along with** a plan or decision when you agree with it and support it: *I'll go along with anything you might suggest.* □ *I think you're simply going along with what he wants, and frankly that's out of character.*

○ **go around**
1 Something such as a rumour or an illness **is going around** or (*BrE*) **round** when it is being passed from one person to the other: *Have you heard the rumour that's going round that the Prime Minister is thinking of resigning.* □ *There's a tummy bug going around the*

office. □ *One idea going around is that French troops might be mixed in with brigades from Britain and other NATO countries.* [*same as* **go about**] **2** If there is enough to **go around** or (*BrE*) **round** there is enough for everyone: *Would you mind having white wine? There isn't enough champagne to go around.* □ *With less capital to go around, banks must make fewer loans.*

○ **go around with**
You **go around with** someone, or (*BrE*) **go round with** them, when you are often in their company in public: *'Perhaps there isn't all that much fun in going around with a married bloke, after all?'* □ *He goes round with a very strange crowd.* [*same as* **go about with**]

○ **go away**
1 You **go away** when you leave a place: *They've gone away on holiday.* □ *I hated the idea of her going away to school.* □ *Now he must go away and I daresay I shall never see him again.* □ *Unable to go away for weekends or holidays, she never goes out at night to dinner parties, discos or evening classes.* **2** When you tell someone to **go away** you are telling them to leave, especially to leave your presence: *He came round to see me but I told him to go away.* □ *'Fenna, it's over, go away.'* □ *The men motioned me to go away.* □ *So they asked him to go away and come back in a week.* **3** Something **goes away** when it disappears: *The issue would not go away.* □ *The recession they have caused and which so nearly ditched them will not go away automatically.* □ *The rash seems to be going away now.*

○ **go back**
1 You **go back** when you return to a place or position that you have been in before, or a method that you have used before: *She should go back home. She's old.* □ *I'll go back tonight and see what's to be done.* □ *They have gone through too much to go back now.* □ *The doctors told me to go back to Cambridge and continue the research.* □ *I go back into her room and have a look around.* □ *Go back down the road for half a mile.* □ *When I retire I want to go back to the Highlands.* □ *The teacher told him he hadn't done any of*

the work properly so he had to go back to the beginning. **2** Something **goes back** to an earlier time when it has its origins in that earlier time: *Go back a few hundred years and look around.* ❑ *Their quarrel goes back to the time when they fought over the same girl at school.* ❑ *His family tree goes back to just after the Norman Conquest.*

○ **go by**

1 Someone or something **goes by** when they pass along in front of you: *I saw a number 88 bus go by with a bright yellow ad proclaiming 'Britain needs its universities'.* ❑ *He sat on the verge and watched the traffic go by.* **2** You **go by** a place when you pass it: *If you're going by the chemist's would you drop in and collect my prescription?* ❑ *Melanie felt a shudder of dread as she went by every door.* **3** Time **goes by** when it passes: *As time went by they became closer and closer.* ❑ *Twenty years went by before he saw his homeland again.* ❑ *The Broomielaw Quay was enlarged as years went by.* [*same as* **elapse**] **4** You **go by** something, *eg* someone's advice, when it influences your actions or decisions: *You shouldn't go by what you read in the paper; sometimes journalists get their facts wrong.* ❑ *Local music appears to be on the wane, if recent developments are anything to go by.* ❑ *Isn't my word enough to go by, after all these years.* **5** You **go by** a particular name when that is the name you are generally known by: *A singer who goes by the name of Rocking Ronnie.*

○ **go down**

1 Someone or something **goes down** when they move or travel from a higher level or position to a lower one: *He's always wanted to go down the Cresta Run.* ❑ *His office is the first on the right as you go down the stairs.* ❑ *Go down to reception and ask if there have been any messages for me.* ❑ *Men went down the main shaft and tried to clear it.* **2** The sun **goes down** when it sinks below the horizon and it begins to get dark: *I watched the sun go down in the trees behind Thornfield.* **3** Something **goes down** when it falls, reduces or gets lower: *The water level in the lake has gone*

down during the drought. ❑ *The value of the company's shares has been going down for the last few days.* ❑ *Our supply of food is going down rather quickly.* ❑ *The quality of life will go down.* **4** A ship **goes down** when it sinks; its crew **goes down** with the ship when they are drowned: *The suction of the ship going down could pull the lifeboat under.* ❑ *The trawler went down in heavy seas.* ❑ *Only two crew members were rescued; the rest are believed to have gone down with the ship.* **5** Someone **goes down** when they fall to the ground, usually after receiving a stunning blow: *The bottle hit him on the forehead and he went down like a stone.* ❑ *Limeking went down as if shot, and his rider desperately tried to get him to his feet.* [*same as* **fall down**, **collapse**] **6** A sportsman or sporting team **goes down** when they are defeated in a match or competition: *Lendl went down by five sets to three in a thrilling final.* ❑ *He produced one of best performances by an Irish horse when going down narrowly to Garrison Savannah at Cheltenham.* **7** Something like a remark or piece of humour **goes down** well when people like it or enjoy it: *His jokes didn't go down very well with the older folks.*

○ **go down with**

You **go down with** an illness when you begin to suffer from it: *At the start of the holiday they all went down with measles.*

○ **go for**

1 You **go for** someone when you attack them, physically or with words: *You should keep that brute of a dog under control. It went for me when I opened the gate.* **2** You **go for** someone or something when you like or are attracted by them: *She goes for him in a big way.* ❑ *We don't go much for classical music, I'm afraid.* **3** You **go for** something when you choose it: *There were lots of unusual desserts but in the end I went for the chocolate mousse.* ❑ *Parke thought the old version was 'a bit Seventies' and went for something 'more authoritative'.* **4** (*informal*) You also **go for** something when you decide to try to achieve it: *There's definitely a market for this type of ser-*

vice. I think we should go for it. □ *'I'm thinking of becoming a professional jockey.' 'That's a good idea, go for it.'*

○ **go in**
1 You **go in** when you enter a building or room; you **go into** a building or room when you enter it: *Please do go in.* □ *It's got cold; I'm going in.* □ *They all went into the dining room for lunch.* □ *If you go into the cupboard under the stairs, you'll find a stepladder.* **2** Something that **goes in**, or **goes into** a space, fits, or fits into, that space: *He tried to put his new car into his garage but it was too wide to go in.* □ *Where does this piece of the jigsaw go in?* □ *The old key went into the lock surprisingly easily.* **3** (*BrE; informal*) A piece of information or news **goes in** when you understand it: *I told him that his mother was dead but I don't think it went in.* [*compare* **take in**] **4** The sun, moon or stars **go in** when they disappear behind a cloud or clouds: *The moon went in and we were left stumbling along in the dark.*

○ **go in for**
1 (*BrE*) You **go in for** a contest when you enter it: *Are you going in for the sculpture competition?* **2** You **go in for** an activity or occupation when you enjoy it and do it regularly: *Schools went in for a lot of physical education, which involved jumping about in a draughty hall with your shirt tucked into your knickers.* □ *He doesn't go in for outdoor sports much.*

○ **go into**
1 a You **go into** a job or profession when you choose it as a career: *I'd never thought of going into the police force.* **b** Someone **goes into** business when they offer their services or products to customers in the hope of making a profit: *He's thinking of going into business for himself.* **2 a** You **go into** hospital when you are admitted as a patient. **b** Someone **goes into** lodgings when they go and live in someone else's house and pay them rent. **3** You **go into** something when you discuss or explain it in detail: *There isn't time to go into the precise reasons for the decision.* **4** You **go into** something when you examine it thoroughly to find out all you can about it: *Have you gone into all the risks associated with taking this drug for long periods?* [*see also* **go in**]

○ **go off**
1 Someone **goes off**, or **goes off** somewhere, when they leave: *He went off in a rage.* □ *They are going off to the Canaries for a fortnight's holiday.* **2** A bomb or gun **goes off** when it explodes or is fired: *The gun went off accidently.* [*compare* **set off**] **3** (*BrE*) Food **goes off** when it becomes rotten and unfit to eat: *The fridge broke down, and all the milk went off.* **4** An electrical device such as a light, or a system controlled by an electrical switch, **goes off** when it stops functioning: *He set the timer so that the TV would go off after 30 minutes.* □ *At midnight all the lights and heating went off.* **5** (*BrE*) You **go off** someone or something when you stop liking them: *It sounds like she's beginning to go off Simon.* □ *I've gone off the idea completely.* **6** An event **goes off** well when it is successful: *The party went off really well.*

○ **go on**
1 You **go on** doing something, or **go on** with something, when you continue to do it: *Mark went on working while the others were out.* □ *I'll just go on with my guitar practice.* □ *He went on talking after most of the audience had left.* □ *If you had gone on with your studies you might have been able to get a better job now.* **2** You **go on** in a particular direction when you continue travelling or moving in that direction: *Go on until you reach the church and then turn left.* **3** You **go on** when you continue to talk or tell a story, often after an interruption or pause: *'I'm sorry for interrupting you; please go on,' he said.* □ *She went on to tell them how it was she had become a painter.* **4** You say '**Go on!**' to someone when you want to encourage them to do something: *'This cake is delicious. Go on, try a piece.'* **5** People sometimes say '**Go on!**' to someone to show that they don't believe them: *'Go on! That surely can't be true!'* **6** Something **goes on** when it continues to happen: *Do you think this will go on much longer?*

❑ *He didn't want it to stop. He wanted it to go on and on for ever.* ❑ *Do you think this hot weather will go on for much longer?* ❑ *The strike went on for another two months.* **7** Time **goes on** when it passes: *As time went on she got more used to his funny little habits.* **8** An actor or other performer **goes on** when they make their entrance on stage: *She didn't go on till the second act.* **9** You **go on** somewhere when you go there after being somewhere else: *Do you think he'll go on to university when he leaves school?* ❑ *We've all decided to go on to Archie's after the play.* **10** You **go on** to do something when you do it after doing something else: *He started his acting career in rep, and went on to star in several successful West End productions.* **11** When you ask what **is going on** you want to know what is happening, or what the people you are talking to are doing, especially if you suspect they are doing something wrong: *Someone's moved my desk. Would someone please tell me what's going on?* ❑ *Right, what's going on in here?* **12** When you have something to **go on**, you have some piece of evidence or information to support your theory or opinion: *From what I've been able to gather, the police don't have much to go on.* **13** An electrical device such as a light, or a system controlled by an electrical switch, **goes on** when it starts to function: *I heard a click and the security lights went on.* [compare **come on**] **14** You **go on** a course of drugs when you start taking them: *She said she might go on the Pill.* **15** A supply of something **goes on** something else when it is used for that thing: *Most of his money goes on feeding the animals.* ❑ *All his wages go on paying back his debts.*

○ **go out**
1 You **go out** when you leave the room, building or other place you have been in: *Will you be going out today?* ❑ *We went out into the garden.* ❑ *No-one dared go out at night.* ❑ *Beyond, go out of the square by the left exit, Via Baracchini.* ❑ *I went out and slammed the door behind me.* **2 a** A light **goes out** when it is switched off or no longer shines: *The*

lights suddenly went out. ❑ *The stars lost their sheen and went out as the first strain of light eased away the darkness.* **b** A fire or something that is burning **goes out** when it stops burning: *There was a sudden draught and the candle went out.* **3** The tide **goes out** when the level of the sea falls back and the water reaches a lower point on the shore: *The tide in the estuary went out as fast as it came in and it wasn't unusual for large fish to be stranded.* [opposite **come in**] **4** You **go out** when you do something socially, such as visit the cinema or the theatre or go to a restaurant: *Before the children were born we went out two or three times a week.* ❑ *We don't seem to have the money to go out any more.* ❑ *They dress up then and go out to dinner in some restaurant.* **5** Something **goes out** when it is no longer fashionable or popular: *That hairstyle went out in the Seventies.* **6** A message or news **goes out** when it is announced; a letter **goes out** when it is sent: *The call went out for volunteers to help clear up the flood damage.* ❑ *From the leadership, the word went out quickly: no triumphalism.* **7** (especially BrE) A radio or television programme **goes out** when it is broadcast: *The programme will be going out all over Britain.* **8** The money that you have **going out** is the money that you spend on bills and other expenditure: *We'll have to cut down on our spending; we've got more going out that we have coming in.* [= we are spending more than we are earning] **9** (AmE) You **go out** for a sports team when you try to join it by showing your athletic skills: *More than 40 students went out for the football team, but only six were selected.*

○ **go out with**
You **go out with** someone when you have a romantic or sexual relationship with them, but are not living with them: *So I promised I wouldn't go out with him again.* ❑ *They've been going out together for years.* [same as **go together**]

○ **go over**
1 You **go over** something when you cross it, or move from one side of it to the other: *You go over one stile from one field*

then onto another. ❑ *It was flattened as if a steamroller had gone over it.* ❑ *He went over the Tay to Aberfeldy.* **2** You **go over** something when you examine or check it carefully, or discuss it in detail: *It's worth going over her story again to prevent others from falling into the same trap.* ❑ *We need to go over these accounts again.* ❑ *They went over the main points of his scheme again to decide whether or not it was really practical.*

○ **go round** *see* **go around.**

○ **go through**

1 To **go through** an object or place is to travel or pass in at one side and out at the other: *His head went through the windscreen.* ❑ *Will you be going through Edinburgh on your way to the Borders?* ❑ *The path goes through fields.* ❑ *The 5th Brigade had gone clean through enemy lines.* **2** You **go through** an amount or supply of something when you use it all up: *He can go through ten pairs of shoes in a year.* ❑ *We went through a week's supply of food in three days.* [*same as* **get through**] **3** You **go through** something such as a room or container when you check the contents carefully: *She'd gone through her briefcase twice, and the letter wasn't there.* **4** You **go through** a number of things when you examine or consider each one carefully: *Would you go through these old clothes and see if there are any you want to keep.* **5** You **go through** an unpleasant experience when you suffer or endure it: *Looking back, it was a serious situation that I wouldn't wish to go through again.* ❑ *You must have gone through hell when your husband's affair was made public.*

○ **go through with**

You **go through with** something when you decide to do it even though it may be difficult or unpleasant: *She threatened to sue, but I doubt if she'll go through with it.* ❑ *He asked Madge if she wanted to go through with it, which of course she didn't.*

○ **go together**

1 Two or more things **go together** when they match or fit together well, or are closely associated: *I don't think red lip-* stick and green eyeshadow go together. ❑ *It is often observed that misogny and homophobia go together.* [*same as* **go with**] **2** Two people **are going together** when they are having a romantic or sexual relationship, but are not living together: *They've been going together for six months now.* [*same as* **go with**]

○ **go towards** *or* **go toward**

1 You **go towards** someone or something when you move in their direction: *He neither went towards her nor withdrew.* **2** An amount of money **goes towards** something when it is used to pay part of the cost: *My bonus can go towards the cost of a holiday.* ❑ *The money given will go towards nutritional programmes in the poorest areas of Cairo.*

○ **go under**

1 You **go under** something when you pass beneath it or move so that you are under it: *Smoke was blown into the carriages when the train went under a bridge.* ❑ *The mouse has gone under that cupboard.* **2** Something that has been floating on the surface of water **goes under** when it sinks below the surface: *The ship struck a rock and went under.* **3** A business **goes under** when it fails: *They'll lose everything if the company goes under.*

○ **go up**

1 Something **goes up** when it moves to a higher position: *He went up the stairs.* ❑ *The lift attendant asked me if I was going up.* ❑ *The rocket went straight up.* ❑ *I'm going to go up into the attic and look for my old school photographs.* [*opposite* **go down**] **2** To **go up** is also to increase or rise: *The temperature went up into the nineties.* ❑ *The price of fresh vegetables goes up when they are in short supply.* ❑ *Interest rates are going up again.* [*opposite* **go down**; *compare* **come down**] **3** (*informal*) People talk about something **going up** when it explodes or is destroyed by fire: *If you lit a match in our kitchen, it'd go up with a roar.* **4** Something **goes up** to a certain point when it extends as far as that point: *Her legs were so long they seemed to go up to her armpits.* ❑ *There's a damp patch on the wall that goes up to the* *ceiling.*

○ **go with**

1 One thing **goes with** another when they match or compliment each other: *That tie doesn't go with that shirt.* ❑ *This claret will go nicely with the beef.* **2** (*informal*) You **are going with** someone when you are having a romantic or sexual relationship with them: *She's been going with him for a couple of months as far as I know.* **3** (*informal*) You **go with** something when you allow it to happen, or decide to use it or put it into action: *We didn't think much of the name at first, but somehow came round to it and decided to go with it.*

○ **go without**

You **go without** something, especially something needed or expected, when you have to manage without it: *Our parents didn't have the money for Christmas presents, so we went without.* [*same as* **do without**]

grow /grəʊ/: **grows**, **growing**, **grew** /gruː/, **grown** /grəʊn/

○ **grow out of**

1 Children **grow out of** clothes when their body grows so much that the clothes no longer fit properly: *Niall seems to grow out of new shoes in less than a month!* [*same as* **outgrow**] **2** You **grow out of** something such as a hobby or interest when you gradually stop liking it or wanting to do it, especially when you come to think that it is too childish: *I've rather grown out of late-night parties.*

○ **grow up**

1 A person **grows up** when they gradually change from a child into an adult, or they reach the stage of being an adult: *Young Peter is really growing up fast.* ❑ *She's grown up so much since I last saw her.* [*same as* **mature**] **2 a** You can also say that someone **grows up** or **is growing up** when they start to behave in an adult way, no matter how old they are: *He's grown up a lot since he went away to school.* **b** You can tell someone to **grow up** when you want them to behave in a more mature or less childish way: *Oh, grow up, Martin!*

hack /hak/: **hacks**, **hacking**, **hacked**

○ **hack around** (*AmE*; *informal*)

You **hack around** when you wander around wasting time: *Those hoodlums are always hacking around the town.* [*same as* **jack around**]

hand /hand/: **hands**, **handing**, **handed**

○ **hand back**

You **hand** something **back** when you return it to the person you took or borrowed it from: *Following Portugal's revolution in 1974, Lisbon tried to hand back Macao to China; Peking wasn't interested.* [*same as* **give back**]

○ **hand down**

Things that **are handed down** are given or left to people who are younger, or to people who come after: *Traditional storytelling skills were handed down through the generations.* ❑ *Each government hands its failures down to the next lot.* [*same as* **pass on**, **pass down**]

○ **hand in**

1 You **hand** something **in** when you give it to someone, especially someone in authority: *I stopped off at the library to hand in some books.* ❑ *We're giving all young people at risk of offending the chance to hand their weapons in to their local police station.* [*same as* **give in**] **2** You **hand in** a piece of work when you give it to the person who has the responsibility of judging it: *You must have a good reason for handing essays in late.* [*same as* **submit**] **3** You **hand in** your notice or your resignation when you give your employer a letter stating that you are giving up your job.

○ **hand out**

You **hand** things **out** when you give one to each of several people: *The class pre-*

fect would hand out books and pens to the others. [*same as* **give out**, **dish out** (*informal*)]

○ **hand over**

1 You **hand** something **over** to someone when you give it to them to own or keep: *The BBC have refused to hand over film of the event without a court order.* [*same as* **turn over**, **surrender** (*formal*)] **2** You also **hand** something **over** to someone when you give them the responsibility of dealing with it or looking after it: *Who are you going to hand the presentation over to after you've given the introduction?* [*same as* **turn over**]

hang /haŋ/: **hangs, hanging, hung** /hʌŋ/

○ **hang about** (*informal*)

1 You **hang about**, **hang around** or (*BrE*) **hang round** somewhere when you spend a long time there doing nothing, or waiting for someone or something: *I don't know why he had come hanging about here instead of hearing his own minister preach.* □ *Many young prostitutes are preyed upon by men who hang around railway stations waiting for runaways to arrive.* □ *French students had been hanging round the fringes of the course all week, trying to pick up girls at the college doors.* □ *Tony had just left university and was hanging round, not trying very hard for a job.* **2** The people you **hang about**, **hang around** or (*BrE*) **hang round** with are your friends, the people you spend a lot of your time with: *Charlie spends time with his family while the rest of the band hang about together.* **3** You can tell someone to **hang about** or **hang around** when you want them to wait: *The wolf says to the rabbit, 'Hang about 'til 8pm and I'll eat you for supper'.* [*same as* **hang on** (*informal*), **hold on** (*informal*)]

○ **hang back**

Someone who **hangs back** says or does nothing, because they are nervous, cautious or afraid: *She mentally urged him not to hang back, but she didn't want to make the first move.* □ *We must all join in; there is no room for anyone to hang back.* [*compare* **hold back**]

○ **hang in** (*AmE*; *informal*)

You **hang in** when you keep trying to survive a difficult time or position: *They tried to force me to retire, but I intend to hang in.* □ *The largest waves are still coming, so hang in there!*

○ **hang on**

1 (*informal*) You can tell someone to **hang on** if you want them to wait or stop: *Hang on a minute; that's not fair!* [*same as* **hold on** (*informal*)] **2** You **hang on** when you grip something tightly to prevent yourself from being thrown or bumped around: *We all hung on for dear life as the boat plunged into the rapids.* **3** You **hang on** to something when you keep it: *I'd hang on to the old shoes; you could use them in the garden.* □ *It's frustrating for them to see the old leaders hanging onto power.* [*same as* **hold on**]

○ **hang out**

1 You **hang out** washing when you hang it on a line outside, to dry: *Some residents fled with such haste that their washing is still hanging out.* **2** (*informal*) You **hang out** somewhere when you spend a lot of time there; you **hang out** with the people you spend a lot of time with: *In LA, you hung out with your contemporaries; over here, I hang out with traditional musicians from the folk scene.*

○ **hang up**

1 You **hang up** things such as clothes when you store them by hanging them on a hook, rail or other fitting: *She kicked off her shoes and hung her suit up.* **2** You **hang up** when you end a telephone conversation by replacing the receiver: *I tried to reason with her but she hung up on me.* □ *If they call back, just hang up the phone.* **3** You can say that you **hang up** the equipment you use for a job or activity when you stop using it because you are giving up the job or activity: *I think it's probably time he hung his boots up.* □ *The baseball player hung up his spikes.*

hash /haʃ/: **hashes, hashing, hashed**

○ **hash over** (*AmE*; *informal*)

You **hash over** something when you talk about it for a long time in detail, especially when you review something: *The committee took the whole meeting to* *hash over the school's budget.* ◻ *The two women hashed over their early days in London.*

haul /hɔːl/: **hauls, hauling, hauled**

○ **haul in**

Someone who **is hauled in** by the police is arrested by them: *The three suspects were hauled in before daybreak.* ◻ *The police hauled Simon in for questioning.*

head /hɛd/: **heads, heading, headed**

○ **head for**

1 You **head for** a place when you travel or move towards it: *We decided to abandon fishing and head for home before I froze to death.* **2** You can also say that you **are heading for** something, or **are headed for** it, when it is going to happen to you: *He warns that the Arab world is headed 'for a period of turbulence like never before'.*

○ **head off**

1 You **head off** when you leave, often in a particular direction: *I'm afraid we'll have to head off soon; we both have an early start tomorrow.* ◻ *I watched her head off towards the Tube.* [compare **clear off, set off**] **2** You **head** someone or something **off** when you prevent them from reaching a place by blocking their path towards it: *They sent two riders around the rocks to the north, to head the cattle off.* **3** You **head off** something unpleasant when you prevent it from happening: *Another rise in VAT was rumoured, but recent economic surveys suggest the Treasury may have headed it off.*

hear /hɪə(r)/: **hears, hearing, heard** /hɜːd/

○ **hear about**

You **hear about** something when someone tells you about it: *I hear about these artists who work all day and all night.* ◻ *A few days after he died, they came to the house and said they were sorry to hear about my husband.*

○ **hear from**

1 You **hear from** someone when they send you a letter or telephone you: *If you haven't heard from the firm within 28 days, write to their head office.* **2** You can also say that you **hear from** someone when they speak or say something: *Let's*

hear more from Mr Bridges before returning to the audience for their views.

○ **hear of**

1 You **hear of** something when someone tells you about it: *When the king heard of the revolt he was seized by an epileptic fit.* ◻ *You hear of actresses being temperamental; this girl isn't.* **2** You can say that you **have heard of** something or someone when you recognize their name, or when you know that they exist: *Charsky mentioned Ivan Sakulin; we've heard of him before.* ◻ *Le Bugue is a place you've probably never heard of before.* ◻ *Whoever heard of apprentices as old as that?* **3** (*formal*) People sometimes say they won't **hear of** something to mean that they refuse to allow it: *She is advised to rest but won't hear of it, saying the summer will restore her strength.*

heat /hiːt/: **heats, heating, heated**

○ **heat up**

1 You **heat** something **up** when you cause it to become hot or hotter; something **heats up** when it becomes hot or hotter: *It'll only take a few seconds to heat up the milk.* ◻ *The car was beginning to heat up and I was worried about possible damage to the animal's health.* [compare **warm up**] **2** You can also say that a situation **heats up** when it becomes more angry or violent: *That will make the East Germans feel even more imprisoned and could heat up resentment against the government.*

help /hɛlp/: **helps, helping, helped**

○ **help out**

You **help out** when you give someone help that they need; you can also say that you **help** them **out**: *Marie could help out with the baby and I could help out by going to the shops.* ◻ *If we're ever stuck for money I'm sure my parents would help us out if they could.*

hem /hɛm/: **hems, hemming, hemmed**

○ **hem in**

You are **hemmed in** when things prevent you from doing what you want or need to do, or prevent you from moving around freely: *It's quite natural for Western women to feel that Muslim traditions hem them in.* ◻ *It was an oblong pile of barrack building with a narrow paved yard, hemmed in by high walls* *spiked on top.*

hide /haɪd/: **hides, hiding, hid** /hɪd/, **hidden** /'hɪdən/

○ **hide out**

You **hide out** somewhere when you stay there so that people don't find you, especially people you are escaping from: *Is there anywhere you know of where he might go to hide out until the fuss dies down?*

hit /hɪt/: **hits, hitting, hit**

○ **hit on** *or* **hit upon**

You **hit on** something, or **hit upon** it, when you discover it or realize it: *Looking for trousers, he hit on a pair of corduroy breeches.* □ *They exhibited all the satisfaction of someone who has just hit upon a method of causing water to flow uphill.*

○ **hit out**

You **hit out** when you attack someone, especially with criticisms or insults: *They in turn hit out at the festival organizers, claiming not enough has been done to promote the city.*

○ **hit up** (*AmE; informal*)

You **hit** someone **up** when you ask them for money or a favour: *Larry hit me up for $20 to buy his brother a birthday present.*

hold /hoʊld/: **holds, holding, held** /hɛld/

○ **hold against**

You **hold** something **against** someone when you deal with them harshly or unfairly because you disapprove of or dislike something about them: *Her father says, 'So, you married an Englishman. We won't hold it against you.'* □ *Perhaps their lack of computer competence will be held against them.* [*compare* **count against**]

○ **hold back**

1 You **hold** something or someone **back** when you prevent them from moving or leaving: *I would like to have seen the guard holding back the tourists with an old sword.* [*same as* **keep back**] **2** To **hold** something **back** is to prevent or delay its progress; to **hold** someone **back** is to prevent them from making good or proper progress, usually in their career: *Smoking can affect the developing baby by holding back its growth.* □ *Transplant programmes have been held back*

because of a shortage of donor organs. □ *I'm sure your parents never meant to hold you back in any way.* [*compare* **cut back**] **3** You **hold back** information when you don't tell everything you know: *The Inspector feels Evans is holding something back.* [*same as* **withhold**] **4** You **hold back** something such as tears or laughter when you prevent yourself from crying or laughing when you feel you want to: *I could see Moira working hard to hold her anger back.* **5** You **hold back**, or **hold back** from doing something, when you don't do what you intended or wanted to do: *It is necessary to be patient, to hold back and do nothing.* □ *This was something Poindexter could hardly hold back from revealing.*

○ **hold down**

1 To **hold** something **down** is to keep it at a low level and prevent it from rising or increasing: *There are too many market-makers in these areas, which holds down everyone's earnings.* [*same as* **keep down**] **2** You can say that someone **holds down** a job when they manage to keep it, when you might have expected them to lose it: *Peter had never held any job down for longer than a couple of months.* **3** You **hold** feelings or emotions **down** when you prevent yourself from expressing them: *It isn't easy for people like Janey to hold down the waves of panic that surge up inside them every time they have to deal with confrontation.* [*same as* **hold back, keep back, stifle**] **4** Someone who can't **hold down** food vomits after they've eaten: *At least she's managed to hold her breakfast down.* [*same as* **keep down**] **5** To **hold** people **down** is to use force to control their behaviour, giving them no rights or freedoms: *It was to be expected that the African peoples, after being held down for so long, would rise up against their oppressors.*

○ **hold off**

1 You **hold off**, or **hold off** doing something, when you delay doing it; something **holds off** when it doesn't happen, when you expected it would: *The pilot knows he will eject, but holds off until the aircraft is clear of habitation.*

❏ *Could you hold off announcing it to the press until the family has been informed?* ❏ *We just need the rains to hold off for another few days, until we can get the wheat in.* **2** You **hold off** someone who is attacking you, or **hold off** their attack, when you prevent them from defeating you: *If they can hold the Madrid side off until half time, they'll consider that an achievement in itself.*

○ **hold on**

1 (*informal*)

People often say '**Hold on!**' when they want you to wait: *Tell them to hold on a few seconds until we get the rest of the cartons unpacked.* [*same as* **hang on**] **2** You **hold on** when you support yourself by holding something; you **hold on** to something when you hold it in order to support yourself: *You tight-rope walk on the single strand below and hold on to the other two lines for balance.* ❏ *Two tired men were holding on to each other for support.* ❏ *The ride can be a bit bumpy, so you're advised to hold on tight.* **3** You **hold on** to something when you keep it; you can also say that you **are holding on** when you manage to continue doing something: *Mr Quiles is probably more concerned to hold on to his job.* ❏ *There will be more battles like this in the coming years, whether or not the Conservatives hold on to power.* ❏ *I felt a twinge in my leg and eased down, just holding on for the silver medal.* [*same as* **hang on**]

○ **hold out**

1 You **hold** something **out** when you hold it at some distance in front of your body, often in a gesture of offering: *You lie flat on the bench with the weights held out above your chest.* ❏ *I approached and held a piece of chicken out to him.* ❏ *The Syrian soldier nearest the door held out his arms in friendship.* ❏ *They held out the possibility of talks with the government as an incentive to call off the demonstration.* **2** You **hold out** when you manage to resist attacks made against you over a period of time: *I'm not sure how long the Arsenal defence can hold out against such sustained pressure.* ❏ *The Hussites took the territory and managed to hold out successfully until*

1436. [*same as* **last out**; *opposite* **give up**, **give in**] **3** A supply of something **holds out** when it lasts: *We weren't even sure that our stock of firewood would hold out.* [*same as* **last out**] **4** You **hold out** hope of something when you still hope that it will happen: *Few of us at that stage held out much hope for eventual rescue.*

○ **hold together**

1 Something that **holds together** stays in good order, and does not collapse or break: *I'm just hoping my old moped will hold together for another winter.* **2** People or groups who **hold together** stay in agreement or in partnership with each other; you **hold** them **together** when you persuade them not to disagree or end their partnership: *It's difficult to see how the party can hold together in light of such public declarations of discontent.* ❏ *The King encouraged MacDonald to hold the government together and to fight the election as a government.* [*compare* **stick together**]

○ **hold up**

1 You **hold** something **up** when you lift it into a position in front of you, and perhaps slightly above you, often in a gesture of showing: *Agnes was now holding up the coat before her.* **2** Something **is held up** by what supports it or prevents it from collapsing: *The rocks below seemed to be wobbling under the strain of holding the building up.* [*same as* **prop up**] **3** To **hold** something **up** is also to prevent it from failing: *The company's financial fortunes had been shaky and we needed a prop to hold us up.* **4** You **hold** something **up** when you stop or delay its progress: *The object was not to provide refreshment but to hold up the party for a few minutes.* ❏ *Spot checks cannot be carried out without holding other traffic up.* [*compare* **set back**] **5** You can use **hold up** to talk about how effective something remains after it has been used or tested: *The Goretex jackets tended to hold up better in winter conditions.* ❏ *None of their theories would hold up under close examination.* [*same as* **stand up**] **6** You can use **hold up** to talk about the way someone or something is referred to or described by others: *Singers like LL Cool J are held up as authentic voices of teenage youth.* □ *She was embarrassed by the teachers' habit of holding her up to be some sort of model pupil.* **7** To **hold up** people, or places such as banks, is to steal money from them using threats of violence, *eg* with guns: *Trains carrying tourists are regularly held up north of the mountains.*

home /hoʊm/: homes, homing, homed

○ **home in on**
1 Something such as a missile **homes in on** a target when its electronic aiming device fixes it on a direct course that it travels along towards the target: *Enemy vehicles can home in on our signals if we don't use a scrambler.* □ *From distances of up to half a mile, the young hyenas home in on the scent of blood.* **2** You **home in on** something when you concentrate all your attention or efforts on it: *Ministers always seem to home in on fraud at the lower or poorer end of the scale.*

hunt /hʌnt/: hunts, hunting, hunted

○ **hunt down**
You **hunt** someone **down** when you finally find them after a long search: *The image is of drunken, crazed locals hunting down interlopers and murdering them in the night.* □ *Green will hunt you down, both of you, wherever you go.* [*same as* **track down**]

hurry /'hʌrɪ/: hurries, hurrying, hurried

○ **hurry up**
1 You tell someone to **hurry up** when you want them to move or act more quickly: *Hurry up, Bill; people will be standing in line for the loo.* □ *If the kids don't hurry up we'll still be here at teatime.* **2** You **hurry** someone **up** when you make them move or act more quickly: *Miss Jones stood in the corridor hurrying up the stragglers.* **3** You **hurry** something **up** when you make it progress faster or happen sooner: *I wrote them a letter begging them to hurry up the settlement of our claim.*

iron /'aɪən/: irons, ironing, ironed

○ **iron out**
You **iron out** difficulties or problems when you solve them or get rid of them: *We were determined to iron it out before the end of the day.* [*same as* **sort out**, **clear up**]

jack /dʒak/: jacks, jacking, jacked
○ **jack around** (*AmE*; *informal*)
1 You **jack around** when you wander around wasting time: *We decided to jack around after the game.* [*same as* **hack around**] **2** You **jack** someone **around** when you harrass them or treat them badly: *The players walked out because the manager was always jacking them around.*

job /dʒɒb/: jobs, jobbing, jobbed
○ **job out** (*AmE*)
A company or person **jobs out** work by assigning it to other companies or workers: *The construction company jobbed out the plumbing to Thomas.*

join /dʒɔɪn/: joins, joining, joined
○ **join in**
You **join in** when you become involved in something that other people are doing: *She used to watch the other children playing but wouldn't join in.* □ *Soon everyone was joining in the discussion.*

[*same as* **participate**; *opposite* **shy away**]

○ **join up**

1 You **join** things **up** when you connect or attach them to each other: *If you join up these three photos you get a panorama effect.* ❑ *Shorter lengths had been joined up to make one long pipe.* [*same as* **link up**; *opposite* **break up**] **2** Someone **joins up** when they become a member of one of the armed forces: *She joined up in 1940 and was immediately posted abroad.* [*same as* **enlist**; *compare* **call up**]

jump /dʒʌmp/: jumps, jumping, jumped

○ **jump aboard** *or* **jump on board** (*AmE*)

You **jump aboard** when you join an organization or activity that already exists: *The manager invited me to jump on board his successful computer company.* ❑ *After I heard the candidate speak, I jumped aboard his campaign.*

○ **jump at**

You **jump at** a suggestion or offer when you accept it eagerly: *He'll jump at the chance to spend a bit of time in the country.* [*same as* **seize upon**]

○ **jump out**

1 Someone **jumps out** when they suddenly appear from a hiding place: *I opened the door and a gang of children in Hallowe'en masks jumped out.* [*same as* **leap out**] **2** Something, such as a word on a page of writing, **jumps out** at you when you notice it immediately because it is very striking or obvious: *A name from the past jumped out at me from the page.* [*same as* **leap out**]

keep /kiːp/: keeps, keeping, kept

○ **keep away**

1 You **keep away** from somewhere when you don't go there: *In the afternoons, when the shops were busiest, I tended to keep away.* [*same as* **avoid**] **2** You might tell someone to **keep away** when you don't want them to come near: *She threatened to turn the dogs on him if he didn't keep away.* ❑ *Keep those children away from the fire.*

○ **keep back**

1 You **keep** something **back** when you don't tell others everything: *He seemed frank and sincere, but I got the impression he was keeping something back.* ❑ *She had kept back important evidence, which obstructed police investigations.* [*same as* **hold back**, **withhold**; *opposite* **give away**, **confess**] **2** You **keep back** emotions when you control them and don't show others how you feel: *I was finding it hard to keep back the tears.* ❑ *He's been used to keeping his feelings back.* [*same as* **hold back**, **stifle**, **suppress**; *opposite* **let go**, **reveal**, **disclose**] **3** You **keep back** when you stand some distance away: *Keep back and let the ambulance through.* ❑ *Marshals are employed to keep spectators back.* [*same as* **stand back**, **stay back**] **4** You **keep** part of something **back** when you don't give or use all of it now, but save some for later: *Remember to keep back a little of the meat juices to make a gravy with.* ❑ *They insisted on keeping back £4000 of our mortgage until we had carried out some repairs.* [*same as* **reserve**, **retain**; *opposite* **use up**, **give up**, **surrender**]

○ **keep down**

1 You **keep** things such as costs or prices **down** when you prevent them from rising or increasing: *We have introduced sensible economic policies to keep down inflation.* [*same as* **hold down**, **control**, **contain**, **curb**] **2** You can't **keep down** what you eat or drink when you vomit it back up because you are ill: *She's kept her breakfast down, so far at least.* [*opposite* **throw up** (*informal*)]

○ **keep in with**

You **keep in with** someone when you do things that make them continue to like you, usually for selfish reasons: *Your uncle is the kind of powerful man every young boy should keep in with.* [*opposite* **alienate**, **antagonize**]

○ **keep off**

1 You **keep** someone or something **off** an area when you don't let them enter it; you **keep off** when you don't enter it yourself: *If you don't keep your dog off my land, next time I'll shoot it!* ❑ *I just think bikes should be kept off the roads in busy cities.* ❑ *People using the park are requested to keep off the grass.* ❑ *A large sign read: Private Estate. Keep Off.* [*same as* **keep away**; *opposite* **give access to**] **2** You **keep** something unwanted **off** something else when you stop it from touching, harming or spoiling it: *There didn't seem to be any way we could keep the insects off our baby.* ❑ *We'll light a fire, to keep off the cold.* [*same as* **keep away, deter, repel**; *opposite* **attract, invite**] **3** You **keep off** something when you no longer eat or drink it, *eg* because you know it would make you ill: *The doctor has told me to keep off alcohol of any kind.* ❑ *His wife was instructed to keep him off the cigars.* [*same as* **lay off** (*informal*), **go without**; *compare* **give up**] **4** You **keep off** something when you avoid talking about it: *Thank God we managed to keep off the subject of politics.* [*same as* **steer clear of**] **5** Rain or snow that **keeps off** doesn't come, when you expected it would. [*same as* **hold off**; *opposite* **come on**]

○ **keep on**

1 You **keep on** doing something when you continue to do it or do it repeatedly: *They kept on walking in spite of their hunger and tiredness.* ❑ *She keeps on talking about her childhood, as if she wants to return to the past.* ❑ *As I keep on telling you, your parents know best.* [*same as* **carry on**; *opposite* **stop, give up**] **2** Someone **keeps** you **on** when they continue to employ you: *If you're a good worker, they might keep you on for another few weeks.* ❑ *Most of them will go when the office closes; the best will be kept on in other jobs.* [*same as* **retain**; *opposite* **get rid of, sack, give the sack**]

○ **keep out**

You tell someone to **keep out** when you don't want them to enter a place or an area: *A handwritten sign on the door said 'DANGER. KEEP OUT!'.* ❑ *We tried all sorts of ways of keeping the neighbour's dogs out of our garden.* [*same as* **keep away**; *opposite* **bring in, go in, come in**]

○ **keep to**

1 You **keep to** something when you follow its line or course and don't go away from it: *Keep to the path and you won't get lost.* ❑ *Our discussion time is limited, so we must keep to the subject.* ❑ *When you work shifts, it's difficult to keep to a regular routine.* ❑ *There'd be no problems if they'd kept to the original plan.* [*same as* **stick to**; *opposite* **go off**] **2** You **keep** something **to** a certain amount when you limit it to that amount: *Pocket money should be kept to about £5 per child per week.* ❑ *We try to keep waste to an absolute minimum.* [*same as* **restrict**; *compare* **keep down**] **3** You **keep** someone **to** a decision or promise when you make them do what they have decided or promised: *He had said he was willing to marry the girl and they were determined to keep him to it.* ❑ *Patrick was kept to his word by pressure from close friends and family.* **4** You **keep** something **to** yourself when you don't tell others about it: *I'd like you to keep our little discussion to yourself.* ❑ *She'd always kept her feelings to herself.*

○ **keep up**

1 One person or thing **keeps up** with another that is moving or progressing when they move or progress at the same speed as the other: *She walked so fast that I had to trot to keep up with her.* ❑ *Salaries are increased regularly to keep up with inflation.* ❑ *One or two of the pupils are finding it difficult to keep up with the rest of the class.* ❑ *You'll have to work a little faster if you want to keep up.* [*same as* **keep pace**; *opposite* **fall behind, get left behind, drop back**] **2** You **keep up** with things that are happening if you make sure you know about them: *I do try to keep up with the latest developments in world politics.* ❑ *So many changes are being made all the time that it's impossible to keep up.* [*same as* **stay abreast, keep in touch**; *opposite* **lose touch, lose track of**]

3 You **keep** something **up** when you continue to do or achieve it, not letting it decline or stop: *I knew he couldn't keep that pace up for long.* ❑ *Her work has improved greatly in recent weeks; let's hope she can keep it up.* ❑ *They kept up the attack for most of the game, but without creating a single real scoring chance.* ❑ *It's important that academic standards should be kept up.* ❑ *Marching soldiers would sing to keep their spirits up.* ❑ *The doctor says you must eat to keep your strength up.* ❑ *If this hot weather keeps up, there could be a drought.* [*same as* **maintain, sustain, persist**; *opposite* **drop off, let up**] **4** You **keep** someone **up** when you cause them not to go to bed until later than usual or later than they would like: *A phone call from Floyd kept her up past her normal bedtime.* ❑ *I must apologise for keeping you up so late.*

kick /kɪk/: **kicks, kicking, kicked**

○ **kick in** (*AmE*; *informal*)

You **kick in**, or **kick in** money, when you pay for your share in something: *The office wanted to buy her a wedding present, so I had to kick in.* ❑ *Joe kicked in £10 for the party.*

○ **kick off**

1 A football match **kicks off** when play begins: *One of their players arrived late, so we didn't kick off until quarter past.* **2** (*informal*) To **kick off** is also to start or begin anything: *The course kicked off with coffee and an introductory chat.* ❑ *I suppose we should kick off by learning one another's names.* ❑ *They kicked off the concert with a couple of their best-known songs.* [*same as* **open, commence**] **3** You **kick off** your shoes when you casually push each shoe off with the opposite foot: *She flopped into a chair and kicked her boots off.* **4** (*AmE*; *informal*) If you **kick off**, you die: *My uncle always said he would kick off before he reached 40.*

○ **kick out** (*informal*)

To **kick** someone **out** of somewhere is to force them to leave: *A group on a table in the corner got a bit rowdy and the manager kicked them out.* ❑ *He's been kicked out of his job.* ❑ *She was expelled from two schools, and later managed to*

get herself kicked out of college. [*same as* **throw out, turn out**]

○ **kick over** (*AmE*)

If a vehicle or its motor **kicks over**, it starts to operate: *It was so cold, my car took 15 minutes to kick over.* ❑ *The engine kicked over twice and died.*

kill /kɪl/: **kills, killing, killed**

○ **kill off**

You **kill** something **off** when you destroy it completely: *Early frosts killed off most of the fruit.* ❑ *Any opposition to the scheme would have to be killed off in the early stages.* [*same as* **wipe out**]

kiss /kɪs/: **kisses, kissing, kissed**

○ **kiss up to** (*AmE*; *informal*)

When someone is trying to flatter another person, you can say disapprovingly that they are **kissing up to** that person: *I can't stand the way Maria kisses up to the professor.*

knock /nɒk/: **knocks, knocking, knocked**

○ **knock out**

1 Someone **is knocked out** when they are made unconscious by being hit on the head, or made sleepy or unconscious by drugs or alcohol: *The blow seemed to have knocked him out.* ❑ *A whisky before bedtime usually knocks me out.* [*opposite* **bring round**] **2** (*BrE*)

A competitor or team **is knocked out** of a competition when they are defeated at one of its stages and do not take any further part in it: *We were knocked out in the third round.* [*same as* **beat, eliminate**; *opposite* **go through**] **3** You **knock** something **out** when you force it out by a sharp blow: *She walked into a door and knocked one of her teeth out.* **4** (*informal*) You **knock** something **out** when you produce it quickly and with little or no effort or care: *You can spot the students who just knock out their essays in a couple of hours.* [*same as* **knock off, churn out, crank out, rattle off**] **5** (*informal*) You might say that something **knocks** you **out** when you are very impressed by it: *The poems just knocked me out; I'd never read anything like them before.* [*same as* **bowl over**]

○ **knock up**

1 (*BrE*; *informal*) You **knock** something **up** when you make it quickly: *She was* *one of those people who could knock up a dress in an evening.* **2** (*BrE*) You **knock** someone **up** when you wake them by knocking on their door: *We asked John and Betty, who were early risers, to knock us up around 7.30.* [*same as* **get up, rouse**]

lag /lag/: **lags, lagging, lagged**
○ **lag behind**
A person or thing **lags behind** another or others when they move or progress more slowly and become left behind: *Mum strode out purposefully, with Dad and the kids lagging behind.* ▫ *Salaries in Britain lag behind those in many other European countries.* [*same as* **fall behind**]

land /land/: **lands, landing, landed**
○ **land in**
Someone or something **lands** you **in** a difficult situation when they cause or create it for you: *Comments like that could land the whole government in trouble.* ▫ *You're going to land yourself in an intolerable mess if you don't assert yourself now.* [*same as* **get into**]

○ **land on** (*AmE*; *informal*)
You **land on** someone when you criticize them harshly: *When I saw the teacher's look, I knew he was going to land on me.*

○ **land up** (*informal*)
You **land up** in a particular place or situation when you arrive there, especially without particularly intending to, after a journey or a series of events: *After months of travelling she landed up in Istanbul.* ▫ *I didn't want to land up teaching English in some remote place.* ▫ *Over half of them will land up in prison by the time they're twenty.* [*same as* **end up, wind up** (*informal*)]

○ **land with** (*BrE*; *informal*)
Someone **lands** you **with** a problem or something unwanted when they leave you to deal with it: *I found myself landed with the bill for the whole meal.* ▫ *She always seemed to get landed with the clumsiest dancers.* [*same as* **lumber with** (*informal*), **saddle with** (*informal*)]

last /lɑːst/: **lasts, lasting, lasted**
○ **last out** (*especially BrE*)
1 A supply of something **lasts out** when it is not used up too soon: *A pile of firewood that size should last out the winter.* ▫ *I wasn't sure how long our oil reserves would last out.* [*same as* **hold out, subsist** (*formal*); *opposite* **run out, dry up**] **2** To **last out** is to survive, especially to remain strong or in good working order for a certain period or as long as is necessary: *He wasn't sure he could last out the whole evening without a whisky.* ▫ *Mexico was only another twenty miles or so, and I was sure my horse would last out.* [*same as* **hold out, hang on, come through**; *opposite* **break down, crack up** (*informal*)]

laugh /lɑːf/: **laughs, laughing, laughed**
○ **laugh off**
You **laugh off** a problem or difficulty when you treat it as unimportant or as a joke: *Actors learn to laugh off criticisms in the press.* ▫ *If anyone said anything nasty about her, she would laugh it off.* [*same as* **shrug off, make light of**; *opposite* **take seriously, take to heart**]

lay /leɪ/: **lays, laying, laid**
○ **lay aside**
1 You **lay** something **aside** when you keep or save it to use later: *We always have some spare cash laid aside for emergencies.* ▫ *Could you lay it aside for me if I promise to collect it next week?* [*same as* **lay by, set aside, put aside**] **2** You **lay aside** something you are using or doing when you put it down and take a break or rest: *It must have been three o'clock before I finally laid my books aside.* [*same as* **set aside, put aside**] **3** You **lay aside** your feelings or opinions when you take a decision to abandon them and adopt new ones: *It was hard to see how they could lay aside years of*

mutual dislike. ❑ *She will have to lay her old fears aside and get on with the future.* [*same as* **cast aside**, **set aside**, **dismiss**]

○ **lay down**
1 You **lay** something **down** when you put it down, *eg* on a table or on the floor: *The gunmen were then ordered to lay down their weapons.* [*same as* **set down**; *opposite* **pick up**, **take up**] **2** A rule, or a person in authority, **lays down** what should be done when they state officially what must be done: *The government have issued a new booklet laying down guidelines for safety at work.* ❑ *Conditions for membership are laid down in the club rules.* [*same as* **set out**, **stipulate**] **3** Someone **lays down** their life when they die fighting for a cause or to save someone else. [*same as* **sacrifice**] **4** Wine **is laid down** when it is stored, to be drunk in the future: *All too often, people who have laid down a cellarful of expensive wine feel obliged to prepare a feast to go with it.* **5** When something is being built on an area of land, people sometimes say that it **is being laid down**: *Where before there was only wasteland, beautiful gardens have been laid down.*

○ **lay off**
1 A company **lays** people **off** when it stops employing them, permanently or often only temporarily: *They'll be laying off another fifty employees in the new year.* ❑ *We've been laid off indefinitely until business picks up.* [*opposite* **take on**, **hire**; *same as* **sack**, **pay off**] **2** (*informal*) People sometimes tell someone who is annoying them or attacking them to **lay off** when they want them to stop: *He'd been warned to lay off, but was too drunk to take notice.* ❑ *Lay off him, Tom; he's just a kid.* [*same as* **leave off**, **give over** (*informal*), **quit**] **3** (*informal*) You **lay off** something when you stop doing, using or consuming it: *The doctor's told him to cut out the big lunches and lay off the beer and whisky.* ❑ *It's a good idea to lay off the chemical fertilizers and make your own organic compost.* [*same as* **stay off**, **give up**]

○ **lay on**
1 You **lay** something **on** when you provide or supply it: *Up till now the management has always laid on a Christmas party for the staff.* ❑ *They even laid a car on, to take him to the airport.* **2** People often use **lay on**, or **lay upon**, where 'put on' would be used in a general sense: *They tried to lay the blame on us.* ❑ *Emphasis was always laid upon the importance of classical training.*

○ **lay out**
1 You **lay** things **out** when you arrange them in a neat, ordered way: *She laid all her photographs out on the floor.* ❑ *He would methodically lay out all his clothes for the morning.* [*same as* **set out**, **spread out**] **2** Things such as gardens, towns and streets **are laid out** when they are designed and arranged according to a certain plan: *splendidly laid-out gardens.* **3** Things such as ideas or plans **are laid out** when they are described or presented in detail: *The inspector's recommendations are laid out in a paper entitled 'Options for Improvement'.* [*same as* **set out**] **4** (*informal*) You **lay out** money on something when you spend a lot of money on it: *The company simply wouldn't be prepared to lay out sums of that kind.* [*same as* **fork out** (*informal*), **shell out** (*informal*)] **5** (*informal*) A person **is laid out** when someone hits them and knocks them to the ground, usually making them unconscious: *The blow laid him out flat on the floor.* [*same as* **knock out**]

○ **lay to** (*AmE*)
You **lay to** when you make a great effort or work hard: *This book has a deadline, so everyone needs to lay to.*

○ **lay upon** *see* **lay on**.

lead /liːd/: **leads**, **leading**, **led** /lɛd/

○ **lead on**
Someone **leads** you **on** when they make you believe something that is not true, *eg* by telling you a series of lies or giving you false impressions: *The boy, it seems, was really in love, but Eleanor was just leading him on.* ❑ *Are we just being led on by the advertisers?* [*same as* **string along** (*informal*), **deceive**, **lead up the garden path** (*informal*)]

○ **lead up to**
1 A series of events **lead up to** a particular situation if one develops from another so as to cause or create that situation: *Let's examine the events leading up to World War I.* **2** You **lead up to** a particular subject in a conversation when you carefully direct the conversation towards it: *I wondered what you were leading up to.*

lean /liːn/: **leans, leaning, leaned** *or* (*especially BrE*) **leant** /lɛnt/
Leaned and **leant** are both used as the past tense and past participle of the verb.

○ **lean on** (*informal*)
1 Someone **leans on** you when they use threats or other forms of pressure to try to make you do what they want: *If he won't pay up, we'll have to lean on him a bit.* [*same as* **coerce, pressurize**] **2** You **lean on** someone when you need their help or support, and you expect them to give it whenever you ask for it: *The youngest boy has always leant a lot on his parents.* ▫ *For too long the company has been leaning on its reputation and its past glories, forgetting that in the modern world you have to earn your business.* [*same as* **rely on, depend on**]

○ **lean towards** *or* **lean toward**
American speakers of English usually use **toward** instead of **towards**.
People often say that they **lean towards** something that they support or prefer, or something that they are in favour of: *It is clear that NATO is leaning increasingly towards a military solution.* ▫ *If anything, I lean towards the Liberals on this issue.* [*same as* **tend towards, incline towards** (*formal*); *opposite* **be against, oppose**]

leap /liːp/: **leaps, leaping, leaped** /liːpt/ *or* /lɛpt/, **leapt** /lɛpt/
Leaped and **leapt** are both used as the past tense and past participle of the verb.

○ **leap at**
You **leap at** something when you accept it eagerly: *I imagine she would leap at the chance to spend her summer working in Australia.* [*same as* **jump at, grab**]

○ **leap out**
1 Someone **leaps out** when they suddenly appear from a hiding place: *At the moment the camera stopped, the dog was to leap out and start barking.* [*same as* **jump out, emerge**] **2** Something **leaps out** at you when you notice it immediately because it is very striking or obvious: *Bad grammar and punctuation leapt out at him from every page.* [*same as* **jump out**]

leave /liːv/: **leaves, leaving, left** /lɛft/
Left is used as both the past tense and past participle of the verb.

○ **leave behind**
1 You **leave** someone or something **behind** when you don't take them with you, whether by accident or on purpose: *The passenger jets off happily to the sun while their luggage is left behind in London.* ▫ *They frequently go off by themselves and leave the children behind with Granny.* [*opposite* **take, bring**] **2** You use **leave behind** to talk about things, often unpleasant or unwanted things, that remain in a place as a result of someone or something having been there: *Gigantic tankers ply coastal waters and leave a trail of oil and debris behind them.* ▫ *She has taken care not to make herself responsible for any business debts that may be left behind after his death.* ▫ *The Romans departed, leaving behind them a network of roads that was to form the backbone of our transport system for centuries.* **3** Someone who **is left behind** fails to progress or advance as well as others: *The child who can already read doesn't leave his classmates behind; rather he is held back while they struggle to bring themselves up to his level.* [*same as* **outstrip**; *compare* **fall behind**]

○ **leave out**
1 You **leave** something or someone **out** when you don't include them: *After such a poor performance, he risks being left out of the squad for the winter tour.* ▫ *I told her what you'd said, leaving out the bit about her husband.* [*same as* **omit**; *opposite* **put in, add**] **2** (*BrE; informal*) People sometimes say **leave it out** as a way of telling someone to stop doing something, especially to stop

telling lies or pretending: *'This has been one of the greatest days of my life!' 'Oh, leave it out; it's not been that exciting.'* [*same as* **turn in**]

let /lɛt/: **lets, letting, let**
  Let is used as the past tense and past participle of the verb.

○ **let down**
  1 Someone **lets** you **down** when they fail to do what they agreed or promised they would do, or what you expected they would do: *That would be letting down my whole family; I could never do that.* ▫ *It's understandable that people feel let down by a government that said it would bring taxes down.* **2** (*BrE*) You **let down** something that is filled with air, such as a tyre, when you allow the air inside it to escape: *They'd let one of the teachers' tyres down.* [*same as* **deflate**; *opposite* **blow up, pump up, inflate**] **3** To **let down** garments such as skirts and dresses is to make them longer by unfolding material that forms their bottom edge: *For my sister, who was taller, we had to let the coat down by a good couple of inches.* [*opposite* **take up**; *see also* **let out**] **4** (*AmE*) If you **let down**, you relax or do not keep up an effort: *We almost have this game won, so don't let down.* ▫ *We can't let down before all the furniture is moved.*

○ **let in on** (*informal*)
  You **let** someone **in on** something that is secret, or is reserved for a few people only, when you tell them about it, or allow them to take part in it: *I'll let you in on a little secret; I'm going to go for that job at the Sorbonne.* ▫ *If they'd let anyone else in on the scam it would have meant smaller shares for everyone.*

○ **let off**
  1 Someone who **is let off** is given a punishment less severe than they deserve, or no punishment at all: *I'll let you off this time; next time it'll be no football for a week.* ▫ *The papers reported it as a rapist being let off with a fine.* [*compare* **get off**] **2** Someone who **is let off** a duty or task is allowed not to do it: *The beauty of a holiday is being let off cooking and housework.* ▫ *Some teachers would let you off homework if you played in the orchestra.* **3** To **let off** a gun is to

fire it; to **let off** a bomb or other exploding device is to make it explode: *They dress up in bright costumes and let off fireworks.* ▫ *He wouldn't have dared let the gun off inside the house, for fear someone would hear it.* [*compare* **go off, set off**] **4** Smoke, gases or fumes **are let off** when they are released: *The steam that the boiler lets off could be harnessed to produce electricity.* [*same as* **give off, emit**] **5** The driver of a vehicle you are travelling in **lets** you **off** when they stop to allow you to get out: *We made an unscheduled stop at Igoumenitsa, to let off a couple of sick passengers.* ▫ *She said she had errands to run; I let her off at the post office.* [*same as* **drop off, put off, set down**]

○ **let out**
  1 You **let** someone **out** when you allow them to leave, usually by opening or unlocking a door: *There was opposition to the policy of letting prisoners out for Christmas.* ▫ *Food and drink are brought in to her; she's never let out of the room for anything.* ▫ *Don't interrupt your meal; I can let myself out.* **2** To **let out** something such as air or water is to allow it to escape or flow out: *Lift the baby out before you let the water out of the bath.* ▫ *Try to let the breath out slowly and evenly.* [*same as* **release**] **3** You **let out** sounds or noises when you make them: *Tristan squeezed the damaged paw and the dog let out a yelp.* [*same as* **emit, utter**] **4** You **let** something **out** when you say something that should be kept secret: *It seemed clear that a member of the team had let out the details of our meeting.* [*same as* **let slip**; *compare* **come out, get out**] **5** (*informal*) Something **lets** you **out** when it allows you to avoid doing something or to escape something, usually something unpleasant: *The meeting has been fixed for next Wednesday, which lets me out as I'll be in Amsterdam.* ▫ *'They're looking for talented young musicians.' 'That lets you out, then!'* **6** (*especially BrE*) You **let out** a house or other property that you own when you rent it to other people: *They could easily let a couple of rooms out to students, to make a bit of extra money.*

[*same as* **rent out**] **7** To **let out** a garment is to make it wider by repositioning the joins at its sides, bringing out material that was inside the original joins: *I let it out a couple of inches when I was pregnant.* [*opposite* **take in**; *see also* **let down**]

○ **let up**

Something **lets up** when it becomes less strong or intense, or when it stops altogether: *There'll be serious flooding if the rain doesn't let up soon.* ❑ *The good interviewer puts the pressure on with the first couple of questions and never lets up for the whole interview.*

▶ *noun* **let-up**: **let-ups**: *There's been no let-up in fighting in the two days since the agreement was signed.*

○ **let up on** (*AmE*)

You **let up on** someone when you stop criticizing them or treating them severely or badly: *His mother would not let up on Frank until he made better grades.* ❑ *Not once did the lawyer let up on the witness.*

level /'lɛvəl/: **levels**, **levelling** (*AmE* **leveling**), **levelled** (*AmE* **leveled**)

○ **level off** *or* **level out**

1 You **level off** a surface when you make it smooth or level: *Once the concrete begins to set you can level it off with a square edge, or a plasterer's float, for a really smooth finish.* **2** Something that is rising or falling in number, amount, degree or extent **levels off** or **levels out** when it stops rising or falling and remains steady or level: *Student intake had reached over 25,000 before it began to level off.* ❑ *The road climbed steeply and then levelled out.* **3** An aircraft **levels off** or **levels out** when it begins to fly horizontally after flying up or down: *We levelled out at 35,000 feet.*

○ **level with** (*informal*)

You **level with** someone when you're honest with them and tell them the whole truth: *I don't think they're levelling with me about their plans for the land.* [*same as* **be straight with** (*informal*)]

lie /laɪ/: **lies**, **lying**, **lay** /leɪ/, **lain** /leɪn/

○ **lie down**

1 You **lie down** when you get into a flat or horizontal position, especially to sleep or have a rest: *I lay down on the*

grass *and went to sleep.* ❑ *We were ordered to lie down and place our hands behind our heads.* **2** Someone who refuses to **lie down** is determined not to stop fighting or struggling: *Local protesters say they will not lie down over the issue of the proposed bridge.* [*same as* **give in**, **give up**, **yield**; *opposite* **fight on**]

○ **lie in** (*BrE*)

You **lie in** when you intentionally stay in bed until after the time you usually get up in the mornings: *The twins slept on until after nine, which gave us a rare opportunity to lie in.* [*compare* **sleep in**]

lift /lɪft/: **lifts**, **lifting**, **lifted**

○ **lift off**

A spacecraft **lifts off** when it rises up from the ground at the beginning of a flight.

light /laɪt/: **lights**, **lighting**, **lit** /lɪt/, **lighted**

Lighted and **lit** can both be used as the past tense and past participle of the verb, though **lit** is more usual.

○ **light up**

1 To **light** something **up** is to shine lights on it or make it bright with light; something **lights up** when a light inside it is switched on: *Fires all along the hillside lit up the night sky.* ❑ *It makes a difference having public buildings lit up at night.* ❑ *The control panel lights up automatically when you go through a tunnel.* [*same as* **illuminate**] **2** People's faces or eyes **light up** when an expression of happiness or excitement comes into them: *Young eyes light up at the mention of Christmas.* **3** (*informal*) Someone **lights up** when they light a cigarette or pipe and begin to smoke it: *You see the smokers lighting up as soon as they get off the coach.*

lighten /'laɪtən/: **lightens**, **lightening**, **lightened**

○ **lighten up** (*especially AmE*; *informal*)

You can tell someone to **lighten up** if you think they are too serious or tense and should relax more: *The whole damn deal might be blown if Rizzo doesn't lighten up a little.*

line /laɪn/: **lines**, **lining**, **lined**

○ **line up**

1 People **line up** when they form a straight line or queue; you **line** them **up** when you put them into a straight line or queue. **2** You **line** one thing **up** with another when you make it straight, or in the right position, in relation to the other: *Skoda, now a member of the Volkswagen group, is lining up right alongside companies such as BMW and Mercedes in the pursuit of motoring excellence.* ❑ *Don't rush the shot; take time to line up the camera.* ❑ *The casual effect of a dry-stone wall is ruined if you try to line stones up with each other perfectly.* **3** (*informal*) You **line** something **up** when you organize or arrange it: *She's got a job lined up for the summer.* ❑ *A singer has been lined up for the party.* [*same as* **fix up**, **lay on**] **4** People often use **line up** to say whom, in a dispute or conflict, they give their support to and whom they oppose: *A number of prominent backbenchers were lining up against the Cabinet.* **5** (*AmE*) In American football, players **line up** for a kick-off or to begin a play: *Denver is lining up with the ends split wide.*

link /lɪŋk/: **links, linking, linked**

○ **link up**

You **link up** two people, places or things when you connect or join them in some way: *The Edinburgh office is linked up with the London office by computer.*

listen /'lɪsən/: **listens, listening, listened**

○ **listen in**

1 You **listen in** to a private conversation, *eg* on the telephone, when you listen to it secretly: *Her parents sit outside the door to listen in on her conversations with friends.* ❑ *We can't talk about anything without your father listening in.* [*same as* **eavesdrop**] **2** You **listen in** to a radio programme when you listen to it: *If you were listening in last week, you'll remember that Eric Clapton was in the studio.* [*compare* **tune in**]

○ **listen out**

You **listen out** for something when you prepare to hear and identify the sound of it when it comes: *I lie awake, listening out for the sound of her key in the door.* [*compare* **look out for**]

live /lɪv/: **lives, living, lived**

○ **live down**

You'll never **live down** something you've done when it is so very foolish, embarrassing or wrong that people will never forget it or forgive you for it: *I'll never live it down if I fail my driving test again.*

○ **live off**

1 You **live off** a certain kind of food when it is the only kind you eat, often because no other kinds are available: *We slept on the ground and lived off whatever was growing on the trees and in the fields.* [*same as* **live on**] **2** People use **live off** to say where they get the money they need to live: *The interest from his UK investments alone is enough for them to live off.* ❑ *We were made to feel that we'd lived off our parents long enough.*

○ **live on**

1 People use **live on** to say how much money they have to buy food, clothes and other things they need: *I wasn't sure the family could live on one wage only.* **2** You **live on** a certain kind of food when that is the only kind of food you eat, perhaps because there are no other kinds available: *Health problems of one sort or another are inevitable in children who live predominantly on fried food and sweets.* [*same as* **live off**] **3** You can use **live on** to talk about what still exists, or what people in general still remember: *His widow lived on into her nineties.* **4** Something **lives on** if people go on remembering it: *The disaster lives on in people's memories, kept alive perhaps by its frequent treatment in film.*

○ **live up** (*informal*)

Someone who **is living** it **up** is having a wild, exciting time full of pleasures, especially the kind of pleasures that cost a lot of money: *He said he had worked long and hard for years and now he was going to live it up a bit.*

○ **live up to**

Something that **lives up to** expectations is as good, or sometimes as bad, as you expected it to be: *Barry spent the evening living up to his reputation as a ladies' man.* ❑ *Very few of the products lived up to the claims of their manu-*

facturers. [*same as* **match up to**, **measure up to**]

long /lɒŋ/: **longs, longing, longed**

○ **long for**

You **long for** something when you have a very strong desire to have it: *The cold wet winters depressed her; she longed for balmy Mediterranean evenings.* [*same as* **be dying for, yearn for** (*formal*), **hunger for, hanker for**]

▶ *adjective* **longed-for**: *It can be pretty upsetting when a much longed-for holiday goes disastrously wrong.*

look /lʊk/: **looks, looking, looked**

○ **look after**

1 You **look after** someone, usually a child or someone ill, when you do and give what they need and keep them safe and well: *Women, as much as men, are surprised to learn that fathers are capable of looking after their babies.* [*same as* **care for, take care of**] **2** You **look after** something when you keep it in good condition: *A reliable car, well looked after, should last you at least six years.* [*same as* **take care of**] **3** Someone who **looks after** something is responsible for doing it, dealing with it or making decisions about it: *This company books the venue and the band, and even looks after the catering.* □ *You often find that cleaning is looked after by an outside contractor.* [*same as* **see to**, **attend to, take care of**] **4** You **look after** something for someone when you make sure that it is not damaged, lost or stolen, perhaps while they are away: *Would you look after my cases while I go to the toilet?* □ *We're looking after the house next door while the neighbours are on holiday.* [*same as* **watch, mind, keep an eye on**] **5** You say you can **look after** yourself to tell someone you are able to protect yourself from people who try to harm or deceive you: *He said I wasn't to worry about John, that he was a big boy now and could look after himself.*

○ **look ahead**

You **look ahead** when you consider the future, and perhaps prepare for what you expect will happen: *Looking ahead ten years, we can see the South East Asian countries dominating the market.*

○ **look back** *or* **look back on**

1 You **look back**, or **look back on** something, when you think about the past: *She looks back on her childhood with fond memories.* **2** You say someone has **never looked back** if they have been very successful: *She opened her first shop at the age of twenty and never looked back.*

○ **look down on**

Someone who **looks down on** you thinks you are not very important, or less important than they are: *It's amazing to think how goods from Japan were once looked down on.* [*same as* **sneer at, look down one's nose at, turn one's nose up at**]

○ **look forward to**

You **look forward to** something that is going to happen when you feel happy because you know you are going to enjoy it: *She's looking forward to the birth of her baby.* □ *Are they looking forward to going to Australia?* □ *I think we can look forward to a period of sustained economic growth.*

○ **look into**

You **look into** something when you investigate it: *I've offered to look into the problem for him.*

○ **look on**

1 You **look on** when you watch something without taking part: *The boys were presented with their medals as proud parents and friends looked on.* **2** You can use **look on** or **look upon** to talk about the way you regard or consider something: *Some men do look upon marriage as an unnecessary restriction on personal freedom.* □ *They made it clear that they would not look kindly on applications from Blacks.*

○ **look out**

1 You say '**look out!**' to warn someone of danger: *Look out! There's a car coming!* [*same as* **watch out**] **2** (*BrE*) You use **look out** to talk about looking for something when you're not sure where it is because you haven't used or seen it for a long time: *Chris and Dave came down, and we looked out some old photos from our schooldays.* □ *There's a hand drill in the garage; I'll look it out for you.* [*same as* **dig out**]

○ **look out for**

1 You **look out for** something when you are ready to notice and identify it when it comes or when it becomes available: *I've got Tom looking out for one in the Edinburgh secondhand shops.* ❑ *Look out for a sign on the right.* [*same as* **watch out for**] **2** You **look out for** someone when you are ready to give protection when they need it: *With a close-knit extended family, they all look out for each other.*

○ **look over**

You **look over** something, or **look** it **over**, when you examine it: *We've looked over several flats in this part of town.* ❑ *Could you briefly look over this report for me?* ❑ *Why don't you let the doctor look you over to make sure you haven't broken anything?*

○ **look through**

1 You **look through** things when you examine them one by one: *I looked through my clothes but found nothing suitable for the funeral.* ❑ *Neil asked me to look through all the cupboards again, but I knew we wouldn't find anything.* [*same as* **go through**] **2** You **look through** something written or printed when you read it briefly: *I only get about ten minutes at breakfast to look through the morning's headlines.*

○ **look to**

1 You **look to** someone for something when you rely on or expect them to do or provide it: *She has always looked to her parents for support.* ❑ *It would seem fanciful to look to poetry to inspire a revolution of any kind.* [*same as* **turn to**] **2** You **look to** the future when you consider it: *He said they had put all the bad times behind them and were now looking to the future with confidence.*

○ **look up**

1 You **look** information **up** when you look for it in books or other printed material where it may be found: *I had to look up the spelling in a dictionary.* ❑ *They gave me the street-name and I looked it up on the map.* **2** (*informal*) You **look** someone **up** whom you haven't seen for a while when you visit them: *Look us up if you're ever in Edinburgh.* **3** (*informal*) You can say that a

situation **is looking up** when it is improving: *The weather is beginning to look up.* ❑ *With cuts in interest rates, things are beginning to look up for small businesses.*

○ **look upon** *see* **look on**.

○ **look up to**

You **look up to** someone that you admire and respect: *Because students automatically look up to you, you have a responsibility not to talk rubbish.*

lose /luːz/: **loses, losing, lost** /lɒst/

○ **lose out**

You **lose out** as a result of something if it causes you to suffer a loss or other disadvantage: *A spread of investments safeguards you if you lose out on any single investment.* ❑ *With indirect taxes like VAT, it's always the people at the bottom of the scale who lose out.*

lunch /lʌntʃ/: **lunches, lunching, lunched**

○ **lunch out** (*AmE*)

You **lunch out** when you have lunch away from your home or office: *The secretaries always lunched out on Friday to discuss their weekend plans.*

make /meɪk/: **makes, making, made** /meɪd/

○ **make for**

1 You **make for** a place when you move towards it: *We didn't tell them we were really making for Athens.* ❑ *He jumped up and made hastily for the door.* [*same as* **head for**] **2** Something **makes for** a certain situation if that situation is likely to occur as a result: *Fine weather made for an enjoyable holiday.*

○ **make of**

What you **make of** something is the opinion you form of it, or the impression you get of it, or what you understand it to mean: *So, what did you make of the new manager?* □ *I didn't know what to make of her strange response.*

○ **make off** (*informal*)

1 You **make off** when you leave, especially hurriedly: *The thieves made off in a yellow Transit van.* [*same as* **take off**] **2** Someone **makes off** with something when they steal it: *Anyone might walk in and make off with the family silver.*

○ **make out**

1 You can **make** something **out** when you are able to see or hear it, usually with difficulty: *I could make out the faint outline of a car in the fog.* □ *I couldn't make out all the words of the song.* [*compare* **pick out**] **2** You can **make** something **out** when you can understand it, usually with difficulty: *I couldn't make out whether he was pleased or not.* □ *From his account of events, it was difficult to make out how it had happened.* [*same as* **work out**, **figure out**] **3** You can't **make** someone **out** if you can't decide what kind of person they are, or you can't understand why they behave the way they do: *None of us could really make Phil out; he had every reason to be happy.* [*same as* **figure out**] **4** You **make out** that something is so when you try to convince people that it is: *She's been making out that checking windows was not her responsibility.* □ *The programme made her out to be concerned only with holding on to power.* □ *It's not as difficult as some people make out.* **5** You can use **make out** to talk about the way you describe someone or something, or the impression you give of them, particularly when it is a false or wrong impression: *The press had made him out to be a shameless philanderer who trifled with unsuspecting women's hearts.* □ *The situation is not as black as it is made out to be.* □ *She makes herself out to be something of an expert in the field.* **6** You **make out** things such as cheques and receipts when you write the necessary details on them: *Could you make the cheque out to Breakages Ltd?* [*same as* **write out**; *compare* **fill in**] **7** (*infor-*

mal) You can ask how someone **is making out** when you want to know how they are, or what progress they are making; someone who says they **are making out** means they are dealing successfully with the situation they are in: *I don't know how they'll make out in the big city.* □ *You shouldn't worry about Clancy; he'll make out all right on his own.* **8** (*slang*) To **make out** is to engage in sexual activity: *I could see a couple of kids making out in the back of my truck.* [*same as* **get on**, **get along**, **cope**, **manage**]

○ **make up**

1 The things that **make up** something are its parts, or the things that form it: *The potting compost is made up of moss peat, sharp sand, garden soil and fertiliser.* □ *Blacks still make up only 2% of our representation nationwide.* [*same as* **comprise**, **constitute**] **2** You **make up** something that is not true when you invent it, perhaps to deceive others: *She made up some feeble excuse to do with washing her hair.* □ *They had accused him of making the whole thing up.* [*same as* **cook up** (*informal*), **trump up** (*informal*), **concoct 3** You **make** something **up** when you prepare it by putting various things together: *The kitchen staff will be happy to make up packed lunches for guests that require them.* **4** You **make up** something when you add the number or amount of things that are missing, to make it complete: *We need another player to make up the team.* **5** You **make up** your mind when you make a firm and final decision or choice: *I couldn't make up my mind whether he was lying or not.* □ *She made her mind up to get on the first train that came in.* **6** Someone **makes** themselves **up** when they put cosmetics on their face. **7** People who have quarrelled **make up**, or **make** it **up**, when they settle their differences and become friends again: *Have you made it up with Janice yet?* **8** You **make up** a bed when you prepare a bed that is not currently being used, *eg* for an unexpected guest: *Don't go to the bother of making the camp bed up; I'm just as happy on the sofa.*

map 55 **mess**

○ **make up for**

1 Something **makes up for** something else that is lacking or lost if it replaces it and restores the balance: *We'll have to work hard to make up for lost time.* **2** You **make up for** something bad or wrong that you have done when you do something good or right as an apology or to restore a good relationship with someone: *I hoped this would make up for my earlier rudeness.* ❑ *She wanted to do something to make up for coming home late the previous evening.* [*same as* **compensate for, atone for**]

○ **make with** (*especially AmE; informal*) Someone who tells you to **make with** something wants you to bring or produce it: *Hey, waitress! Let's make with the coffee over here!*

map /map/: **maps, mapping, mapped**

○ **map out**

You **map out** future plans, intentions or schemes when you decide or explain how they will happen: *Her parents appear to have her career all mapped out for her.* ❑ *We took a number of options and mapped them out for the students to consider.* [*same as* **set out, lay out**]

match /matʃ/: **matches, matching, matched**

○ **match up**

Things **match up** when they are the same or similar, when they are suited to each other, or when they fit together correctly: *If you can match up the names with the faces, you can win a faulous prize.* ❑ *Genetic fingerprinting techniques confirmed that crime and suspect matched up.*

max /maks/: **maxes, maxing, maxed**

○ **max out** (*AmE; informal*)

If someone or somebody **maxes out**, they do or reach a maximum or limit: *Henry was the type of worker who could max out on anything you gave him.* ❑ *The plane soared upward, maxing out at 30,000 feet.*

meet /miːt/: **meets, meeting, met** /mɛt/

○ **meet up**

1 You **meet up** with someone when you each go to the same place at the same time by arrangement, to do something together: *We parted in Cologne, arranging to meet up in Venice a week later.* **2** Things **meet up** at the point where they connect with or join each other: *An extra signal box was positioned where the old track meets up with the new.* [*same as* **link up, join up, come together**]

○ **meet with**

1 You **meet with** people when you come together for a discussion: *She is meeting with her solicitors this morning.* [*same as* **meet**] **2** Something **meets with**, or **is met with**, a certain response or reaction if that is the way people respond or react to it: *My suggestion met with contempt.* ❑ *Reports of atrocities had initially been met with disbelief.* ❑ *Her first novel met with considerable success.* **3** You can use **meet with** to talk about what happens to you, or what you experience: *If patients meet with an accident whilst in your care, you want to be sure your insurance will cover it.* [*same as* **encounter**]

melt /mɛlt/: **melts, melting, melted**

○ **melt away**

1 Heat **melts** something **away** when it causes it to melt and eventually disappear: *The old layers of paint were quickly melted away.* ❑ *The addition of oil will help the residue to melt away.* **2** You can say that anything **melts away** when it slowly or gradually disappears: *Any support he once had amongst his colleagues had melted away.* [*same as* **fade away, die away, peter out, dwindle**] **3** (*literary*) You can say that people **melt away** when they move away quietly or secretly: *When Derek launched into his salesman routine, most of the guests melted away.* [*same as* **disperse**]

○ **melt down**

To **melt down** an object, especially one made of metal, is to heat it until it melts and can be reshaped or re-used: *Environmental groups opposed plans to melt the structures down.*

mess /mɛs/: **messes, messing, messed**

○ **mess up** (*informal*)

1 You **mess** something **up** when you make it dirty or untidy: *Don't mess up my dress; I've just ironed it.* [*same as*

muck up (*informal*)] **2** You **mess** something **up** when you spoil or damage it: *This strike has really messed up our plans.* [*same as* **muck up** (*informal*), **foul up** (*informal*, **screw up** (*vulgar slang*)] **3** (*AmE*) Someone **messes up** when they make a mistake or do something badly: *This is your last chance; don't mess up.* [*same as* **foul up** (*informal*, **screw up** (*vulgar slang*)]

miss /mɪs/: **misses, missing, missed**
○ **miss out** (*BrE*)
1 You **miss** something **out** when you fail to include it or decide not to include it: *When I read through the form, I noticed that he'd missed out his date of birth.* ❑ *Have I missed anyone out?* [*same as* **leave out**, **omit**] **2** You **miss out** on something that others enjoy when you don't receive it or don't take part in it: *You mustn't miss out on all the free food.* ❑ *I don't want my children to feel that they're missing out not having the toys the others have.*

mix /mɪks/: **mixes, mixing, mixed**
○ **mix up**
1 You **mix up** two people or things when you identify them wrongly and think one is the other: *I always mix him up with his brother.* ❑ *Even now, after knowing them for years, I still sometimes get them mixed up.* [*same as* **muddle up**] **2** You **mix** things **up** when you upset their usual or correct order, whether deliberately or by accident: *Your papers fell on the floor, and I may have mixed them up in retrieving them.* [*same as* **muddle up**, **jumble up**] **3** You **mix** something **up** when you prepare it by combining different ingredients: *Mix up another barrowload of concrete.* ❑ *Sheila mixed up a salt and lemon solution and soaked the area with it.* [*same as* **prepare**] **4** You are **mixed up** in something, such as a crime or other dishonest activity when you are involved in it: *This is the kind of scandal that no government minister wants to get mixed up in.*

move /muːv/: **moves, moving, moved**
○ **move in**
1 You **move in** when you start to live in a new or different house: *We get the keys on Friday and will begin moving in at the weekend.* [*opposite* **move out**; *compare* **settle in**] **2** Someone **moves in** with you when they come to live in your home: *Then she told us her boyfriend wanted to move in.* **3** People who **move in** arrive in order to take action or take control: *The order was given and officers with riot shields moved in.* ❑ *Rival ice-cream sellers moved in on each other's territory.* **4** To **move in** on someone is to approach them in order to attack them: *The boys moved in on him from all sides.* ❑ *Interviewers like Humphries soften you up a bit before they move in for the kill.* [*same as* **close in**]

○ **move off**
A vehicle **moves off** when it starts moving after being stationary: *Don't move off until I've got the children safely strapped in.* [*compare* **set off**]

○ **move on**
1 You **move on** when, after stopping or staying for a while, you leave, often to continue a journey: *No job could keep her for longer than a year; she would get itchy feet and feel it was time to move on.* ❑ *We packed up the trailer and moved on down the coast to Montpelier.* [*compare* **go on**] **2** You **move on** from one thing to the next when you stop doing one thing, or finish doing it, and begin dealing with the next: *Moving on to the question of the concert, we still need volunteers to sell tickets.* [*same as* **go on**] **3** A police officer or other person in authority **moves** you **on** when they order you to leave the place you are standing or sitting in: *A bloke in a uniform said we had to move on.* [*same as* **move along**] **4** You **move on** when you change to something, *eg* a job or a house, that is better than the one you had before: *If he does well, they might move him on to a sales position.* ❑ *He moved on from a late-night slot on Radio Stoke to a high-profile show on national radio.* [*same as* **progress**] **5** Things such as ideas and methods **move on** when they become more modern or more advanced: *Surgical techniques have moved on astonishingly fast in the last five years.* **6** You can say that time **moves on** when it passes, often suggesting that it seems to pass quickly: *We'd better order the*

dress soon; time is moving on.

○ **move out**

1 You **move out** when you leave your house to go and live elsewhere: *We're moving out of the flat in April.* ❑ *They've moved out of this area altogether.* **2** People **are moved out** of a place when they are taken from it or ordered to leave: *We will not be satisfied until the British government moves its troops out of Northern Ireland.* **3** To **move out** of a particular activity or business is to stop being involved in it: *It seemed prudent at the time to move out of sheet metal products altogether.* ❑ *We were certainly taking risks picking up our share of the market at a time when all the big companies were moving out.* [*opposite* **move in**, **move into**]

○ **move up**

1 People in a row or line **move up** when they move so that they are standing or sitting more closely together, usually so as to make room for others: *If we all moved up a little Phil could get on the end.* [*same as* **move along**] **2** You **move up** or **are moved up** when you progress to a higher grade, rank, level or position: *He moves up to the senior school next term.* ❑ *If he's moved up a class now, he'll only be sixteen in his final year.*

muster /ˈmʌstə(r)/: **musters**, **mustering**, **mustered**

○ **muster in** (*AmE*)

A military force **musters** someone **in** when they enlist that person: *Walker was mustered in the Army on his 21st birthday.*

○ **muster out** (*AmE*)

A military force **musters** someone **out** when they discharge that person: *I plan to marry when I'm mustered out.*

name /neɪm/: **names**, **naming**, **named**

○ **name after** (*BrE*)

A child **is named after** another person when they are given the same first or Christian name as that other person, often as a way of showing respect or affection for them; something **is named after** someone or something when it is given the same name as that person or thing: *They named the baby after her mother's father.* ❑ *Peter is named after his maternal grandfather.* ❑ *Behind the apse of the Duomo the visitor passes the Palazzo dell'Orologio, named after the clock at the top.* ❑ *Thrushcross Grange, named after the mansion in Wuthering Heights.* [*same as* **call after**]

○ **name for** (*AmE*)

Name for is mainly used in American English and means the same as **name after**: *He was named for John Edward Grant, his maternal grandfather.* ❑ *the Hoover Dam, named for Herbert Hoover.*

narrow /ˈnaroʊ/: **narrows**, **narrowing**, **narrowed**

○ **narrow down**

When you **narrow down** a number of choices or possibilities you reduce their number so that you are left with only those that are most likely or most appropriate: *The police have narrowed down the number of possible suspects to two.* ❑ *This one is too expensive, and this one is shoddy-looking. That narrows the choice down a bit.* [*same as* **restrict**]

nod /nɒd/: **nods**, **nodding**, **nodded**

○ **nod off** (*informal*)

You **nod off** when you go to sleep, especially without intending to and when you are somewhere other than in bed: *'Would you like to lie down, lass. You* were just about to nod off there.' □ I settled down in a pew at the back and nodded off. [same as **doze off**, **drop off** (informal)]

noise /nɔɪz/: **noise, noising, noised**

○ **noise about** or **noise around** (*AmE*)

You **noise about**, or **noise around** when you talk a lot, especially when you spread a rumour: *Joanne is probably in town noising around with her girl friends.*

note /nəʊt/: **notes, noting, noted**

○ **note down**

You **note down** something, or you **note** it **down**, when you write it quickly on paper, often in an abbreviated form, so that you can refer to it later: *A couple of pressmen were following him, noting down everything he said.* □ *I'm just noting down the registration number of that car.* □ *Are you noting this down?* [same as **jot down**, **take down**, **write down**]

open /'əʊpən/: **opens, opening, opened**

○ **open out**

1 You **open out** something that is folded when you unfold it or spread it out: *He took out a folded sheet of paper, opened it out, and smoothed it flat on the table.* □ *Opening out the map, he began to look for a route that led to the nearest village.* **2** A flower or flower bud **opens out** when the petals unfold and spread out: *The buds had formed but for some unknown reason they didn't open out.* **3** Something narrow such as a corridor, road, valley or river **opens out** when it gradually widens: *A deep grove in the rock opened out into a chimney in which he could brace his feet against the sides.* □ *He saw that the vaulted passageway opened out into a large courtyard.* **4** A

view or prospect **opens out** when you are able to see more of it because there is in nothing in the way: *It's worth taking the funicular railway just to experience the journey and marvel at the views opening out below.* □ *The whole panorama of life was opening out in front of him.* **5** (especially *BrE*) Someone **opens out** when they begin to express their feelings or thoughts more freely: *After some hesitation, she opened out and told us a bit more about her life in the secret service.* [same as **open up**]

○ **open up**

1 You **open up** a building or room when you unlock the door or doors so that people can come in: *Father had gone on ahead to open up the house.* □ *He hammered on the door and shouted that he'd wake the whole hotel if I didn't open up.* **2** A new shop or business **opens up** when it begins trading; the shops **open up** when they open their doors so that customers can come in and buy things: *She's opening up a boutique in the high street.* □ *They often came past the shop to see when it was going to open up again.* □ *He knew that by the time he'd walked into town they'd have opened up the covered market.* **3** You **open up** a package, or a locked container, when you unwrap it or unlock it so that you can see inside or take something out: *Using a huge old key, he opened up the trunk and took out what looked like a jewelled mask.* □ *The dogs bounded across the drive to their master who was opening up the car boot to remove his luggage.* **4** A gap or passageway through something **is opened up** when the things that have been blocking it are removed allowing people or things to pass through: *I've been campaigning to open up the unofficial footpath bordering the golf course.* **5** A region or territory **is opened up** when it is made easier to get to, or easier to have trading links with: *opening up new territories like China* □ *Thomas Cook opened up the world to men and women who had never dreamed of travelling before.* **6** Opportunities **open up**, or a circumstance **opens up** opportunities to you, when it creates opportunities for you to make progress or experience new things: *They all thought that the value of the course was in the career opportunities it opened up.* ❑ *Far from ruining his life, he found it had opened up all sorts of undreamt-of opportunities.* **7** You **open** yourself **up** to criticism or abuse from others when you make yourself vulnerable to it: *When stepping forth with an idea, an individual may open himself up to personal rejection.* ❑ *'Be careful! You may be opening yourself up to ridicule, or even worse.'* **8** (*informal*) Someone previously unwilling to talk about themselves or their feelings **opens up** when they begin to talk more freely: *We had a couple of glasses of wine, and she opened up a little after that.* ❑ *He played the role of my psychoanalyst by helping me to open up.* [*same as* **open out**] **9** (*informal*) A surgeon **opens** you **up** when he or she cuts into your body so that a diseased or damaged organ or part can be repaired or removed: *What worries me is that when the surgeon opens me up he might find something nasty, like a tumour.* [*same as* **cut open**] **10** (*informal*) Someone with a gun **opens up** when they begin firing: *He burst through the doors and just opened up on innocent by-standers.* ❑ *The German guns then opened up and bombarded our positions.* [*same as* **open fire**] **11** (*informal*) You **open** the vehicle you are driving **up** when you make it go much faster, or as fast as it will go: *Once you get out on the autobahn you can open her up and really see how she performs.* [*same as* **accelerate**] **12** A game such as football **opens up**, or the players **open** it **up**, when it begins to be played in a more exciting way with the players moving around a lot and playing less defensively. **13** A competitor in a race **opens up** a lead when they get well ahead of their opponents: *Arkle swept past Mill House and opened up an unassailable lead.*

option /'ɒpʃən/: **options, optioning, optioned**

○ **option out** (*AmE*)

A major league baseball team **options out** a player when they transfer him to a lower league but have the option of

recalling him: *The Yankees optioned out three of their young pitchers as the season began.*

order /'ɔːdə(r)/: **orders, ordering, ordered**

○ **order about** *or* **order around**

When someone **orders** you **about**, or **orders** you **around**, they tell you to do things in a rude and unpleasant way and don't allow you to make your own decisions or choices: *She ordered her daughters about and made their lives impossible with hundreds of petty rules.* ❑ *'Stop ordering me about!'* [*same as* **boss about, push around**]

own /oʊn/: **owns, owning, owned**

○ **own up**

Someone who has done something wrong **owns up** when they admit that they did it; someone **owns up** to something wrong or illegal when they admit that they did it: *'Come on, own up. I know you did it.'* ❑ *He said he wasn't going to own up to something that would get him expelled.* [*same as* **confess, come clean** (*informal*)]

pack /pak/: **packs, packing, packed**

○ **pack in**

1 You **pack** things **in** when you put them in a container or space so that they fit tightly and neatly; people or things **are packed into** a space or container when they are fitted into it tightly with little or no space between them: *Dolly had opened the case and was packing in the neatly-ironed shirts.* ❑ *The investigators said the explosive could have been illegally packed into the hold as part of the cargo.* ❑ *Simmer the pears in the syrup and pack into sterilised jars.* **2** You **pack** a lot **in**, or you **pack** a lot **into** a relatively short period of time, when you succeed in doing a great many things in that time: *If you are well organized, you can pack a lot into a single weekend.* **3** (*informal*) People sometimes say that an event or performance, especially one in a theatre, **is packing** them **in** when it is attracting very large crowds or audiences: *The tiny island theatre has been packing them in every week since it opened.* **4** (*especially British; informal*) **a** You **pack** something **in** when you stop doing it, especially suddenly or abruptly: *After a couple of weeks working in those terrible conditions, I felt like packing it in and going home.* **b** When someone tells you to **pack** something **in** they are telling you rudely or angrily to stop doing it: *You had better pack that nonsense in if you don't want to end up being sent out of the room!* **5** (*BrE; informal*) People say that a machine **has packed in** when it has stopped working altogether; they also sometimes say that an organ or organs in someone's body, such as the liver or the kidneys, **has** or **have packed in** when they have stopped functioning altogether: *Don't tell me the generator's packed in again!* □ *It's not surprising that his liver packed in after thirty years of heavy drinking.* [*same as* **pack up** (*informal*)]

○ **pack into** *see* **pack in.**

○ **pack off** (*informal*)
You **pack** someone **off** somewhere when you send them there without wasting any time, even though they may not want to go: *After Mario had been packed off to be charged with attempted murder, the police started to search the apartment.* □ *part of a scheme to brush the whole racial problem under the carpet by packing the black majority off to rural 'homelands' dotted around the country.* [*same as* **bundle off** (*informal*), **send off**, **dispatch** (*formal*)]

○ **pack out** (*BrE*)
You can say a place **is packed out** if it is as full of people as it is possible to be; people **pack** a place **out** when they crowd into it and fill it completely: *They gave a series of special concerts and the village hall was packed out every evening.* □ *Jostling and shoving, they*

packed the Assembly Rooms out, and still more people tried to get in. [*same as* **mob**]

○ **pack up**
1 You **pack up** your belongings when you put them in a suitcase, bag or other container so that you can take them with you when you are leaving: *I gave her a hand packing up her clothes.* □ *She packed up her car as if about to go away for the weekend.* **2** You **pack up** at the end of the working or school day when you tidy your desk or work area and put everything away before you leave: *By the time the bell rang, the kids had cleared their desks, packed up, and put on their outdoor clothes.* **3** (*BrE; informal*) You **pack up** some activity, or you **pack** it **up**, when you stop doing it: *If I had a cough like that I'd pack up smoking right away!* [*same as* **pack in** (*informal*)] **4** (*BrE; informal*) People say that a machine or an organ in the body **has packed up** if it has broken down or stopped working altogether: *'Do you have a torch? This one's packed up.'* □ *We're hoping he gets a transplant before his kidneys pack up completely.* [*same as* **pack in** (*informal*)]

pad /pad/: **pads, padding, padded**
○ **pad down** (*AmE*)
You **pad down** when you go to sleep or go to bed: *You look dead tired. Why don't you go pad down?* □ *Three of us padded down on the floor.*

part /pɑːt/: **parts, parting, parted**
○ **part with**
You **part with** something when you give or sell it to someone else, especially when you do so reluctantly: *Thomas just couldn't bear to part with his toy rabbit.* □ *Bingham appeared happy to part with the money.* □ *Few farmers can now afford to part with such valuable by-products as manure without charging for them.* [*same as* **give up, let go of, relinquish** (*formal*)]

pass /pɑːs/: **passes, passing, passed**
○ **pass around** *see* **pass round.**
○ **pass as** *see* **pass for.**
○ **pass away**
1 Something **passes away** when it gradually disappears; something that **has passed away** is no longer there or

no longer exists: *When at last the pain passed away, Norma was able to open her eyes again.* ❏ *a powerful nostalgia for the world that has passed away.* **2** (*euphemistic*) People often say that a person **has passed away** when that person has died: *A police spokesman said: 'It seems Mrs Soper died and then her husband passed away a short time later.'* [*same as* **pass on**, **pass over**]

○ **pass by**

1 People or things **pass by** when they go past; you **pass by** a place when you go past it on your way to somewhere else: *He backed into a doorway to allow the boisterous crowd to pass by.* ❏ *Through the café window I watched London nightlife pass by.* ❏ *I would, of course, have to write to Miss Kenton to tell her I might be passing by.* **2** Time **passes by** when it elapses: *A day, a week, then a month passed by, and still there was no news.* **3** You **pass** things or people **by** if you go past them without stopping; someone or something **passes** you **by** when they ignore you or avoid you, or go on their way without involving or coming into contact with you: *I simply can't pass the island by without a further look at its highlight, the Black Cuillin.* ❏ *Women in her position can have that desperate feeling that life has passed them by.* ❏ *He said firmly that he wouldn't let such an opportunity pass him by again.*

○ **pass down**

Things such as stories, customs, physical characteristics or skills **are passed down** when they are taught to, or reappear in, the next and subsequent generations: *The craft of metalworking was passed down from father to son.* [*same as* **hand down**, **pass on**]

○ **pass for**

Someone or something **passes for** or **passes as** something else when they appear to be that thing, or are a reasonable substitute for it: *With a new outfit and hairstyle, she felt she could almost pass for human.* ❏ *Is this then what passes as witty conversation amongst the younger generation?* [*same as* **be taken for**]

○ **pass on**

1 You **pass on** something, or you **pass** it **on**, when you give or tell it to another person or other people: *She wants to pass on the message that the world is still a great place despite everything.* ❏ *You can pass on the infection without knowing.* ❏ *Those fugitives who congregated on the Omsk railway passed on spotted typhus to 60% of the regional railway workers.* ❏ *Radiation is absorbed by the living material, and thus passes on its energy to it.* **2 a** You **pass on** things such as skills, customs or wealth when you teach them or give them to the next generation: *The farm will be passed on to the eldest son when he dies.* ❏ *He sees it as part of his responsibility to the game to pass his skills on to the next generation of players.* [*same as* **hand on**, **hand down**, **pass down**] **b** You **pass on** your genes, or a specific gene, when you have children and they have some of your genes, or when that particular gene appears in one or all of your children, and in subsequent generations of your family: *Haemophilia doesn't appear in the carrier mother, but is, instead, passed on to her male children.* [*same as* **transmit**] **3** You **pass on** from one place, activity, subject or stage to another when you progress or move from one to the next: *With so little space available in newspapers, the critic only has time to mention a painter or sculptor, make a brief observation, and pass on.* [*same as* **go on**, **proceed** (*formal*)] **4** You **pass** someone **on** to someone else when you refer them to or put them in touch with that other person so that they can deal with them or give them the help they want: *'I'm going to pass you on to my colleague, Mr Adams, who knows all about your case.'* **5** (*euphemistic*) Sometimes people say that a person **has passed on** when that person has died: *She passed on two weeks ago.* [*same as* **pass away**] **6** Increased costs or financial savings **are passed on** to a business company's customers when the company adjusts the price they charge for their goods, either upwards or downwards, to take account of any rise or fall in their production costs: *A threefold increase* *in the price of our raw material will have to be passed on to our customers somehow.*

○ **pass out**
1 People or things **pass out** of an opening when they move through it to the outside: *Cars passed out of the iron gates, one by one, and sped after the hearse.* **2** People you have known **pass out** of your life when you no longer have any contact with them: *At New Year, I think about the year that's gone past, and perhaps, people who've passed out of my life.* **3** You **pass** things **out** when you give or distribute them to a number of people: *The exam papers were passed out and we had a few moments to look at them before we had to begin.* [*same as* **give out**, **hand out**] **4** Someone **passes out** when they become unconscious for a short time: *If your attacker tries to strangle you, you can pass out in a matter of seconds.* □ *It was so hot I was near passing out at times.* [*same as* **black out**, **faint**] **5** (*BrE*) Students or cadets being trained at a military or police college **pass out** when they finish their course successfully.

○ **pass over**
1 Something **passes over** something else when it moves above or across it, or follows a route from one side of it to the other: *Two beautiful night herons passed over our heads.* □ *The train passed over huge bridges that looked as if they were made of matchsticks.* □ *a coast path that passes over National Trust property.* **2** Someone **is passed over** for a job or promotion if they are not selected for it, especially when a younger or less experienced person is chosen instead: *Why were the first and second prize-winners in the competition passed over and Scott appointed instead?* □ *She has been passed over for promotion yet again.* [*same as* **overlook**] **3 a** You **pass over** something when you fail to mention it or notice it: *This is the sort of CD that the ordinary music-lover is likely to pass over in favour of something better known.* [*same as* **ignore**, **disregard** (*formal*)] **b** You **pass over** some unpleasant fact when you de-

liberately avoid mentioning it or dealing with it: *He passed quickly over the section of the report that criticized his department.* [*same as* **gloss over**, **skirt around**, **skate around**; *opposite* **confront**] **4** Some people say that someone who has died **has passed over** meaning that their spirit has left their body and entered the spirit world or 'gone over to the other side'.

○ **pass round** (*BrE*) or **pass around** (*AmE*)
1 People **pass** something **round** when they give or hand it to one another in turn; something **is passed around** when one person gives or hands it to another person, who gives or hands it to the next person, and so on: *Traditionally, African beer is drunk from a large cup, passed round the group of drinkers.* □ *We passed books around, swapped the names of authors, and discussed the latest writing in literary magazines.* □ *Copies of their first report were being passed around, and avidly perused.* [*same as* **hand round**, **circulate**] **2** You **pass** something such as a length of rope or yarn **round** something else when you form it into a loop or circle around that other thing: *Pass the elastic round your fingertip, then slip the end through the loop.*

○ **pass up** (*informal*)
You **pass up** an opportunity or chance, or you **pass** it **up**, when you don't use it or take advantage of it: *Surely you wouldn't pass up a chance to study in France?*

patch /patʃ/: **patches**, **patching**, **patched**
○ **patch up**
1 You **patch up** a quarrel or disagreement that you've been having with someone, or you **patch** things **up**, when you both agree not to quarrel or disagree anymore: *I'm glad to hear they've patched things up and are friends again.* **2 a** You **patch up** something that has been broken or damaged, or you **patch** it **up**, when you do a quick temporary repair on it so that it can be used again: *The garage patched up the bodywork but it really isn't a very satisfactory job.* **b** (*informal*) A doctor or surgeon **patches up**

a wounded or injured patient when they give them temporary treatment *eg* by cleaning, stitching and bandaging their wounds or performing an emergency operation at the scene of an accident to repair as much damage as possible.

pay /peɪ/: **pays, paying, paid**
○ **pay back**
1 You **pay back** money that someone has lent you when you return it to them; you **pay** someone **back** when you return the money that you owe them: *Grants intended to help meet the cost of extra fuel in very cold weather do not have to be paid back.* ❑ *Budgeting loans are paid back by weekly deductions from benefit.* ❑ *I can lend you something as long as you pay me back this week.* [*same as* **repay**] **2** You **pay** someone **back** for something bad they have done to you when you get your revenge on them or punish them for it: *'It was awful what he did to you!' 'Don't fret, I'll pay him back; make his life a misery.'* [*same as* **pay out**]
▶ *noun* **payback** (*AmE*; *informal*) You give someone a **payback** when you do something bad to them to get revenge for something bad they have done to you.
○ **pay down** (*AmE*)
You **pay** money **down** as the first payment on an item you are buying with regular monthly payments: *Nick paid $700 down on his new car and then $200 a month.*
○ **pay for**
1 You **pay for** something when you give money in exchange for it: *By far the safest way to pay for mail order goods is by credit card.* ❑ *The inclusive tour, in which every item of travel arrangement was paid for in advance, was Thomas Cook's invention.* **2** Someone **pays for** something they have done wrong when they are punished for it or are made to suffer because of it: *He paid for his mistake with his life.* **3** Something you have bought, especially something that may have cost you a lot of money at the time, **pays for** itself when its use saves you more money than it cost because it enables you to do things more cheaply or efficiently: *The machine is so cheap*

to run it'll have paid for itself in a couple of years.
○ **pay off**
1 You **pay off** a debt when you return to the lender all the money you owe them: *The crunch came when my bank asked me for my credit card back and demanded I pay off the overdraft at once.* ❑ *Never borrow more money to pay off existing debts.* [*same as* **repay**, **settle**, **discharge**] **2** A business or organization **pays off** workers when it makes them redundant, paying them the wages or salary that they are entitled to up to the time of redundancy; a worker **is paid off** when their employer makes them redundant: *Another slump in the construction industry meant that most companies were paying off men.* ❑ *It came as a very nasty shock when he heard he was being paid off.* [*opposite* **take on**] **3** Something you do **pays off** if it has profitable results: *It was at this stage that the intensive training in navigation paid off.* ❑ *My persistence paid off when the RCA allowed me to take up my place on a joint MA course in the departments of Environmental Media and Design Education.* **4** You **pay** someone **off** when you bribe them with money in order to get rid of them, usually because they have been threatening you or blackmailing you: *If you pay him off this time, he'll just come back for more.*
○ **pay up** (*informal*)
1 You **pay up** when you give someone the money you owe them, especially when you do so unwillingly: *It became obvious that Mrs Schofield wasn't going to pay up without a struggle.* **2** (*informal*)
You **pay** something **up** when you pay for it in instalments: *You can put down 20% now and pay the rest up over six months.*

phone /fəʊn/: **phones, phoning, phoned**
○ **phone back**
Someone **phones back** or **phones** you **back** when they contact you by telephone sometime after you have telephoned them, or they telephone you for a second time: *I waited to hear from him again, but he didn't phone back.* ❑ *Sorry, I can't speak to you just now; I'll phone you back later.* [*same as* **call**

back, ring back]

○ **phone up**

You **phone** someone **up** when you dial their telephone number and talk to them on the telephone: *The man from the council told me I could phone up anytime and ask for rubbish to be collected.* ❑ *Sometimes he would phone her up and threaten her.* [same as **call up, ring up**]

pick /pɪk/: **picks, picking, picked**

○ **pick off**

1 You **pick off** something, or you **pick** it **off**, when you remove it from the place where it is attached using your fingers or fingernails: *A hair was stuck to the helmet. Philip picked it off carefully.* ❑ *If you pick off the scab the wound might get infected.* **2** Individuals in a group of *eg* soldiers **are picked off** by a gunman or gunmen when they are shot down one by one: *It was known as 'sniper alley' where both civilians and soldiers were regularly picked off.* ❑ *The men inside would then be fired on through the roof, picked off like pigeons in a cote.*

○ **pick on**

1 You **pick on** someone when you select them from a group: *The teacher always seems to pick on one of the girls to read aloud.* ❑ *I was picked on to lead the singing.* [same as **pick out, choose**] **2** Someone **picks on** you when they choose you, often unfairly and repeatedly, as a target for criticism or bullying: *Because he was different, he was picked on by the other boys.*

○ **pick out**

1 You **pick** something **out** when you select it from a group: *She picked out the most expensive engagement ring in the display.* [same as **choose**] **2** You **pick** someone or something **out** from a crowd or mass when you recognize or identify them: *It was hard to pick out faces he knew from the swaying mass of heads.* ❑ *My eyes became accustomed to the semi-darkness, so that I could pick out shapes about seventy-five yards away.* [same as **make out, distinguish**] **3** You **pick out** certain things from a mass or group when you remove them: *Wash the lentils and pick out any that look discoloured.* **4** A detail **is picked out** in a separate colour when it is

painted or given a different colour from the background to emphasize it or make it more noticeable: *The room had a chimney-piece picked out in false stone-effect.* **5** You **pick out** a tune on a musical instrument when you play it slowly note by note: *By the age of two, she could pick out a tune on the piano.*

○ **pick up**

1 You **pick** something **up** when you take hold of it and lift it, usually with your hands or fingers; something **is picked up** when someone or something lifts it off the ground: *Stanley picked up a newspaper and started to read.* ❑ *He saw an envelope on the floor, and bending down, picked it up.* ❑ *Women in brown shawls picked up their babies and shouted to their children to come inside.* ❑ *a machine with great gaping jaws that could pick up cars and move them around the junk-yard.* **2 a** You **pick** yourself **up** when you stand up again after falling: *Astonishingly, after tumbling headlong down the steps, she picked herself up and walked away as if nothing had happened.* **b** You **pick up** your feet when you lift each foot off the ground as you walk, instead of dragging or scuffing your feet along the ground: *Major Vine snapped at the men to pick up their feet and straighten their shoulders.* **3** You **pick** someone or something **up** when you go and fetch them from the place where they are waiting to be collected: *You can pick me up about half past two.* ❑ *Next night he remembered to pick up the video on the way home from work.* **4** You **are picked up** by a passing car, helicopter or boat when it stops to give you a lift or take you on board: *The crew of the stricken tanker were picked up by the Peterhead lifeboat.* **5** You **pick up** something such as a skill or language when you learn it casually through observation and practice, rather than through formal teaching or training: *You may know only a few German phrases now, but you'll soon pick it up.* **6** You **pick up** a habit, especially a bad one, when you copy other people who do it: *He'd picked up a few nasty little habits since I last came across him.* **7** You **pick up** an infectious disease when you get it by coming into contact with the thing that infects you: *Paul's picked up a throat infection that proving very difficult to get rid of.* [*same as* **catch**, **contract** (*formal*)] **8** You **pick up** things like news or ideas when you gather them from various sources or hear about them through casual contact with other people: *Along the way you pick up little techniques that help you control your behaviour, or get your own way.* ▫ *I wonder where he picks up ideas for new recipes?* **9** You **pick** things **up** when you get them or buy them cheaply: *You can pick up all sorts of bargains at car-boot sales.* **10** You **pick up** points or penalties when you gain them during a match or competition: *Hull picked up their first win of the season against Leeds on Sunday.* ▫ *The Republicans also picked up an estimated 14,000 votes from the Social Democrats.* ▫ *You will pick up penalties for stepping out of the area.* **11** You **pick up** a radio or television transmission when you receive it on your equipment: *The only programme our radio would pick up was Soviet propaganda, in English.* ▫ *TV programmes picked up by the satellite on Bykov's roof.* **12** Someone **is picked up** by the police when they are arrested and taken to the police station: *Never before have so many young men been picked up for questioning in one day.* **13** A individual or organization **picks up** the bill for something when they pay for it: *It doesn't seem fair that the taxpayer should have to pick up the bill for their incompetence.* **14** You **pick up** when you recover from an illness, or your health improves; something that has been in a bad or poor state **picks up** when it improves: *Iain wasn't at all well, but thankfully he's beginning to pick up now.* ▫ *Trade picked up slowly towards the end of the year.* ▫ *He reckons the economy will soon pick up again.* [*same as* **get better**] **15** You can say that something **picks** you **up** when it makes you feel better or more cheerful: *It was the only hangover remedy that really did pick him up the morning after.* **16** A vehicle or vessel **picks up** speed when it starts going faster; the wind **picks up**

when its force increases: *As they picked up speed along the main tarmac road, it was already 3 am.* ▫ *We steered clear of the crashing waves off Rubha Dubh Tighary as a Force 5 gale picked up from behind.* ▫ *The wind has picked up a bit.* **17** You **pick up** a story that someone else has left unfinished, or cannot finish because they do not know what happened next, when you continue with it: *Anton picked up the story from the point when I had left the group to do some shopping.* **18** (*informal*) Someone who tries to **pick** you **up** tries to get to know you in the hope of having a sexual relationship with you: *Maybe he's taken a course in French film as a way of learning to pick up girls.* ▫ *A couple of American sailors tried, unsuccessfully, of course, to pick us up.* **19** (*AmE*) If you **pick up** a room, you tidy it up: *Greg's mother made him pick up his room.*

○ **pick up on**
1 You **pick up on** something when you return to it after doing or discussing something else for a time: *He has a habit of picking up on topics discussed in previous conversations.* **2** You **pick up on** something when you notice it and draw others attention to it by beginning to discuss it or challenge it: *Neither of these points were picked up on in the debate.* **3** (*informal*) Someone **picks** you **up on** something that you have said when they point out that it is wrong: *The interviewer failed to pick him up on the obvious contradictions in his argument.*

piece /piːs/: **pieces, piecing, pieced**
○ **piece together**
1 You **piece together** something such as a story or the truth when you gradually collect all the relevant facts and understand how they fit together: *Police piecing together the events of Tuesday night have discovered that the killer robbed another couple a few minutes earlier.* ▫ *It's difficult to know what of the last few days I remember, or have pieced together, or have been told by Nathan.*
2 To **piece together** something broken or torn into fragments is to mend it, or re-

form it, by fitting all the pieces together again: *Piecing together and gluing the broken shards is a job for an expert.* ◻ *Eliot's poem seems at times to be attempting to piece together some new religion out of the fragments of the old.*

pile /paɪl/: piles, piling, piled
○ **pile up**
1 You **pile** things **up** when you put them one on top of the other in a pile: *Clean plates were piled up on the draining board.* ◻ *an old lady with silvery hair piled up high and a pale, invalid's face.* [*same as* **stack up**] **2** Things **pile up** when they accumulate so that there is a great amount or number of them in one place; work **piles up** when it accumulates so that there is a large amount to deal with: *There was a long halt as the traffic jam piled up ahead.* ◻ *Rotting rubbish was piling up in the streets.*

pin /pɪn/: pins, pinning, pinned
○ **pin down**
1 Someone **is pinned down** when they are trapped because someone or something is preventing them from moving, progressing or escaping: *They found themselves pinned down by snipers in a narrow gully.* ◻ *Firemen battled to free the man from the steel beam that was pinning him down.* **2** You can **pin** something **down** if you are able to describe or identify exactly what it is: *She had an eerie sense that she was acting out something she had done before, but she couldn't pin it down.* [*same as* **put one's finger on**] **3** You **pin** somebody **down** to something, or to a specific time, when you force them to decide to do it, or do it at that time: *He wasn't too keen to commit himself to an exact time, but I managed to pin him down to the next afternoon at 3 pm.*
○ **pin on** *or* **pin upon**
1 You **pin** something **on** or **upon** something else when you fasten it to that other thing with a pin or pins: *A distinctive gold badge was pinned on her chest.* **2** You **pin** the blame for something **on** someone when you say that they are responsible for it: *We were trying to pin the blame on each other for messing up the day.*

plan /plan/: plans, planning, planned
○ **plan on**
When you **plan on** doing something you decide in advance to do it: *When organizing a jumble sale, don't plan on selling too much at more than 10 pence an item.*

play /pleɪ/: plays, playing, played
○ **play along**
1 You **play along**, or **play along** with someone, when you keep them happy by cooperating or agreeing with them, or pretending to do so: *He was the one who masterminded it. I just played along because I was scared of him.* ◻ *Perhaps if we play along with them they might let us go.* **2** You **play** someone **along** when you make them believe that you will eventually do what you have no intention of doing: *She's been playing him along for years, but doesn't have the least intention of marrying him.*
○ **play down**
You **play** something **down**, or you **play down** its importance or significance, when you try to make it seem unimportant or of no significance: *The government had tried to play down the dangers of pollution.* ◻ *She talks about her beauty as a fact which she will neither boast about nor play down.*
○ **play off**
Two sporting teams **play off** when they play against each other to decide which will be the winner.
○ **play on**
1 Light **plays on** an object or surface when it falls on or is directed towards it, often moving back and forth across it: *The sergeant's torch played on a single figure ten yards away.* **2** Someone or something **plays on** or **upon** your feelings when they have a strong effect or influence on them; someone **plays on** or **upon** your good nature or weaknesses when they take advantage of them for their own benefit: *The condition of his sister still played on his mind.* ◻ *music that plays on the emotions* ◻ *The Tories played on the electorate's fears that Labour was the 'tax and spend' party.*
○ **play out**
1 An event **is played out** when it is acted

or happens as if it were a play or a scene in a play: *Though every second customer is probably just like me, this charade is going to be played out on the basis that I'm being difficult.* ◻ *This initially provincial dispute was played out on the national stage.* **2** (*informal*) Someone or something **is played out** when they are exhausted or finished, or have no further usefulness or relevance: *The notion that women can't function without a man is played out.*

○ **play up** (*BrE*; *informal*)
1 A machine **is playing up** when it is not working properly: *Suspecting that the compass was playing up again, Wood altered course by 5 degrees.* [*same as* **act up** (*informal*)] **2** A part of your body, especially a diseased or injured part, **is playing up**, or **is playing** you **up**, when it is giving you a lot of pain: *I see the Major's limping again. His old wound must be playing him up.* **3** Children who **are playing up** are behaving badly and refusing to cooperate: *Some of the older boys were playing up and wouldn't sing.* [*same as* **act up** (*informal*)]

○ **play upon** *see* **play on.**

point /pɔɪnt/: **points, pointing, pointed**
○ **point out**
1 a You **point** something **out**, or you **point** it **out** to someone when you indicate it to them in some way: *The islands of Capri, Procida and Ischia had been pointed out to her.* ◻ *He can take you to the loch and point out precisely where you will be sure to catch fish.* **b** You **point** a particular person **out** when you identify them from amongst a group, especially by pointing your index finger in their direction: *I don't know who the director is. Can you point him out to me?* **2** You **point out** something when you mention it to people for consideration, or draw it to their attention: *I examined my contract and pointed out a minor discrepancy in it to Personnel.* ◻ *Sceptics point out that the Conservatives' share of the vote is less than it was in the 1960s.*

police /pəˈliːs/: **polices, policing, policed**
○ **police up** (*AmE*)
Soldiers **police up** a military base when they make the ground or buildings clean and tidy: *The commander was returning, so 20 men were sent to police up the parade ground.*

polish /ˈpɒlɪʃ/: **polishes, polishing, polished**
○ **polish off** (*informal*)
You can say that you **polished** something **off** when you finished it quickly and easily: *He watched her polishing off the final remains of her large meal.* ◻ *He'd polished off his first two matches in three sets.*

○ **polish up**
1 You **polish up** an object or piece of furniture when you rub it with polish so that it shines: *Will you be polishing up your medals for the big parade?* **2** You **polish up** a skill or technique when you improve it by practising: *If you're going to camp out on the mountain, you'd better polish up your survival skills.* ◻ *The cast were polishing up their lines.*

pony /ˈpəʊni/: **ponies, ponying, ponied**
○ **pony up** (*AmE*; *informal*)
You **pony up**, or **pony** money **up**, when you pay money to someone, especially to settle an account: *I suppose someday I'll be able to pony up and start over again.* ◻ *The mob said it was time for Lou to pony up $2,000 for his gambling debts.*

poop /puːp/: **poops, pooping, pooped**
○ **poop out** (*AmE*; *informal*)
1 You **poop out** when you stop or quit because you are very tired or out of breath: *We climbed up 3,500 feet before I pooped out.* **2** Something **poops out** when it stops working: *The car radio suddenly pooped out after six years.*

pore /pɔː(r)/: **pores, poring, pored**
○ **pore over**
You **pore over** something such as a book when you study it carefully and with great concentration: *Alicia found him pouring over the documents, his brow furrowed with concentration.*

pour /pɔː(r)/: **pours, pouring, poured**
○ **pour down**
Rain **pours down** when it falls very heavily: *The rain poured down in Carmarthen and the streets were like rivers.*

print /prɪnt/: **prints, printing, printed**
○ **print out**

You **print out** data from a computer when you produce a printed copy of it: *You can print out what's on the screen at any time.* □ *Parish records are available in printed-out form from a microcomputer.*

prop /prɒp/: **props, propping, propped**
○ **prop up**
1 You **prop** something or someone **up** when you support them or keep them upright by leaning them on or against something: *She propped herself up on one elbow.* □ *The roof had to be propped up before the damage could be assessed fully.* **2** One person or group **props up** another when they support or help the other financially: *a benefit system that will prop up the rich in temporary difficulty but is reluctant to help people who are literally out on the streets* □ *The industry had to be propped up with government money.*

pull /pʊl/: **pulls, pulling, pulled**
○ **pull away**
1 A vehicle or its driver **pulls away** when it starts moving after being stationary, *eg* at the side of the road or at traffic lights: *James Hunt pulled away from the start line.* □ *The two policemen gave chase but the white car pulled away before they could reach it.* **2** Something, especially a vehicle, that is moving ahead of you **pulls away** when it moves more quickly than you are moving so increasing the distance between you and it: *The boat was pulling swiftly away towards a distant ship.* **3** A person **pulls away** from someone who is holding them or touching them when they move back and away from that person suddenly in alarm or surprise: *'Leave me alone, it wasn't me!' I cried, trying to pull away.* **4** You **pull** yourself **away** from something when you force yourself to leave, though you are very reluctant to do so: *It was all she could do to pull herself away from such a fascinating spectacle.*
○ **pull back**
1 Troops **are pulled back** when they are moved away from the front line: *The German forces had pulled back towards the Seine taking all their equipment with them.* **2** You **pull back** from something that you had been thinking of doing

when you decide not to do it or be involved in it: *They've pulled back from all-out confrontation with the unions.* **3** You **pull** yourself, someone or something **back** from a difficult situation you have got yourself into when you succeed in doing something that makes the situation better than it was: *They were a goal down when the captain scored, pulling them back from almost certain relegation.*
○ **pull in** *or* **pull into**
1 A vehicle or its driver **pulls in**, or **pulls into** a place, when the vehicle leaves the road it has been travelling on and turns off and stops, *eg* at the side of the road or at a filling station: *We stopped and the police car pulled in behind.* □ *I pulled into the driveway of the third house on the right.* **2** A train **pulls in**, or **pulls into** a station, when it arrives there: *We tried to get a clear view of the platform and the hundreds of people watching the troop train pull in.* □ *At 6.30 am the next morning the train pulled into Central Station, Glasgow.* [*opposite* **pull out, leave**] **3** (*informal*) People sometimes say that someone **is pulling in** a large amount of money or large profits when they are earning it, often from various sources: *After a couple of successful shows in the Big Apple, you'll soon be pulling in the cash.* [*same as* **rake in** (*informal*)] **4** An event **pulls in** the crowds when a lot of people go to it: *He said he was getting out of the business; circuses weren't pulling in the crowds like they used to.* [*same as* **attract**]
○ **pull off**
1 You **pull** something difficult **off** when you succeed in it or manage to achieve it: *He is backing his old club to pull off the first Premier League title.* [*compare* **bring off**] **2** A vehicle **pulls off** when it starts moving forward after being stationary: *The guard blew his whistle and we pulled off in clouds of steam.* [*same as* **pull away**] **3** A vehicle or its driver **pulls off** the road when the vehicle leaves the road and parks, or joins another road: *Ellwood saw them pull off the road into the driveway of a hotel.*

○ **pull out**
1 You **pull** something **out** when you take hold of it and remove it with a rapid movement of you hand from a container or the place where it is kept; you **pull out** something that has been embedded in something else when you remove it with a quick forceful movement: *He opened one of his desk drawers and pulled out a little tin box.* ❑ *He pulled a wad of hundred-dollar bills out of his pocket.* ❑ *a claw hammer, which can pull nails out as well as drive them in.* **2** A vehicle or its driver **pulls out** when it moves out from the side of the road, or moves to the centre of the road in order to overtake another vehicle going in the same direction: *He was struck by a van pulling out of a side street.* **3** A train **pulls out** when it leaves a station: *Several minutes before the express was due to pull out, there was no-one on the platform.* [*same as* **leave**; *opposite* **pull in**] **4** A person or organization **pulls out** of an agreement, undertaking or previously-arranged event when they withdraw from it: *He pulled out of the tournament with a sprained wrist.* ❑ *His chance for gold was gone when the US pulled out of the Moscow Olympics.* **5** An army **pulls out** or **is pulled out** when it leaves the place that it has been occupying or fighting in: *some of the British forces being pulled out of Northern Ireland.*

○ **pull over**
1 A vehicle or its driver **pulls over** when the vehicle moves closer to the side of the road, usually to park or to let other vehicles overtake: *We pulled over at a roadside café to have a cup of coffee.* **2** When the police **pull** you **over** they signal to you to move your car to the side of the road and stop: *The police can pull you over and check that your vehicle is roadworthy.*

○ **pull through**
Someone **pulls through** when they recover from a serious illness or injury so that their life is no longer in danger; someone **pulls through** when they survive or overcome their personal troubles and difficulties; you **pull** someone **through** when you give them the

help or support they need in order to recover or survive: *He's a fighter, and hopefully he will pull through.* ❑ *It was the love and support of our family that pulled us through.*

○ **pull together**
1 People **pull together** when they work together to achieve a common aim or purpose: *'France and England never really pulled together, for all they might find themselves on the same side.'* **2** You **pull** the various elements of some scheme or plan **together** when you succeed in making it work: *I hope we can pull it together, but sometimes I have my doubts.* **3** You **pull** yourself **together** after being shocked or upset by something when you get your feelings under control so that you are able to act more rationally: *I saw him go pale and then visibly pull himself together before proceeding.* ❑ *Slowly the tears subsided and gradually I began to pull myself together.*

○ **pull up**
1 You **pull** yourself **up** when you are sitting or lying down when you bring your body into a more upright position using your arms: *The baby can pull himself up using the sides of the cot.* **2** You **pull up** a chair when you move it closer to someone or something: *Maggie pulled up a chair to be close to the fire.* **3** You **pull up** plants when you remove them from the ground by their roots: *Vandals had pulled up all the tulips and strewn them over the grass.* **4** A moving vehicle or its driver **pulls up** at a certain place when the vehicle comes to a stop there: *By the time he pulled up she was beginning to feel much better.* **5** You **pull** yourself **up** when you suddenly stop yourself doing or saying something: *He was just about to dive, saw the pool was empty, and pulled himself up just in time.* **6** (*informal*) You **pull** someone **up** when you scold or reprimand them: *He pulled me up about my work, saying it wasn't up to the required standard.*

punk /pʌŋk/: **punks, punking, punked**
○ **punk out** (*AmE*; *informal*)
You **punk out** when you quit because you are frightened: *Joe said he would ask her to marry him, but he punked out.*

[*same as* **chicken out** (*informal*)]

push /pʊʃ/: **pushes, pushing, pushed**

○ **push about** *or* **push around**

1 You **push** something **about** or **around** when you move it across a surface from one place to the other: *Her walking-frame squeaked on the lino as she pushed it about.* □ *He was taken to L'Escargot to eat but just pushed his gourmet food around on his plate.* **2** Someone **pushes** you **around**, or they **push** you **about**, when they bully you or treat you roughly: *'You'd never have stayed around so long if I'd pushed you about.'* □ *I told him he couldn't push me around any more like a football from one job to another.* □ *a public body that felt pushed around by the Tories.*

○ **push by**

You **push by** someone who is blocking your path when you press your body against them roughly or rudely as you go past them: *Her eyes stared unseeingly at the people pushing by her into the Metro.* □ *The woman suddenly crossed the room, pushed by him, and ran down the stairs.* [*same as* **push past**]

○ **push on**

1 Someone or something **pushes on** when they continue in a certain direction: *We stopped at the inn for a mid-day meal and then pushed on to Aubeterre.* □ *There were times when even the thought of the money wasn't enough to push him on to success.* **2** (*informal*) You **push on** with something that you want to complete when you continue to work steadily at it: *Raymond's working at the weekend so that he can push on with the job.*

○ **push through**

You **push through** a proposal or plan, or you **push** it **through**, when you make a determined effort to get it accepted or put into effect: *Bandiera even admitted to doubts about some of the deals he had pushed through.* □ *Important bills were pushed through using the swift but effective parliamentary guillotine.* □ *Gorbachev used his powers to rule by decree to push the reform through.*

put /pʊt/: **puts, putting, put**

○ **put about** (*BrE*; *informal*)

You can say that someone **is putting** themselves **about** when they are making contact with a great many people, often to impress them or to achieve some aim: *You have to put yourself about a bit if you want the right people to notice you.*

○ **put across**

You **put** ideas **across** well, or you **put** them **over** well, if you express them so that they are clearly understood by your listeners or readers: *Keep it simple. Put it across as something they can't do without.* □ *They're increasingly dependent on 'spin-doctors' to put over the party message.*

○ **put aside**

1 You **put** something **aside** when you separate it from other things, often so that you can keep it for use later: *Their gardener put aside some of the best plants to take cuttings for next season.* **2** You **put** money **aside** when you save it, especially for a particular purpose: *Surely you have some money. Have you really got nothing put aside?* [*same as* **save**] **3** (*formal*) You **put** someone or something **aside** when you abandon them: *He'd put his first wife aside to marry a princess whose dowry included large areas of the adjoining province.* [*same as* **discard**]

○ **put at**

If the value or cost of something **is put at** a certain figure that is what it is estimated to be; if someone's age **is put at** a certain number of years that is the age that they are thought to be: *I would put it at nearer a thousand.* □ *The skeleton's age was put at about eighteen or nineteen years.*

○ **put away**

1 You **put** something **away** when you put it into the place where it is to be kept or stored: *'I have put away my paints and brushes for ever,' he said.* □ *The girls had washed and put away the cups and plates.* □ *The dishes had been washed and put away.* □ *It started to rain heavily before he could roll up and put away his prayer mat.* □ *It was time to put away childish things.* **2** (*informal*) You **put** money **away** when you save it: *You don't have to invest large sums; you can put away as little as £10 per month.* [*same* as **put by**] **3** In games such as football, basketball and snooker, a player **puts away** the ball when they kick it into the back of the goal net, put it in the basket or hit it into the pocket: *Shortly afterwards Chandler put away the second.* **4** (*informal*) When people say that you can **put away** food or drink they mean that you can eat or drink a lot: *He was putting away cakes and sandwiches as if he hadn't seen food for a month.* **5** (*informal*) People **are put away** when they are sent to prison or to a secure hospital for people with severe mental illness: *She's a danger to herself and to others. She ought to be put away.* ❑ *The evidence we have should be enough to put him away for at least ten years.*

○ **put back**

1 You **put** something **back** when you return it to its proper place, or to the place it came from: *Iona picked up one of the figures, saw what it cost, and put it back hurriedly.* ❑ *The stones were collected in a trailer and taken away, instead of being put back on the field.* ❑ *You will begin to realize what action you need to take to put everything back on course.* **2** To **put** a planned event or procedure **back** is to delay it until a later time: *Dinner had to be put back an hour.* [*same as* **postpone**]

○ **put behind**

You **put** an unpleasant experience **behind** you when you decide that it will no longer affect you or influence you: *I can put all that fear behind me now.*

○ **put down**

1 You **put** something you have been holding or carrying **down** when you place it somewhere *eg* on the floor or on a table: *Chief Inspector Kuhlman put down the phone and looked at Kurt Meyer.* ❑ *The small boy put down the basket he was weaving.* ❑ *I lifted the receiver, listened to the dialling tone, and put it down again.* **2** The police or army **put down** a revolt or rebellion when they use force to stop it: *The Americans dispatched marines to put down an uprising in Grenada.* [*same as* **crush**] **3** (*informal*) You **put** someone **down** when you criticize them and make them feel stu-

pid: *Some women put her down for working with a man.* **4** (*BrE*) An animal **is put down** when it is killed painlessly, *eg* because it is ill, old, or considered dangerous: *Poor old thing shouldn't be allowed to suffer any longer. I want him to be put down humanely.* [*same as* **put to sleep**, **destroy**] **5** You **put down** *eg* suggestions or ideas when you write them on paper: *I've put down four different headings.* ❑ *He put down whatever came into his head.* [*same as* **set down**, **note down**, **jot down**, **put in writing**] **6** You **put** one thing **down** to another if you think the first is caused by the second: *I'd been having these terrible headaches, but I put them down to stress. It never occurred to me that I might need glasses.* ❑ *The accident could be put down to failure to maintain a safe airspeed at low altitudes.* ❑ *The evening's success should be put down to music that never ceases to delight.* ❑ *The decline of the forest was put down to a condition known as progressive spruce death.*

○ **put forward**

1 You **put forward** an idea when you suggest it for other people's consideration: *The arguments he put forward were very persuasive indeed.* ❑ *In his book Herbert Read took up the categories of types put forward by Jung.* ❑ *The case put forward by the pensions industry was less than persuasive.* **2** You **put** your name **forward** for something when you offer yourself as a possible candidate for a post or role; someone else **puts** your name **forward** when they suggest that you be considered as a candidate for a post or role: *It was then that Gordon Brown decided not to put his name forward for party leader.*

○ **put in**

1 You **put** something **in** a container or other enclosed space when you place it inside it: *She put her thumb in her mouth again as soon as her mother's back was turned.* ❑ *The children were wrapped in blankets and put in the car.* **2** You **put in** time or effort when you spend it on some activity: *He puts in the hours but the standard of his work is still not as good as it should be.* ❑ *Crisp was putting in an astonishing perfor-*

mance. **3** You **put in** a claim when you make it officially or submit it to someone in authority: *Postal workers have put in a claim for a 10% pay rise.*

○ **put off**
1 You **put** something **off** when you delay doing it: *The Mozarts set out for Salzburg to visit Leopold, a visit promised since their marriage but constantly put off.* [*same as* **postpone**] **2** Something **puts** you **off** doing something when it makes you unwilling to do what you wanted or intended to do: *The weather conditions weren't severe enough to put us off going for a sail.* ▫ *The house still had the gaunt, haunted look that had so put Meg off before.* [*same as* **deter, discourage**]

○ **put on**
1 You **put** something **on** something else when you place it on top of that other thing: *Philip took the vase and put it on the table.* **2** You **put** clothes **on** when you put them on your body: *I sprinted back to the changing room to put on my gym shoes.* ▫ *She had put the hat on and taken it off again three times.* **3** You **put on** something such as a light when you press or turn the switch so that it begins to operate: *She led the way into a miniature kitchen and put on the kettle.* **4** You **put on** a record or tape when you place it on or in the record player or tape recorder so that it will play: *She put on another record.* **5** You **put on** a play or other entertainment when you organize it and perform it in public: *The drama society put on a comic sketch.* ▫ *We put on three new plays by Will in the next year, and some plays by other writers.* **6** You **put on** weight when you gain weight: *He's put on a lot of weight since last year.* **7** You **put on** a certain type of behaviour when you deliberately behave in an unnatural way: *Then she puts on her little-girl-lost face.* ▫ *Can you really believe he's that concerned? I think he puts it on.* **8** Stress or strain **is put on** you when something causes you to feel it or suffer from it: *He was aware of the strain it had put on his relationship with George.* **9** (*AmE; informal*) If you **put** someone **on**, you try to make them believe something that is not

true: *Ann said she hated men, but she was just putting me on.*

○ **put out**
1 You **put** something **out** when you take it from inside a place and put it outside: *He put the cat out, locking the back door before he came to bed.* **2** You **put out** a light when you switch it off; you **put out** a fire when you extinguish it: *'Would you put out the light, please, dear?'* ▫ *Firemen who were called to put out the fire discovered the child's body.* **3** Someone or something **puts** you **out** when they inconvenience you: *Don't do it unless you have time. I don't want to put you out.* **4** You **are put out** by something when it causes you to feel anxious and upset: *He had to admit he was a little put out by her reaction.* ▫ *The Commandos in the trench with me didn't seem to be put out by the noise of the explosions.* [*same as* **disturb**] **5** You **put out** a message, request or warning on the radio when you broadcast it: *We couldn't put a message out on the radio because there was something wrong with the equipment.* **6** (*AmE; informal*) If a woman **puts out**, she has sexual intercourse: *Jim thought Debbie would put out after a few drinks.*

○ **put over**[1] *see* **put across.**

○ **put over**[2] (*AmE*)
You **put over** an action or event, or **put** it **over**, when you delay it to a later time: *Sam was ill, so we put over our reunion until Christmas.* ▫ *It rained so hard, we put the festival over for a week.*

○ **put over on**
You **put** something **over on** someone when you deceive or trick them: *I thought the painting was an original. He really put one over on me.*

○ **put through**
1 Someone **puts** you **through** an unpleasant experience when they make you suffer it: *This is typical of the pain Dustin would put himself through in order to get 'inside' a character.* ▫ *She acted in a very calm manner considering the trauma she had been put through.* ▫ *How could I put the people I love through so much pain?* **2** You **put** a caller **through** on the telephone when you connect them with the person they want to

speak to: *'I'm putting you through now, caller.'* ◻ *She put a call through to Riorbak.* ◻ *The staff were refusing to put calls through to Scotland Yard.*

○ **put together**

1 You **put** people or things **together** when you put them with each other in the same place: *When horses are put together in the same paddock they need to be carefully chosen for their compatibility.* **2** You **put** something **together** when you join a number of separate parts to make a whole or complete thing, or you gather a number of separate things together and make them part of something larger or more complete: *The way sleeping bags are put together is one of the main factors affecting their efficiency.* ◻ *Now that he'd put the facts together the story sounded absolutely ridiculous.* ◻ *Our buying power with the major hotel chains means we can put together an excellent package, complete with rail and coach fares.* ◻ *Hopefully, he'll be interested in being in this band that we're trying to put together.* **3** You **put together** a piece of work when you create it bringing together all the necessary elements: *She knows how to put a business letter together all right.* ◻ *The company was fully prepared to give her the freedom necessary to put together the type of programme she truly wanted to make.* **4** You **put together** an event when you organize all the different elements into a workable whole: *They're putting together an exhibition of post-war British painting.* **5** You can say that one thing excels or is worth several other things **put together** if even in combination they cannot beat it: *He seemed to have more money than all the rest of us put together.*

○ **put towards** *or* **put toward**

You **put** money **towards** something when you use it to meet part of the total required: *The money I was going to save on rent could be put towards a deposit on a house.* ◻ *He wanted to earn a higher salary so that he would have something to put towards his eventual retirement.*

○ **put up**

1 To **put up** a building or other structure is to build or erect it: *Her parents had put up a marquee in the garden.* **2** You **put up** something such as an umbrella when you unfold it and raise it ready for use: *Lucia took her umbrella with her but didn't put it up despite the light drizzle.* **3** You **put up** something such as a poster or notice when you attach it to a wall or noticeboard: *He took a hand in the redecorating, splashing on paint and putting up wallpaper.* **4** (*especially BrE*) Prices **are put up** when they are increased: *Most high-street banks have put up their charges to customers who go into overdraft.* **5** You **put up** money for some cause when you provide money for it: *No-one is willing to put up the funds for a proper training course.* **6** You **put** property **up** for sale when you make it available to be bought: *On the way they stopped at a farmhouse that was about to be put up for sale.* **7** You **put up** a struggle or fight when you resist an attack or fight in a determined way: *He decided it wasn't worth putting up a fight and risking a beating.* ◻ *The Nissan of Bailey and Blundell put up a strong challenge and took second.* **8** You **put** someone **up** when you give them accommodation in your house, especially by providing them with a bed for the night: *Would your brother be willing to put us up for a few nights?* **9** A political party **puts up** a candidate in an election when they choose that candidate to contest the election: *The Republicans put up candidates in about half the constituencies.* [*compare* **stand for**]

○ **put up to**

One person **puts** another **up to** something wrong, silly or dishonest when they tell them or encourage them to do it: *It wasn't something he'd have thought of by himself. Someone must have put him up to it.* [*compare* **egg on**, **urge on**]

○ **put up with**

You **put up with** something unpleasant or unsatisfactory when you accept or tolerate it: *Over the years, Anne had put up with an awful lot from me.* ◻ *Violence in the home is as much a crime as violence from a stranger, so don't put up with it.*

queue /kjuː/: **queues, queuing, queued**

◻ **queue up** (*BrE*)
People **queue up** when they stand one behind the other in a queue, *eg* because they are waiting to get into a place or are waiting for service in a shop or post office: *At noon things get busy as customers queue up for sandwiches and take-away meals.* ◻ *I wouldn't mind betting people will be queuing up for these products as soon as they come on the market.*

quiet /'kwaɪət/: **quiets, quieting, quieted**

◻ **quiet down** (*AmE*)
Quiet down is used in American English and has the same meaning as **quieten down**: *When things had quieted down a little, we went into the garden to look at the stars.*

quieten /'kwaɪətən/: **quietens, quietening, quietened**

◻ **quieten down** (*BrE*)
You **quieten** someone or something **down** when you calm them or do something to make them less noisy; someone or something **quietens down** when they becomes quiet or calm: *Four months in France had quietened her down and given her a veneer of sophistication quite lacking before.*

rain /reɪn/: **rains, raining, rained**
◻ **rain down**
Things **rain down** when a great many of them fall from above at the same time, like raindrops: *As soon as they announced they were to have a baby loads of letters of congratulation, bibs and baby boots rained down on them.* ◻ *Bombs were raining down on the city day and night.*

rake /reɪk/: **rakes, raking, raked**
◻ **rake over**
Someone **rakes over** something from the past, especially something that people would prefer to forget because it is upsetting or unpleasant, when they talk about it again in detail: *The press will insist on raking over all the details of his past indiscretions.*
◻ **rake up** (*informal*)
1 You **rake up** the past when you talk about unpleasant things that happened some time ago, that people would prefer to forget: *It may be regarded as of historical interest by some, but as far as I'm concerned its just raking up a past that is best forgotten.* **2** You **rake up** the people or things needed for a particular purpose when you look in various places for them, find them and bring them all together: *I think I might be able to rake up enough people to make two 5-a-side football teams.* [*same as* **dredge up**]

ram /ram/: **rams, ramming, rammed**
◻ **ram through** (*AmE*)
A government or legislature **rams through** a bill or law, or **rams** it **through**, when they use their political power to force it through: *The Republicans were able to ram the tax bill through the Senate.*

reach /riːtʃ/: reaches, reaching, reached

○ **reach for**

You **reach for** something when you stretch out your hand and arm as far as you can so that you can grasp it: *Reaching for a cup, her hand accidentally brushed his arm.*

○ **reach out**

1 You **reach out** when you stretch your arm out in a particular direction so that you can touch or grasp something that is some distance away from you: *He reached out and switched on the lamp.* **2** You **reach out** to people in need when you try to give them help or comfort: *Charities and support groups reaching out to the needy and victims of injustice of all kinds.*

read /riːd/: reads, reading, read /red/

○ **read into**

You **read** something **into** what someone says or does when you find some extra meaning in it, often one which they did not intend: *No matter what he does now, the press will read something sinister into it.* ❑ *Those are the facts; read into them what you will.*

○ **read out**

You **read** something **out** when you say it aloud as you read it: *They had all been there when Moran read out the telegram.* ❑ *His statement was read out in court.*

○ **read up** or **read up on**

You **read up on** a subject, or you **read up** for something such as an exam, when you find out as much as you can about it or learn as much as you can by reading: *Ray is reading up on the history of Crete before we go on holiday.* ❑ *We recommend that applicants read up on the company and prepare a list of questions about it for their interviews.*

reason /ˈriːzən/: reasons, reasoning, reasoned

○ **reason with**

You **reason with** someone when you talk to them and use logical and sensible arguments to try to persuade them to do or not do something, or to convince them about something: *They tried in vain to reason with the gunman.* ❑ *He tried to reason with her but she wouldn't be reasoned with.*

reel /riːl/: reels, reeling, reeled

○ **reel off**

You **reel** things **off** when you say them quickly and without having to think; you also **reel** things **off** when you get through them quickly and easily: *She can reel off the relevant statistics at the drop of a hat.* ❑ *Miss Cross began the match well, reeling off the first four games for the loss of only four points.*

refer /rɪˈfɜː(r)/: refers, referring, referred

○ **refer to**

1 You **refer to** something when you mention it: *Who exactly were you referring to when you talked about people being marginalized?* ❑ *He referred repeatedly to the 'special relationship' that existed between their two countries.* **2** You **refer to** someone or something as a particular thing when that is the name you give them when you are talking to or about them: *He's in the habit of referring to his wife as his old woman.* ❑ *Don't you think it's rather unjust to refer to him as 'that young thug'.* **3** You **refer to** a book or other source of information when you read it or look at it in order to check facts or find something out: *Check your spelling by referring to your dictionary.* ❑ *For guidance on grammar refer to the appendices at the back of the book.* **4** You **refer** someone **to** a source of information when you tell them to look at it because it may be useful to them: *My tutor referred me to a collection of the author's letters held in the university library.* **5** You **refer** someone or something **to** a specialist or expert when you get the specialist or expert to examine them or give their opinion: *If your GP is unable to make an accurate diagnosis, he should refer you to a consultant.* ❑ *He was referred to a lawyer who specialized in that area.*

relate /rɪˈleɪt/: relates, relating, related

○ **relate to**

1 Something that **relates to** something else is concerned with that other thing or has a direct connection with it: *How does this relate to what we were discussing earlier?* ❑ *all the evidence relating to* *the crime.* **2** You **relate to** another person or their situation when you understand their feelings because you have had similar experiences or feelings yourself: *'I find big crowds terrifying.' 'Yes, I can relate to that.'* □ *She was looking for someone she could relate to.*

rely /rɪˈlaɪ/: **relies, relying, relied**

○ **rely on** *or* **rely upon**

1 You **rely on** or **upon** something when you need it or depend on it to exist or survive: *Smokers ought to give up the habit and stop relying on the NHS as a safety-net.* □ *a form of socio-economic domination from outside that does not rely on direct political control.* **2** You **rely on** someone when you trust them to do what they should do or what you ask them to do: *You can always rely on Adele to help you out in a crisis.* □ *I have my doubts about Gerry. Do you think we can rely on him?*

rent /rɛnt/: **rents, renting, rented**

○ **rent out**

You **rent out** property or land that you own when you make it available for others to use in return for a regular payment or rent: *I'm going abroad for a year so I'll be renting out my flat in Edinburgh.*

rest /rɛst/: **rests, resting, rested**

○ **rest with**

The responsibility for something **rests with** a particular person or organization when they have that responsibility: *A Scottish Office spokesman said responsibility for the repairs rested with the local authority.* [same as **lie with**]

result /rɪˈzʌlt/: **results, resulting, resulted**

○ **result from**

One thing **results from** another when the first thing is caused by or is a consequence of the second: *Scurvy results from a lack of vitamin C in the diet.*

○ **result in**

An action or circumstance **results in** a particular situation or consequence when it causes it to happen: *I predict that the experiment will result in complete disaster for us all.*

ride /raɪd/: **rides, riding, rode** /roʊd/, **ridden** /ˈrɪdən/

○ **ride out**

You **ride out** a difficult or dangerous period when you manage to get through it without suffering a lot of damage or harm: *If we can just ride out the next six months, we should be okay.*

rig /rɪɡ/: **rigs, rigging, rigged**

○ **rig up** (*informal*)

You **rig** something **up** such as a piece of equipment for a particular purpose, when you put together its various parts or some readily-available substitute, and place them in position: *They were able to rig up a sort of temporary hospital on the outskirts of the camp.* □ *Can you rig me up a couple of spotlights?*

ring /rɪŋ/: **rings, ringing, rang** /raŋ/, **rung** /rʌŋ/

○ **ring back** (*especially BrE*)

You **ring** someone **back** when you telephone them for a second time or when you return a call that they have made to you: *Can you ring me back later?* □ *John called and asked if you would ring him back before lunch.* [same as **call back, phone back**]

○ **ring off** (*BrE*)

You **ring off** when you end a telephone conversation and put the receiver down: *I'm going to ring off now, Mum; I can hear the baby crying.*

○ **ring up**

1 (*especially BrE*) You **ring** someone **up** when you contact them by phone: *The cheeky young devil rang me up and asked me out.* [same as **call up, phone up**] **2** A shopkeeper or till operator in a shop **rings up** a sale when they record it on the cash register by pressing the appropriate keys: *Do you want to put this back, sir? I haven't rung it up yet.*

rip /rɪp/: **rips, ripping, ripped**

○ **rip off**

Someone **rips** you **off** when they cheat you *eg* by charging too much for something: *I can't believe they can get away with ripping customers off with these massive bank charges!* □ *He said he didn't mind paying, but really resented* *being ripped off.* [*same as* **cheat**, **overcharge**]

rise /raɪz/: **rises, rising, rose** /rooz/, **risen** /'rɪzən/

○ **rise above**

You **rise above** a difficult or degrading situation when your character is strong enough or you are determined enough not be affected by it: *Jocasta rose above those minor setbacks, and continued*
undeterred with her arrangements.

○ **rise up**

1 To **rise up** is to move upwards: *Smoke rose up in a great black column, obliterating the sun.* ❑ *Their chanting rose up through the vaulted roof of the Cistercian chapel.* **2** Something tall or steep **rises up** when it appears suddenly in front of you: *A massive iceberg rising out of the mist like a floating cathedral.* **3** People **rise up**, or **rise up** against authority, when they rebel and begin to fight against authority: *The peasants rose up against their oppressors.*

roll /rool/: **rolls, rolling, rolled**

○ **roll in** *or* **roll into**

1 (*informal*) You **roll in** somewhere, or you **roll into** a place, when you arrive there in a vehicle; someone **rolls in**, or **rolls in** drunk, when they swagger in casually, or come in moving from side to side unsteadily: *The convoy rolled into Sarajevo just before dusk.* ❑ *Iraqui tanks rolling into Kuwait* ❑ *He rolled in two hours late and seemed surprised at her indignation.* **2** (*informal*) People **are rolling in** somewhere when they are arriving in large numbers; money **is rolling in** when you are receiving large amounts of it: *Visitors to the palace are rolling in at the rate of ten thousand a day.* ❑ *Once we start selling the houses money should start rolling in and we'll be out of the bad patch.*

○ **roll on**

1 Time or a process **rolls on** when it continues steadily and smoothly: *And thus the years rolled on, uneventful but nonetheless happy.* **2** You can say '**roll on**' something when you want to let people know you are impatient for it to happen: '*Roll on tomorrow night,*' he moaned. '*It can't come quick*

enough.'

○ **roll up**

1 You **roll** something **up** when you turn or fold it over again and again so that it forms a roll; you **roll up** your sleeves when you turn the cuffs back until your sleeves are above your elbows, especially as a way of preparing for a spell of hard work: *He was carrying a rolled-up copy of the Evening Standard.* ❑ *He says we need a lot more heavy rain before he can roll up and put away his prayer mat.* ❑ *He rolled up his sleeves immediately and got to work.* **2** (*BrE*) People **roll up** to an event or entertainment such as a circus when they come to it or are attracted to it in large numbers: '*Roll up, roll up! See the greatest show on earth!*'

rope /roop/: **ropes, roping, roped**

○ **rope in** *or* **rope into**

1 You **rope** something **in** or **into** a small area when you confine it there and put up a rope barrier to prevent it getting out: *The bulls may have been tied up and roped in but he was still wary of going too near them.* **2** (*informal*) You **rope** someone **in** when you trick or persuade them into doing something; you **rope** someone **into** doing something by tricking or persuading them: *If we need a driver, we can always rope in Sue.* ❑ *Let's try to rope Bill into taking care of the kids tonight.*

round /raʊnd/: **rounds, rounding, rounded**

○ **round off**

You **round off** something when you do something that has the effect of making it complete: *They rounded off their formal education with a cookery or arts course.* ❑ *Charles finds that a glass or two of port is a very pleasant way to round off a good dinner.*

○ **round up**

1 To **round up** people or animals is to gather them together in a group so that they can be kept in one place or driven elsewhere: *It looks like one of those dogs that round up sheep; a collie or something.* ❑ *Those that have tried to escape have either been killed or rounded up.* **2** You **round up** a figure that includes a fraction when you make the fraction into a whole number: *His official salary is £23,750 but it's been rounded up to £24,000 to make it easier to divide by 12.*

rub /rʌb/: **rubs, rubbing, rubbed**

○ **rub in** (*informal*)

You can say that someone **is rubbing** it **in** when they go on talking about something embarrassing concerning you or a mistake that you have made, that you are already aware of: *'You seem to have put on a bit of weight!' 'Yes, I know; don't go rubbing it in.'*

○ **rub off** *or* **rub off on**

1 You **rub** marks or dirt **off** a surface when you remove them by rubbing with *eg* a cloth: *The teacher had rubbed the examples off the board before I had time to take them down.* □ *Will these marks rub off or will we have to paint over them?* **2** When one person's way of doing things, or the way they are feeling, **rubs off** or **rubs off on** another person, that other person is influenced by them and begins to behave or feel as they do: *We're hoping that some of Lee's enthusiasm will rub off on him.*

○ **rub out**

1 You **rub out** something that has been written in pencil or chalk when you remove it using a rubber or cloth: *She wasn't satisfied with what she had written so she rubbed it out and started again.* **2** (*AmE*; *informal*) If you **rub out** someone, or **rub** them **out**, you murder them: *He talked too much and was rubbed out by the mob.* □ *They rubbed Williams out for talking to the police.*

rule /ruːl/: **rules, ruling, ruled**

○ **rule out**

1 You **rule** something **out** when you decide not to consider it or include it: *The French still have interest rates above the German level and they don't rule out a devaluation of the franc.* □ *The Labour leader hadn't actually ruled out proposals on electoral reform.* **2** One thing **rules out** another when the first makes the second impossible or impractical: *A hairline fracture of the finger ruled him out of the match.* **3** You **rule out** a certain type of behaviour when you get rid of it because it is not appropriate or acceptable: *This would rule out*

racial discrimination.

run /rʌn/: **runs, running, ran** /ran/, **run**

○ **run across**

You **run across** someone or something when you meet them or find them by chance: *Did you happen to run across any of my old acquaintances while you were in Oxford?* [*same as* **come across**]

○ **run around**

1 People or animals **run around** or **about** when they move quickly from place to place within an area in an excited or energetic way: *No-one seemed to know what to do. They were all running around in a blind panic.* □ *When she got to the park she let the dog off the lead so that it could run around.* **2** You **run around** or **about** doing something when you move quickly from place to place getting the things you need or attending to many different things: *The daily chores fell mainly to the women; shopping, running around to find particular things.* **3** (*informal*) You say that people **are running around** or **about** when they moving about in public going from one place to another in a purposeless or threatening way: *It terrifies me to think of people running around the streets carrying guns.*

○ **run around with**

You **run around with** someone when you have a casual romantic or sexual realtionship with them; you **run around with** a gang or similar group of people when you are involved with them and take part in their activities: *Six months ago she was involved with a known criminal; now she's running around with a married man.* □ *He runs around with some pretty unsavoury characters.*

○ **run away**

1 You **run away** when you get away from someone or something by running: *I ran away as fast as I could.* □ *The boys would ring the neighbours' doorbells and run away.* **2** Someone **runs away** from home when they leave without telling anyone they are going because they are unhappy there: *He ran away to the Army when he was 17.* **3** You **run away** from something that you don't want to deal with when you avoid it or refuse to face it: *You can't run away from the fact that you are ten years older than you were then.*

○ **run down**

1 You **run** someone **down** when you criticize them unfairly: *It won't do much for his confidence if people are always running him down.* **2** A business **is being run down** when it is being reduced in size and in its range of activities, often with the intention of closing it down completely: *The factory is being run down and closure is scheduled for 1997.* **3** A supply **is run down** when it is reduced: *The $25 million reserve fund had been run down to $8 million.* **4** A mechanism or battery **runs down** when it gradually stops working or loses power: *I think the batteries in this radio are running down.* **5** A vehicle or its driver **runs** someone **down** when they hit that person and injure them: *He was about to be run down by the motorcycle.* **6** (*informal*) You **run** someone or something you have been searching for **down** when you eventually find them: *I ran him down in a seedy little hotel on the Left Bank.*

○ **run for** (*AmE*)

When someone decides to become a political candidate, you say he **runs for** a certain position or office: *Everyone knew Bush would run for President.* ❑ *Hillary Clinton made the decision to run for the Senate.*

○ **run into**

1 You **run into** someone when you meet them unexpectedly: *'Did you run into anyone interesting on your travels?'* ❑ *I stayed outside in case I ran into Father.* [*same as* **bump into**, **run across**] **2** You **run into** difficulties when you are suddenly faced with them and have to deal with them: *One of the residents was a chap about my age who had run into problems after his wife died.* **3** A sum of money **runs into** a stated amount if it reaches that amount: *The cost to government, employers and insurance companies could run into millions.* **4** A vehicle **runs into** another, or **into** a stationary object such as a wall, when it hits it: *The Benetton ran straight into*

the front of the Williams. ❑ *The Hurricane was badly damaged and ran into a parked aircraft on landing.* **5** One thing **runs into** another when the one merges with the other so that there is no distinct division between them: *It was late one night running into horribly early the next morning.* ❑ *red running into purple, then into a deep blue.*

○ **run out**

A supply of something **runs out** when there is none of it left: *What're they going to do when North Sea oil runs out?*

○ **run over**

1 Something that is filling up with a liquid **runs over** when liquid begins to spill over its upper edge: *They found the bath running over, but there didn't seem to be anyone in the house.* **2** A person or animal **is run over** when a vehicle's wheels pass over them, injuring or killing them: *Hundreds of toads are run over every year on Britain's roads.* ❑ *He tried to run me over with his tractor.* [*compare* **run down**] **3** You **run over** something when you practice it or check it to make sure it is correct: *I'd like you to run over these accounts with me sometime.* **4** Something **runs over** its alloted time when it goes on for longer than it should: *We're running over by at least ten minutes.*

○ **run through**

1 You **run through** a place when you pass through it, running: *They ran through the fields waving their arms and shouting to him to stop.* **2** Something such as a road or river **runs through** a place when its route goes through that place: *a long straight road running through agricultural land dotted with occasional clumps   of   trees.* **3** Something that **runs through** something else is found all through it: *What makes it interesting are the various subplots that run through the entire novel.* **4** You **run through** something when you use it all up: *We seem to be running through a huge amount of paper.* ❑ *I predict that they'll manage to run through all the money before Christmas.* **5** You **run through** something when you check it to make sure it is agreed or understood, or is being done properly: *I just want to run through the times of the flights again so that you all know when you should be where.*

○ **run up**

1 You **run up** a debt when you get things without paying for them at the time, or you use other people's money that has to be repaid eventually: *How much debt do you run up on your credit card at this time of year? Too much, that's for sure.* **2** A flag **is run up** a flagpole when it is raised so that it flies from the top: *They ran up the Jolly Roger.*

rush /rʌʃ/: **rushes, rushing, rushed**

○ **rush in** *or* **rush into**

You **rush in**, or **into** something, when you start doing it immediately without thinking about it or preparing for it: *Andy's always getting into scrapes; he just rushes in without thinking.* □ *I wouldn't rush into marriage if I were you.*

sack /sak/: **sacks, sacking, sacked**

○ **sack out** (*AmE; informal*)

You **sack out** when you go to sleep or to bed: *Rosy usually sacks out about midnight.*

sail /seɪl/: **sails, sailing, sailed**

○ **sail through**

You **sail through** a difficult or testing experience when you deal with it easily and successfully: *Oxbridge interviews are supposed to be stiff, but Wilkie sailed through.* [*same as* **romp through, walk it** (*informal*)]

salt /sɔːlt/ *or* /sɒlt/: **salts, salting, salted**

○ **salt away** (*informal*)

To **salt** money **away** is to save it for the future, especially secretly: *We listened open-mouthed as we were told of the thousands she had somehow managed to salt away.* [*same as* **put by, put**

away, stash away (*informal*); *compare* save up]

save /seɪv/: **saves, saving, saved**

○ **save up**

1 You **save up** when you gradually gather a sum of money, made up of all the smaller amounts you haven't spent, so that you can buy something you want; you can also say that you **save up** money, or an amount of money: *I had saved up and gradually built up my set of golf clubs.* □ *She saved up enough money to take a manicuring class.* [*compare* **put away, salt away**] **2** You **save** something **up** when you keep it to be used or dealt with later: *I'd saved up quite a stock of scrap paper for the kids to draw on.* □ *Note down any queries and save them up for the next meeting.*

scale /skeɪl/: **scales, scaling, scaled**

○ **scale down**

To **scale** something **down** is to reduce its size, extent or value: *By the end of the '80s, armies were scaled down enormously and we waited for the peace dividend.*

scare /skeə(r)/: **scares, scaring, scared**

○ **scare away** *or* **scare off**

1 To **scare away** a person or animal, or **scare** them **off**, is to frighten them so that they go away or stay away: *The radio had been left on to scare burglars away.* □ *All the recent police activity scared him off and he left in quite a hurry.* **2** To **scare** someone **away**, or **scare** them **off**, is to make them unwilling to do what they had wanted or intended to do: *An overprotective father is guaranteed to scare off even the most committed boyfriend.* □ *Potential investors had been scared away by rumours of interest-rate rises.* [*same as* **put off, deter, discourage**]

○ **scare up** (*AmE; informal*)

You **scare up** someone or something, or **scare** them **up**, when you have to find them quickly: *See if you can scare up somebody in the back room.* □ *Dorothy had to scare up $10 for the delivery man.*

scarf /skɑːf/: **scarfs, scarfing, scarfed**

○ **scarf down** *or* **scarf up** (*AmE; informal*)

You **scarf down**, or **scarf up**, food or

drink when you eat it eagerly: *Ron scarfed down three hamburgers after winning the game.* ❑ *The kids scarfed up just about everything on the table.*

○ **scarf out** (*AmE; informal*)

You **scarf out** when you eat too much: *We scarf out every time we holiday in America.*

score /skɔː(r)/: **scores, scoring, scored**

○ **score out**

You **score out** something written or printed when you cancel it by drawing a line through it: *The manuscript reveals that he had chosen a much more prosaic title at first, and later scored it out.* [*same as* **cross out**]

scrape /skreɪp/: **scrapes, scraping, scraped**

○ **scrape by**

You **scrape by** when you manage to live on very little money: *We will have to depend on dad for money or else scrape by on Social Security.* ❑ *Those who had possessions pawned them; others did what they could to scrape by.* [*same as* **get by**]

○ **scrape through**

You **scrape through** when you only just manage to pass an examination or test, or survive a difficult or testing experience: *I gather I scraped through the interview on the cut of my suit more than the cut of my wit.* ❑ *The aim is to cut costs enough to scrape through today's recession.*

○ **scrape together** *or* **scrape up**

You **scrape together** an amount of something, usually money, or you **scrape** it **up**, when you only manage to gather or collect it with great difficulty: *I managed to scrape enough together to feed my children and keep my flat going.* ❑ *Watson had succeeded in scraping together eleven players, although two of them were over fifty.*

scratch /skratʃ/: **scratches, scratching, scratched**

○ **scratch about** *or* **scratch around**

You **scratch about** or **scratch around** when you struggle to gather or collect all you need: *He was worrying his head off, scratching about for the rent and weathering one disappointment after another.* ❑ *Although they won the game 60-18, the Barbarians too scratched around*

for fluency.

screen /skriːn/: **screens, screening, screened**

○ **screen off**

You **screen off** part of a room when you separate it from the rest, with something such as a screen or curtain: *He worked in the dining room, at a desk that was screened off.* [*compare* **seal off**]

screw /skruː/: **screws, screwing, screwed**

○ **screw down**

You **screw** something **down** when you fasten it down firmly using screws: *The lid had been screwed down.*

○ **screw up**

1 You **screw up** your eyes when you close them tightly; you **screw up** your face when you twist it out of its normal shape, usually in an expression of disgust: *Stephen screwed his eyes up; nothing could have prepared him for this sight.* ❑ *You put down a lovingly cooked meal and your child just screws up her face at it.* **2** (*BrE*) You **screw up** paper when you squash it into a ball-like shape with your hands: *Jason screwed the letter up nonchalantly and tossed it into a bin.* [*same as* **scrunch up**] **3** You can say that you **screw up** your courage when you make a great effort to deal bravely with something frightening: *Screwing up her courage, Polly turned the handle slowly.* [*same as* **summon up**, **muster up**] **4** (*informal*) You **screw** something **up** when you spoil it or deal with it badly or foolishly; you **screw up** when you make a foolish mistake that spoils something: *The drugs business has screwed up his chances of going to the world championships next summer.* [*same as* **mess up** (*informal*), **foul up** (*informal*)] **5** (*informal*) Something **screws** you **up** when it makes you nervous, uneasy and confused about how you should feel or think: *Outwardly you have to be unemotional and cynical, but inside it can really screw you up.*

seal /siːl/: **seals, sealing, sealed**

○ **seal off**

To **seal off** a place or area is to prevent people from getting in by blocking the entrances to it: *Forensic were on the scene and the whole area had been sealed* *off.* [*same as* **cordon off**; *compare* **screen off**]

search /sɜːtʃ/: **searches, searching, searched**

○ **search out**

You **search out** someone or something when you find them after a long search: *With John in the band, we began to search out new songs.* [*same as* **hunt out**]

○ **search through**

You **search through** numerous things, or **through** what contains them, when you look at each in an attempt to find the thing you are looking for: *He came to London and systematically searched through the various agencies that might have employed her.* □ *We searched through all his bags, but could find no evidence of it.* [*same as* **look through**]

see /siː/: **sees, seeing, saw** /sɔː/, **seen**

○ **see about**

You **see about** something when you take action to have it done, dealt with or provided: *I phoned up to see about having the bed delivered.* □ *They'd left us to see about the broken washing machine.* □ *'So he wants to get rid of the strike leaders, does he? We'll see about that!'* [*compare* **see to**]

○ **see off**

1 You **see** someone **off** when you say goodbye to them as they leave: *She comes out on the terrace to see them off to school.* □ *We've just come down to see off a friend of my sister's.* **2** (*BrE*) You **see off** an opponent when you defeat them: *They defeated Spurs, then saw Chelsea off with ease.* **3** (*BrE*) You also **see** someone **off** when you force them to go away: *The dogs are left in the yard to see off intruders.* [*same as* **chase off**]

○ **see through**

1 You can **see through** something when you can see from one side of it to the other: *The latest radar equipment enables them to see through layers of cloud.* □ *She could see the bones through the skin.* **2** You can **see through** a person, or their behaviour, when you understand what their true intentions are, although they try to hide them: *She presents herself as the victim of men she sets*

out to attract and soon sees through and rejects. **3** You **see** something **through** when you continue with it until it is finished: *It would be a bold attack requiring determination to see it through.* **4** Something **sees** you **through** a difficult time when it helps you to survive it: *The points secured will see England through to the finals.* **5** Something **sees through** a period of time when it lasts until the end of it: *The despised suburban style looks like seeing the century through.* □ *He doubted he would see the winter through, and he died the following spring.*

○ **see to**

You **see to** something when you do it or arrange for it to be done or dealt with: *I would also need to see to the matter of costumes.* □ *Who's seeing to the travel arrangements?* □ *'Would someone please organize some coffee and sandwiches for our visitors.' ' Yes, I'll see to it.'* [*same as* **attend to, deal with, take care of**; *compare* **see about**]

sell /sɛl/: **sells, selling, sold** /sould/

○ **sell off**

Someone **sells** something **off** when they get rid of it by selling it: *They were forced to keep the land because of the problems associated with selling it off.* □ *He was often broke and was gradually forced to sell off his library.*

○ **sell out**

1 A shop **sells out** of something when they have none of it left to sell: *Sega is anticipating selling out within a week of the game's release.* **2** A film, play or other performance **is sold out** when all the tickets have been sold: *The concert sold out two hours after the box office opened for business.* **3** (*informal*) Someone who **sells out** betrays their principles or their friends: *Educationalists have sold out to those who have imposed attainment on the education system.* □ *He didn't want to be accused of selling out to the arts establishment.*

○ **sell up** (*BrE*)

Someone who **sells up** sells everything they have, such as their home or their business: *They didn't sell up completely but granted leases of land wanted for development.* □ *It looked as if they might* *have to sell up and move into rented accommodation.*

send /sɛnd/: **sends, sending, sent** /sɛnt/

○ **send back**

You **send** something **back** when you return it, usually by post: *Send them one of your pieces and ask them to match it and send their sample and yours back.* ◻ *They took the bills away but didn't send back the cheque.*

○ **send for**

1 You **send for** something when you send a letter to the supplier asking them to send it to you: *Before launching out to buy new materials, send for literature from each company.* [*same as* **send away**] **2** You **send for** someone when you send a message asking or ordering them to come and see you: *I advised him to send for the leaders of the other two parties.*

○ **send in**

1 You **send** something **in** when you send it by post to someone who will judge it or deal with it officially: *To win a prize, send in your caption together with any suitable photos.* ◻ *Complete the form opposite and send it in to our Marathon team.* **2** You **send** someone **in** when you invite or order them to enter a room: *Mrs Pygling sent her in to spy on Jane.* **3** People such as police or soldiers **are sent in** when they are ordered to go and deal with a difficult situation: *The banks don't want to send in managers or directors.* ◻ *It's one of these situations where they usually end up sending in a SWAT team.*

○ **send off**

1 You **send** something **off** when you post it: *He hasn't forgiven her for sending it off without telling him.* **2** You **send off** for something when you send a letter to the supplier asking them to send it to you: *She cuts out coupons from magazines and sends off for make-up samples.* [*same as* **send away**] **3** You **send** someone **off** when you ask or order them to leave, especially to go somewhere specific: *They sent us off on a wasteful course of negative research.* ◻ *She wouldn't listen to him and sent him off feeling more bitter and frustrated than ever.* **4** (*especially BrE*) A foot-

baller or other sportsperson **is sent off** when they are ordered to leave the field as punishment for breaking the rules: *He's back from a one-match ban after being sent off against Crystal Palace.*

○ **send out**

1 You **send** something **out** when you post it to someone: *Eleven weeks before departure, we will send out a final invoice showing the balance.* **2** People often use **send out** to refer to something that is produced or created: *The tree sends out shoots from a dry and seemingly lifeless trunk.* [*same as* **send forth**]

○ **send up** (*informal*)

1 (*BrE*) You **send** something **up** when you use humour to make it appear ridiculous: *This is a state which Smith experiences and which he sends up.* ◻ *He sends up politicians and TV personalities brilliantly.* [*compare* **take off**] **2** (*AmE*) You **send** a criminal **up** when you sentence them to prison: *The judge sent Maxie up for seven years.*

set /sɛt/: **sets, setting, set**

○ **set about**

1 You **set about** doing something when you begin to do it, often with energy and enthusiasm: *I took off my jacket and set about clearing the tables.* ◻ *In Africa, the Italian army set about building an empire.* **2** (*informal*) Someone **sets about** you when they attack you; you can also say that you **set about** something when you vigorously or violently tackle it or deal with it: *Then they set about him with sticks.* ◻ *I fetched the iron and set about a pile of shirts.* ◻ *I set about the lump with the woodcarver.*

○ **set aside**

1 You **set aside** something such as time or money when you save it for a special purpose: *I don't know how they had scraped up the money set aside for the roof repairs.* ◻ *The last day had been set aside for a hunting trip.* [*same as* **set apart, put aside**] **2** You **set aside** things such as feelings and beliefs when you disregard them for the sake of something that is more important: *He should set aside his obsession with results and experiment with tactics and* *players.* [*same as* **put aside**]

○ **set back**

1 Something **sets** you **back**, or **sets back** your progress, when it delays or reverses your progress: *A bad training class could have set Toby's development back months.* [*compare* **hold up**] **2** (*informal*) Something that **sets** you **back** a specified amount of money costs you that much: *The white evening gloves set her back the equivalent of two weeks' wages.* [*same as* **knock back** (*informal*)] **3** A building that **is set back** from a road or other landmark is built some distance back from it: *The house is ideally suited, being slightly set back from the busy and noisy seafront.*

○ **set down**

1 You **set** something **down** when you write it down: *An author is taking his revenge in setting down these judgements.* [*compare* **take down, note down, write down**] **2** You can use **set down** to talk about what is stated in laws or official rules: *Many aspects of our proposals are being implemented, such as the need to set down what is meant by 'an acceptable level'.* [*same as* **lay down**] **3** You **set down** something you've been holding when you put it on to a table or other surface, especially carefully or gently: *Little Jane, set down by Dorothy, staggered out to join the others.* [*same as* **lay down**] **4** (*BrE*) You can use **set down** when talking about where a bus or train stops to let people get off: *They asked to be set down in what looked to us to be totally featureless moorland.*

○ **set forth** (*formal*)

1 You **set forth** when you begin a journey: *The two armies finally set forth on the third anniversary of the Battle of Hattin.* ▫ *At once, Richard set forth for Cyprus.* [*same as* **set off, go forth**] **2** You **set forth** things such as opinions, ideas and suggestions when you present or explain them: *This recalls the doctrine set forth in the Old Testament.* ▫ *He sets forth an idealistic view of society.* [*same as* **put forth**]

○ **set in**

An unpleasant condition **sets in** when it begins and seems likely to continue:

Root crops must be dug up before severe frosts set in. ▫ *A sort of bunker mentality quickly sets in.*

○ **set off**

1 You **set off** when you begin a journey: *He collected his offspring and set off home.* ▫ *He could set off to walk south and try to cross enemy lines.* ▫ *She tucked the case under her arm and set off down the alley.* [*same as* **set out**] **2** To **set off** a bomb is to cause it to explode; to **set off** an alarm or other device is to cause it to sound or to function: *Believing that a man is about to set off a bomb won't make our soldier do anything.* ▫ *Exhaust fumes could set off the alarm.* [*same as* **trigger off**; *compare* **go off**] **3** Something **sets off** a process or a chain of events when it causes it to begin: *It can accidentally set off a very volatile and dangerous sequence of events.* [*same as* **trigger off, spark off**] **4** Something **sets** someone **off** when it makes them begin to do something, such as laugh or cry, that they continue to do for some time: *The stop sets one dog off barking and others join in.* ▫ *We'd just calmed her down when a chance remark from Don set her off again.* **5** One thing **sets off** another it is next to when it provides a contrast in shape or colour that makes the other more noticeable and striking: *His luminous head with its burning eyes is set off against a whirlpool of darkness.* ▫ *Soft surrounding plants set off spiky, yellow-bloomed irises.* [*same as* **bring out, show off**]

○ **set on**

1 You **are set on** some course of action when you have firmly decided to do it, or it will definitely or inevitably happen: *Is this a priest who strides towards us, implacably set on some atavistic rite?* ▫ *Within fifteen years, Germany was set on a course of revanche.* ▫ *It was clear that both parties were set on a collision course.* ▫ *He has set the Group on a course for long-term growth.* **2** Someone **sets on** you when they attack you; you can also say that you **are set upon** by them: *Without warning, they set on the ragged marchers with batons.* ▫ *Farrell was set upon by a gang of thugs wielding* *iron bars.* **3** Someone **sets** dogs or other animals **on** you when they cause them to attack you: *The farmer threatened to set his Alsatian on us if we didn't get off his land.*

○ **set out**

1 You **set out** when you begin a journey: *Wycliffe set out along the road which was really a lane.* ❑ *Four horses and riders set out to complete the cross-country course.* ❑ *You are about to set out on an interesting and formative experience.* [*same as* **set off**] **2** What you **set out** to do is the final result you hope to achieve by your actions: *Artists and poets set out to explore their own island in search of inspiration.* ❑ *They did not succeed in doing what they had set out to do.* **3** Something that **is set out** is explained or stated in speech or writing: *In each course, the method of assessment is set out at the beginning of the session.* ❑ *Your attention is drawn to the proviso set out in Clause 3.* ❑ *Its functions and powers are set out in Schedule 1 to the Act of 1986.* [*same as* **set forth** (*formal*)] **4** Something that **is set out** somewhere is placed or arranged there in an ordered way: *Bog plants can be set out in their permanent position.* ❑ *Set the tiles out so that they are centred on the area concerned.* [*same as* **lay out**]

○ **set up**

1 You **set up** equipment when you install it and make it ready to use: *I bought the computer, brought it home and set it up immediately.* **2** You also **set** something **up** somewhere when you build it there, or fix it into position there: *The best solution would be to set a roadblock up at the exit to the estate.* ❑ *They set up two photo-detectors on either side.* [*same as* **erect** (*formal*)] **3** You **set up** something such as a company, an organization or a system when you create it: *Licences were issued to any company wanting to set up a sawmill.* ❑ *There are still those who would advocate setting up a separate Parliament.* ❑ *I set up a little deception plan.* **4** You **set up** in business when you begin to operate a business: *He decided to set up as a psychotherapist.* ❑ *They would contribute to the cost of setting up in*

areas of high unemployment. **5** You **set** something **up** when you cause it, or take action that makes it happen: *The disquiet that he had set up among the brothers would go on echoing for some time.* ❑ *He ended a fine performance by setting up wing Byram for a try.* ❑ *He set up his victory by establishing a new course record in the third round.* ❑ *That victory set the Swede up for a seemingly difficult task against Wheaton in the sixth round.* **6** Something that **sets** you **up** makes you feel healthy and full of energy: *Self-massage sets you up perfectly for the day ahead.* **7** (*informal*) Someone who **sets** you **up** tricks or deceives you, especially by making you appear guilty of a crime or other wrongdoing: *It was then that he realised he'd been set up by Marie.* ❑ *He tried to set us up.*

settle /'sɛtəl/: **settles, settling, settled**

○ **settle down**

1 You **settle down** to do something when you begin to do it, in a calm or serious way: *With its political base ensured, the government could now settle down to enjoy the fruits of recovery.* ❑ *The old hands were less excited and settled down to daydream the time away.* **2** You **settle** yourself **down** somewhere when you make yourself comfortable there and rest or relax: *We settled ourselves down in a first-class compartment.* **3** To **settle down** is to begin to live an ordered life, more or less permanently in the same place or with the same partner: *They're considering building a house and perhaps settling down.* **4** People or situations **settle down** when they become calm or quiet after being noisy, busy or affected by strong feelings: *Things had just settled down when the air-raid siren sounded for a second time.* ❑ *'Settle down now, children. The programme is just about to begin.'*

○ **settle for**

You **settle for** something when you choose or accept it, especially when your preferred choice is not available: *The breakfast on offer looked revolting, so I settled for tea and muesli.* ❑ *He wasn't proposing to settle for just any job.*

○ **settle in**

You **settle in** when you become used to, and begin to feel familiar with, a new situation such as a new house or job: *They had stayed to help her settle in.* [compare **move in**]

○ **settle up**

You **settle up** with someone when you pay them the money that you owe them: *I don't get paid until next week. Can I settle up with you then?* ▫ *You go ahead and I'll settle up the bill.*

shake /ʃeɪk/: **shakes, shaking, shook** /ʃʊk/, **shaken** /ˈʃeɪkən/

○ **shake down** (*AmE*; *informal*)

You **shake** someone **down** when you take money from them using threats or illegal means: *The mafia shook Max down for everything he had.* ▫ *The mafia came around every Monday to shake down the local restaurant owners.*

▶*noun* **shakedown: shakedowns**: *When he showed me the fake police badge, I knew it was a shakedown.*

○ **shake up**

1 Something that **shakes** you **up** shocks or upsets you: *The news from home had really shaken him up.* **2** To **shake up** something such as an organization or a system is to make great changes to it, usually in order to improve it or make it more efficient: *We need some system for shaking things up.*

share /ʃeə(r)/: **shares, sharing, shared**

○ **share out**

You **share** something **out** when you give each of several people a share of it: *She used to count us all and share it all out.* ▫ *Then home we would go and share out the proceeds of our trip.* [compare **give out, dish out**]

ship /ʃɪp/: **ships, shipping, shipped**

○ **ship out** (*AmE*)

You **ship out** when you go to sea, especially with a navy: *John had a month left before he shipped out to the Gulf.*

○ **ship over** (*AmE*)

A sailor **ships over** when they enlist again in the navy: *Carl said he wouldn't ship over if they offered him a million dollars.*

shop /ʃɒp/: **shops, shopping, shopped**

○ **shop around**

1 You **shop around** when, before buying something, you compare the price or quality of it in each of several shops: *This is a bargain time for buyers prepared to shop around.* **2** You can also say that you **shop around** when you examine what is offered by each of several companies or organizations before deciding what to accept: *They encouraged people to shop around among insurers.* ▫ *In the 'internal market', local doctors could shop around for health care.*

show /ʃoʊ/: **shows, showing, showed**

○ **show off**

1 When someone is trying to make others notice how clever or skilful they are, you can say disapprovingly that they **are showing off**: *They speak in English to each other to show off.* **2** You **show off** something you are proud of when you display it to others, expecting them to admire it: *You can acquire a cloth badge to show off your membership.* ▫ *They vie with each other in generosity, showing off their wealth.* **3** To **show** something **off** is to make it seem as impressive or admirable as possible: *She strode forward with that swing in her hips that showed off her tall, slim figure.* [compare **set off**]

○ **show up**

1 (*informal*)

Someone or something **shows up** when they arrive or appear: *Sooner or later the brothers would show up in London.* ▫ *He was supposed to come yesterday but he didn't show up.* [same as **turn up**] **2** Something **shows up** when it can be clearly seen or distinguished: *This was the only medium that showed up against the pattern of the timber.* ▫ *It changes colour so that it doesn't show up against whatever vegetation it happens to be on.* **3** You can use **show up** to talk about what is revealed by a test or investigation: *The analysis shows up imperfections in the processing.* **4** (*BrE*)

Someone **shows** you **up** when their behaviour makes you feel ashamed or embarrassed that you know them or are associated with them: *Promise you'll behave. I don't want to be shown up in front of my colleagues.* **5** (*AmE*) You

show someone **up** when you do something better than they do: *I haven't played chess with you, because I don't want to show you up.*

shuck /ʃʌk/: **shucks, shucking, shucked**

○ **shuck down** (*AmE*; *informal*)

You **shuck down** when you take off your clothes: *We forgot our swimsuits, so we just shucked down and jumped in.*

○ **shuck off** (*AmE*; *informal*)

You **shuck off** your clothes when you take them off: *Dan shucked off his shirt before he cut the grass.* □ *She shucked her coat off and sat down.*

shut /ʃʌt/: **shuts, shuting, shut**

○ **shut down**

1 A business or factory **shuts down**, or **is shut down**, when it closes completely, either permanently or for a limited period: *Any of our pubs can, at a moment's notice, be shut down or altered by uncaring owners.* □ *Many of the firms have shut down.* **2** Machines, usually large industrial machines, **shut down**, or **are shut down**, when they stop working completely for a limited time: *The turbines were shut down until the water supply could be restored.* [*same as* **switch off, shut off**]

○ **shut off**

1 To **shut off** an engine or other large machine is to stop it working by stopping its power supply: *In this case, the engines shut off automatically.* [*same as* **switch off, turn off**] **2** To **shut** something **off** is to prevent it from being seen: *The garden was shut off from the street by a tall screen of conifers.* [*same as* **block out**] **3** You **shut** yourself **off** when you stay away from others and have no contact with them, or when you refuse to speak to them or listen to them: *She never acquired that emotional immunity, that almost instinctive shutting off.* [*same as* **cut off**]

○ **shut out**

1 Something **shuts out** light or sound when it prevents it from being seen or heard: *Heavy brocade curtains were drawn, shutting out all the natural light.* [*same as* **block out**] **2** You **shut out** unpleasant thoughts when you stop yourself thinking them: *She won't admit*

that it ever happened. She's shut it out completely. [*same as* **block out, blot out**] **3** You **shut** someone **out** when you prevent them from entering a place, *eg* by locking doors: *The strikers were shut out of the factory.* **4** You **shut** someone **out** when you deliberately exclude them, or prevent them from communicating with or reaching you: *Hopes are high that the Polish attack can be shut out and the points secured that will see the English team safely through.* **5** (*AmE*) One sports team **shuts out** another team when it prevents the other team from scoring: *Miami shut out San Diego 31 to 0.*

○ **shut up**

1 (*informal*)

Someone who tells you to **shut up** is telling you rudely to stop talking; someone **shuts** you **up** when they do or say something that stops you talking; you **shut up** when you stop talking: *Shut up and listen!* □ *The joke got a laugh but didn't shut the lady up.* □ *A glance from Skinner shut him up.* □ *You find yourself wishing they would shut up.* **2** You **are shut up** somewhere when you are kept there and prevented from escaping: *The dogs had to be shut up in the little room off the kitchen.* [*same as* **shut in, imprison**]

shy /ʃaɪ/: **shies, shying, shied**

○ **shy away**

You **shy away** when you avoid something because you are nervous or afraid: *He confronts problems that other men would shy away from.* □ *Horses are sensible to shy away at the sound of a hiss.* [*same as* **back away**]

sign /saɪn/: **signs, signing, signed**

○ **sign over**

You **sign** something **over** when you give someone else ownership of it by signing a legal document stating that you are doing so: *They found that he'd already signed his house over to his wife.*

○ **sign up**

1 You **sign up** for something, such as a course of study, when you officially join it by signing your name: *Kate signed up for an intensive course at the Berlitz school.* **2** Someone who **is signed up** is acquired as an employee or a team member or joins the military: *The*

Springbok stand-off is not about to be signed up in South Wales.

single /'sɪŋgəl/: **singles, singling, singled**

○ **single out**

You **single** someone or something **out** when you choose them from among others and give them special attention or special treatment: *Four main factors are singled out by Chris Green.* □ *Vichy's anti-Semitism had singled out Jews for contempt and discrimination.*

sink /sɪŋk/: **sinks, sinking, sank** /saŋk/

○ **sink in**

You can say that something **sinks in** when you understand, appreciate or accept it: *I couldn't believe it. It took a while to sink in.*

sit /sɪt/: **sits, sitting, sat** /sat/

○ **sit back**

1 Someone who **sits back** relaxes into a seated position with their back resting against the back of a chair or other support: *Sit back and relax.* □ *Just leave them on the floor and sit back in the chair.* **2** You can also say that someone **sits back** when they take no action, at a time when action is needed or expected: *Steve couldn't sit back while the animals suffered.* [*same as* **sit by**]

○ **sit down**

1 You **sit down**, or **sit** yourself **down**, when you lower your body into a sitting position: *She makes me sit down while she laces my boots.* □ *He sat down at his desk.* **2** You **sit** someone **down** when you tell them or force them to sit down: *She sat Nicandra down on her own chair.* **3** When someone **sits down** to do something they sit so that they can begin to do it, especially with determination: *Representatives of the Cricket Union and the National Sports Congress sat down together in a Johannesburg hotel.* □ *Over 130 people sat down to a five-course meal.*

○ **sit on**

1 Someone who **sits on** something such as a committee is a member of it: *members who'd been appointed to sit on the Commons Select Committee.* **2** You can say that someone **is sitting on** something when they are not dealing with it or allowing it to be used: *It would*

appear that he'd been sitting on the loan application for three weeks.

○ **sit out**

1 You **sit out** when you sit outdoors, rather than indoors: *They would sit out in their deckchairs in brilliant sunshine.* **2** You **sit** something **out** when you stay until the end of it: *They were desperate to get away but had to sit it out until the speeches were over.* **3** You also **sit** something **out** when you don't take part in it: *Tony sat it out in my tent.* □ *If you don't mind, I think I'll sit the next couple of dances out.*

sleep /sliːp/: **sleeps, sleeping, slept** /slɛpt/

○ **sleep in**

You **sleep in** when you continue to sleep past your usual or intended time for waking up: *Her excuse for sleeping in was that her alarm clock hadn't gone off.* [*compare* **lie in**]

○ **sleep together** *or* **sleep with**

1 Two people, usually people who are not married to each other, **sleep together** or **sleep with** each other when they have sex with each other: *She and Jonathan stopped sleeping together.* □ *Angelo offers her a bargain: if she will sleep with him, her brother shall live.* **2** You can also say that two people **sleep together** or **sleep with** each other when they share the same bed: *All four children slept together in one big bed.*

slip /slɪp/: **slips, slipping, slipped**

○ **slip away**

1 You **slip away** when you leave quietly or secretly, without others noticing: *We edged back and managed to slip away without attracting notice.* [*same as* **slip off**] **2** Something that **slips away** disappears quickly and easily: *She opened the window and felt her exhaustion slip away from her.* **3** Things such as chances and opportunities **slip away** when you lose them: *The keeper let two points slip away.* □ *She felt their life together slipping away.*

○ **slip by**

1 Time or an event **slips by** when it passes: *The hours slipped by so quickly that she had no time to brood.* **2** You **slip by** when you move past someone or something without being noticed: *I feel* *as if I can slip by, no-one will notice or comment.*

○ **slip through**
1 Something that **slips through** passes through a barrier or procedure that should not have allowed it through: *Matrons were vetted strictly but a few negligent ones slipped through.* **2** You can say that something such as a chance or opportunity **slips through** your grasp or your fingers when you lose it or fail to take advantage of it: *Norman had let the US title slip through his fingers.*

○ **slip up**
You **slip up** when you make a mistake: *It seemed that they were all waiting for her to slip up.* [*compare* **mess up**]

slow /sloʊ/: **slows, slowing, slowed**

○ **slow down**
1 Something that **slows down**, or **is slowed down**, begins to move or happen more slowly: *A black BMW slowed down and drew abreast of them.* □ *It is used when fermentation begins to slow down.* □ *It was decided to slow down the growth in the UK.* □ *Slow the pace down for two minutes before hiking it up again.* **2** Someone who **slows down** begins to work less hard or become less active or energetic: *I had gone too far and experienced too much, I needed to slow down.* [*same as* **slow up**; *opposite* **speed up**]

○ **slow up**
1 Something that **slows up**, or **is slowed up**, begins to move or happen more slowly: *It slowed things up too much, having to keep putting it away and taking it out.* **2** Someone who **slows up** begins to work less hard or become less active or energetic: *After twenty years of continual hard work, it was inevitable that he should slow up a little once he was financially secure.* [*same as* **slow down**; *opposite* **speed up**]

smash /smaʃ/: **smashes, smashing, smashed**

○ **smash up**
To **smash** something **up** is to destroy it by using violence to break it into pieces: *Simon told me that he'd smashed that kiosk up.* □ *You smash up your opponent's force before he knows what's hit him.*

smell /smɛl/: **smells, smelling, smelled** *or* **smelt**

○ **smell of**
To **smell of** something is to have its smell, or a smell like it: *The whole place smelled of putty and turpentine.* □ *She also had a teething baby, pinched and veined and smelling of milk.*

smooth /smuːð/: **smooths, smoothing, smoothed**

○ **smooth over**
You **smooth over** a situation when you make it easier by dealing skilfully with problems or difficulties: *Don't you think it would make more sense to smooth things over by allowing him some of the freedom he is demanding?*

snap /snap/: **snaps, snapping, snapped**

○ **snap up**
You **snap** something **up** when you buy or take it immediately, before others buy or take it and it becomes unavailable: *So many locations that would before have been snapped up by the professionals are now available to the amateur.* □ *The best roles have already been snapped up.* [*same as* **seize on**, **pounce on**]

snow /snoʊ/: **snows, snowing, snowed**

○ **snow in**
You **are snowed in** somewhere when heavy snow prevents you from leaving: *Almost the entire population of the Shetlands were snowed in for three days.*

○ **snow under**
Someone who **is snowed under** has enormous amounts of work to do: *We're pretty snowed under at work.*

soak /soʊk/: **soaks, soaking, soaked**

○ **soak up**
1 Something such as a sponge **soaks up** liquid when it takes the liquid into itself: *It soaks up water and acts as a reservoir for the plants' roots.* [*same as* **absorb**] **2** Someone who **soaks up** sunshine enjoys having the sun shine on their body: *Thousands of holidaymakers soaking up the sun on the Costa del Sol.* **3** You can say that you **soak** something **up** when give your whole body or mind to experiencing it as fully as possible: *You sit in one of the small*

roadside restaurants and simply soak up the atmosphere. □ *He spends his time painting and soaking up the culture of the land.* [same as **soak in, drink in**] **4** Something that **soaks up** resources such as money or time uses up a lot very quickly: *It'll soak up any contingency fund you may have in no time.* [same as **eat up**]

sort /sɔːt/: **sorts, sorting, sorted**

○ **sort out**

1 People often use **sort out** to refer to action of any kind that solves a problem, corrects a fault, or makes the situation satisfactory again: *Sorting all that out has taken up half the visit.* □ *The history department is trying to sort out its timetable.* □ *We'll hopefully get the bleeper sorted out by then.* [same as **see to, clear up, straighten out**] **2** You also **sort** things **out** when you separate them into different types or groups, or when you identify one type and separate them from the rest: *It takes time to sort out the real issues from the party politics.* [same as **separate out**] **3** (*AmE*) You **sort out** people who are acting in a confused or disorganized way when you show or tell them what to do: *There were some kids trying to push in behind the Germans and he had to go and sort them out.* [same as **organize**] **4** (*BrE*; *informal*) You **sort** someone **out** when you punish them or do something to prevent them doing wrong again: *Someone'll have to sort him out, before he gets involved in worse crimes.* [same as **deal with**]

speak /spiːk/: **speaks, speaking, spoke** /spəʊk/, **spoken** /ˈspəʊkən/

○ **speak for**

1 You **speak for** a person or group when you state their opinions to others and make decisions that affect them: *They pay people like Bobby to speak for them.* □ *Her behaviour could prove dangerous to the causes she speaks for.* [same as **represent**] **2** You **speak for** yourself when you state your own opinions; people often say they **are speaking for** themselves when they want to suggest that others may not have the same opinion as them: *She does often manage to speak for herself.* □ *'I've never seen the point of dieting.'*

'Speak for yourself, most women of our age are obsessed by their weight.' **3** When you say that something **speaks for** itself, you mean that no further proof, information or explanation is needed: *The figures speak for themselves.* **4** Something that **is spoken for** already belongs to someone, and is not available to others; you can say that someone **is spoken for** when they are married or they have a partner: *Is this seat spoken for?* □ *You can't ask Sheila out; she's already spoken for.*

○ **speak out**

Someone who **speaks out** states their opinions openly or publicly: *Carrie dared not speak out, for fear they would question her.* □ *An anonymous female member of the Saudi royal family has spoken out about the reality of life for women in Saudi Arabia.* □ *He did speak out very strongly one evening against it.*

○ **speak up**

1 You **speak up** when you speak more loudly than before: *There were cries of 'Speak up! What did he say?'* **2** Someone who **speaks up** states their support for someone or something openly or publicly: *It is a watchdog organization that speaks up for citizens as well as consumers.*

spell /spɛl/: **spells, spelling, spelled** *or* **spelt**

○ **spell out**

1 You **spell** a word **out** when you say in sequence each letter that forms that particular word: *That's an odd name. Would you spell it out for me?* **2** You **spell** something **out** when you explain it fully or in great detail: *The Special Report spells out the nature and function of the different sections.* □ *It is typical of him to spell things out so literally.* [same as **set out**]

spiff /spɪf/: **spiffs, spiffing, spiffed**

○ **spiff up** (*AmE*; *informal*)

You **spiff up**, or **spiff** a place **up**, when you make it look clean and neat; you can also **spiff** yourself **up**: *Mum always spiffs the bathroom up first when we have guests.* □ *I'll just spiff up the kitchen then I'll be ready to go.* □ *Angie took about an hour to spiff herself up for* *church.*

spill /spɪl/: **spills, spilling, spilled** *or* **spilt**

○ **spill over**

1 Things, usually liquids, **spill over** when they flow out over the sides of their container because the container isn't large enough to hold them: *It was just at the point where the river spills over the weir.* **2** You can say that one thing **spills over** into another when it becomes the other or develops into it: □ *Debates about the problems of the British constitution spill over into a case for resonstructing the constitution itself.*

spin /spɪn/: **spins, spinning, spun** /spʌn/

○ **spin out**

You **spin** something **out** when you make it last as long as possible: *Frankie tried to spin out the discussion as long as possible to allow time for them to arrive.* [*same as* **draw out, drag out**]

spit /spɪt/: **spits, spitting, spat** /spat/ (*AmE* **spit**)

○ **spit up** (*AmE*)

A person or animal **spits up**, or **spits** something **up**, when they vomit: *The cat spat up after I gave her my peanut butter.* □ *Louis spit the oysters up as soon as we left the restaurant.*

splash /splaʃ/: **splashes, splashing, splashed**

○ **splash out** (*BrE*; *informal*)

You **splash out** when you spend a lot of money, perhaps in a carefree way: *It can be tempting to splash out on the first splendid specimen that catches your eye.* □ *Building societies were splashing out on brochures offering fancy loans.* [*same as* **lash out** (*informal*)]

split /splɪt/: **splits, splitting, split**

○ **split up**

1 You **split** things **up** when you divide them into types or groups: *It's the way they are split up that promotes the development of greater strength.* □ *We'll be split up into smaller groups and led through.* [*same as* **divide up**] **2** People who are together **split up**, or **are split up**, when they separate and go to different places or travel in different directions: *They split up again when Gandalf rides off with Pippin and Merry*

sets off with Aragorn. □ *We were split up. I was billeted with a family outside Göttingen. Bruno was sent to stay with a farmer near Weimar.* **3** People who are married or in a relationship **split up** when they end their relationship: *Andy and I had already split up before he met her.* □ *Mum and Dad are splitting up.* [*same as* **break up, separate**]

spread /sprɛd/: **spreads, spreading, spread**

○ **spread out**

1 You **spread out** something that is folded or bundled when you open it fully and lay it flat: *I stripped off and spread my garments out to dry.* □ *A map of the course was spread out over the console before him.* [*same as* **open out**] **2** Things that **are spread out** have gaps or spaces between them: *The permanent jumps are spread out and not in a ring.* [*same as* **space out**] **3** You **spread** your fingers or toes **out** when you extend them fully so that there are spaces between each of them. **4** People who are grouped together **spread out** when they each go or move in a different direction: *We spread out, some diving down to the school of fish below.* **5** You can use **spread out** to emphasize how wide something is or how large an area it covers: *Beyond, the sea spread out like a ploughed field.* □ *The wide sweep of the Bay of Naples spread out far below them.* □ *He was standing alone with the world spread out at his feet.*

spring /sprɪŋ/: **springs, springing, sprang** /spraŋ/, **sprung** /sprʌŋ/

○ **spring on**

You **spring** something **on** someone when you surprise them by presenting or introducing something suddenly and unexpectedly: *They're fond of springing those little surprises on you. It seems to give them some sort of perverted pleasure.*

○ **spring up**

1 Something that **springs up** appears or develops suddenly: *Reform circles were springing up all over the country.* **2** You **spring up** when you stand up suddenly: *Bertha sprang up with surprising alacrity.*

square /skwɛə(r)/: **squares, squaring, squared**

○ **square away** (*AmE*)

1 You **square away** something when you straighten it out or put it in order: *The first thing you need to do is square away that filing cabinet.* **2** You **square** yourself **away** when you get ready for something; you **square** someone **away** when you get them ready for something: *Just let me know when. I can square myself away in a minute.* ❑ *Mom always squared away the kids before church.*

▶*adjective* **squared away**: *I've never seen Uncle Dan when he wasn't squared away like a general.*

○ **square off** (*AmE*)

Someone or something **squares off** to fight by getting into a position to fight: *The two boxers squared off before they entered the ring.* ❑ *The two political parties decided to square off on the issue of European union.*

stamp /stamp/: **stamps, stamping, stamped**

○ **stamp out**

To **stamp out** something unwanted or undesirable is to take firm action, or use force, to get rid of it: *The Church had tried, and failed, to stamp out those ancient pagan customs.* [*same as* **crush**]

stand /stand/: **stands, standing, stood** /stʊd/

○ **stand aside**

1 You **stand aside** when you move to let others pass: *She stood aside to motion him in.* [*same as* **step aside**, **move aside**] **2** You can also say that you **stand aside** when you don't involve yourself in the affairs or arguments of others: *The UN will be standing aside to allow NATO to take over the role of peacekeepers.* [*same as* **stay out of**]

○ **stand back**

1 You **stand back** when you move back and away from something or someone: *He stood back to let us pass.* [*same as* **step back**] **2** You can say that you **stand back** from a situation you are involved in when you try to judge it in the way that someone who is not involved would judge it: *He will have little opportunity to stand back and examine the data.* [*same as* **step back**] **3** A building

that **stands back** from a road or other feature does not lie next to it, but at some distance from it: *Standing some 50 metres back from the main street, the museum was hidden from view until you were right in front of it.* [*same as* **set back**]

○ **stand by**

1 Someone who **stands by** fails to take action to prevent something unpleasant from happening: *Governments stand by while the industry collapses.* ❑ *He would not stand by and watch her implusively throw her life away.* **2** Someone who **is standing by** is ready to take action when asked or when it is needed: *Mr Venables was standing by to offer encouragement.* **3** You **stand by** someone when you remain loyal to them and give them support in a difficult situation: *Think of all the hassle she's had from standing by her father.* [*same as* **stick by**] **4** You can say that you **stand by** something such as a promise or agreement you made earlier to show that you have not changed your mind, even though circumstances may have changed: *I think you have to stand by what you believe.* [*same as* **stick by**, **abide by, adhere to**]

○ **stand down** (*BrE*)

Someone who **stands down** gives up their job or position: *He's about to stand down on grounds of age and health.*

○ **stand for**

1 An abbreviation **stands for** a word or set of words that it represents or refers to: *Somebody writes TNT on the board and says what does that stand for?* **2** You can say that you won't **stand for** something when you won't tolerate it or allow it to happen: *Put him into Mrs McGill's class. She won't stand for any of his nonsense.* [*same as* **put up with, tolerate**] **3** Someone who **stands for** certain principles or values supports them or is regarded by others as representing them: *Guys like him stand for everything that's rotten.* **4** (*BrE*) Someone who **stands for** something such as an election is a candidate in it: *He's standing for the Tories at the by-election.* [*compare* **put up**]

○ **stand in**

You **stand in** for someone when you do their job, or do something that is normally their responsibility, because they are absent: *Barbara Bonney was standing in for an indisposed Lillian Watson.* □ *Would you be able to stand in at short notice if one of the committee doesn't arrive?*

○ **stand out**

1 Something that **stands out** can be seen clearly: *The caravans are painted white so that they stand out against the green landscape.* □ *Mount Kanchenjunga with its bright plume of snow stands out like a triumphal flag.* **2** Something that **stands out** is noticeably much better than others of its kind: *In my opinion, she stands out as being the most confident and self-assured of the four candidates.*

○ **stand up**

1 You **stand up** when you raise your body from a sitting or lying position into a standing position: *Push the hips forward and stand up straight.* □ *We were asked who would volunteer to stand up and read their poem.* **2** You can say that things such as arguments, explanations or excuses **stand up** if they prove to be true or seem likely to be true: *The evidence against him is purely circumstantial and would never stand up in court.* **3** (*informal*) You **stand** someone **up**, especially a boyfriend or girlfriend, when you deliberately don't go to meet them as you had agreed you would: *How dare he stand her up and then get that woman to phone and make his excuses?*

○ **stand up for**

You **stand up for** someone or something, especially when they are being attacked or criticized, when you defend, support or protect them: *They could not be relied on to stand up for British interests.* [*same as* **stick up for**]

○ **stand up to**

1 Something or someone that **stands up to** severe treatment survives it and remains relatively unharmed or undamaged: *This enables them to stand up to heavy wear.* [*same as* **withstand**] **2** You **stand up to** someone who is attacking you when you defend yourself

bravely and with determination: *I would never have thought he had the courage to stand up to her.* [*compare* **face up to**]

start /stɑːt/: **starts, starting, started**

○ **start off**

1 You **start off** by doing something, or **start off** doing it, when that is the first thing you do: *Start off by standing upright with our arms by your sides.* □ *You start off being coy about drinking brandy.* □ *We started off with some introductions.* **2** You **start off** when you begin a journey: *They gave up and started off home.* □ *The signal was given and the train started off.* [*same as* **set off**, **set out**, **start out**] **3** You can use **start off** when talking about the original position, state or nature of something: *Bullens Creek had started off tiny and tedious and gone downhill from there.* □ *The membranes start off positively charged.* [*same as* **start out**] **4** You **start** something **off** when you cause it to begin to happen: *Consider the Big Bang that started off the Universe.* **5** You **start** someone **off**, or **start** them **off** doing something, when you give them the signal to begin something, or when you do or say something that makes them behave in a certain way: *He made this stupid remark about how awful boarding school could be which started her off crying again.*

○ **start out**

1 You **start out** when you begin a journey: *Before you start out, make sure the mountain rescue know when you intend to return.* [*same as* **start off**, **set off**, **set out**] **2** You can use **start off** when talking about the original position, state or nature of something: *A take that started out as three or four minutes long may eventually be edited to a ten-second shot.* □ *He had started out in Cleveland, Ohio playing 3,000 people.* □ *It's a fair achievement having started out on a Youth Training Scheme.* [*same as* **start off**] **3** What you **started out** to do is what you began to do, or what you intended to do: *He had started out to make a rough count of the houses.*

○ **start over** (*especially AmE*)

You **start over** when you do something

again, from the beginning: *The whole thing collapsed and we had to start over.*

○ **start up**

1 You **start up** an engine, vehicle or machine when you switch it on so that it begins working: *They heard an ambulance start up and move off.* **2** You **start up** something such as a business when you begin it: *There was a positive decision against starting up a tourism enterprise.* [*same as* **set up, establish**]

stay /steɪ/: **stays, staying, stayed**

○ **stay away**

You **stay away** when you don't go somewhere: *Many voters simply stayed away rather than vote against the proposals.* □ *We're asking those without tickets to stay away.*

○ **stay on**

You **stay on** when you remain in a place longer than other people or longer than expected: *She had come to Glasgow to nurse her father and stayed on after his death.* □ *The men who were there had no choice but to stay on.*

○ **stay over**

You **stay over** when you spend the night in a place you have been visiting: *John and Mark are welcome to stay over if they want.*

○ **stay with**

1 You **stay with** someone when you live in their home for a time: *Staying with friends can be very disorientating.* □ *Bruno was sent to stay with a family near Weimar.* **2** You **stay with** something when you continue to discuss it, deal with it or use it, rather than changing to something else: *Staying with the economy, is it the Labour Party's intention to increase public expenditure on education?* □ *He'd looked at a few other cars, but in the end decided to stay with Fords.* [*same as* **stick with**]

stem /stɛm/: **stems, stemming, stemmed**

○ **stem from**

You can use **stem from** when talking about the cause or origin of something: *His love of writing stems from his analytical training at university.* [*same as* **spring from**]

step /stɛp/: **steps, stepping, stepped**

○ **step in**

Someone who **steps in** involves themselves in a situation that others have been dealing with: *Some got stranded at the airport but luckily others were on hand to step in.* □ *Television and radio stepped in and killed the art of storytelling.*

○ **step up**

Something that **is stepped up** is increased in amount, extent or intensity: *Lenin appealed to the Ukraine to step up its aid.* □ *The Community's role in this area should be stepped up.* □ *My blood tests were stepped up to once a week.*

stick /stɪk/: **sticks, sticking, stuck** /stʌk/

○ **stick around** (*informal*)

You **stick around** when you stay in a place, often in order to wait for something: *If you find something better, great; if not, stick around.* □ *Just stick around here until we can think of something.* [*same as* **hang around** (*informal*)]

○ **stick by**

1 You **stick by** something you have always believed, supported or used when you continue with it and don't change: *I think you should stick with what I say or get somebody else who can do it better.* **2** You **stick by** someone when you remain loyal to them and give them support in a difficult situation: *Somehow he'd taken it for granted that she would stick by him. She didn't.* [*same as* **stand by**]

○ **stick out**

1 Something that **sticks out** extends beyond the edge of the thing or things that it is next to, and can be easily seen: *His left elbow was sticking out of the window.* □ *The helmeted head of some hero would stick out through the roof.* [*same as* **jut out, protrude** (*formal*)] **2** You can say that anything obvious or noticeable **sticks out**: *Dressed like that you'll certainly stick out in a crowd!* [*same as* **stand out**] **3** You **stick out** a difficult or unpleasant task or situation when you continue to do it, or stay in it, although you might want to stop or leave: *Fordyce stuck it out for as long as he could.*

○ **stick to**

1 You **stick to** laws or rules when you obey them: *Find the rules to work by and then stick to them.* [*same as* **abide by**] **2** You **stick to** something when you continue to do or use it, rather than changing to something else: *It is sometimes best to stick to the familiar, cling to the known.* ▫ *Knighton is publicly sticking to the line that his offer will proceed.* **3** You **stick to** a subject when it is the only thing you talk about or discuss: *I think writers should stick to the facts.* **4** You **stick to** someone when you remain loyal to them and support them in a difficult situation: *Despite the questions about his loyalty, he's sticking to the President, so far at least.* [*same as* **stick by, stand by**]

○ **stick together**

People who **stick together** remain loyal to each other, giving each other help and support in a difficult situation: *All we have to do is stick together and tell the truth.*

○ **stick up**

1 Something that **sticks up** points upwards, or extends upwards beyond the edge of the thing or things next to it: *Some of them had electrodes on their heads that stuck up like a second pair of ears.* **2** (*informal, old*) To **stick up** a place such as a bank is to rob it using a gun or other weapon to threaten violence: *He said jokingly that the only way out of his problems would be to stick up a bank.* [*same as* **hold up**]

○ **stick up for**

You **stick up for** someone when you defend them against attack or criticism: *All the kids stuck up for him.* [*same as* **stand up for**]

○ **stick with**

1 You **stick with** something when you continue to do or use it, and don't change to something else: *Stick with it and you'll get there in the end.* **2** You **stick with** someone when you stay close to them, going where they go: *You stick with me, kid, and I'll show you the ropes.* [*same as* **stay with**] **3** Things stick

with you when you have very clear memories of them: *Their experiences in Burma had stuck with them for all these years.* [*same as* **stay with**] **4** You can say that you **are stuck with** something when you have been forced to keep it or accept it, although you don't want it: *Experimenters are stuck with observing physical events.* ▫ *The Democrats are stuck with Mr Clinton.*

stir /stɜː(r)/: **stirs, stirring, stirred**

○ **stir up**

To **stir up** trouble or unpleasant feelings is to cause them to be produced: *How dare this stranger stir up these doubts in so private an area?* ▫ *This action is commonly attributed to the fear of a working class stirred up by the course of events in France.*

stomp /stɒmp/: **stomps, stomping, stomped**

○ **stomp on** (*AmE; informal*)

1 You **stomp on** something when you bring your foot forcefully down on it, to break or kill it: *Jimmy was badly bitten when he stomped on the ants.* **2** You **stomp on** somebody when you attack, beat or defeat them: *They were bigger kids, but we really stomped on them.* ▫ *We stomp on that team every time we play them.*

stool /stuːl/: **stools, stooling, stooled**

○ **stool on** (*AmE; informal*)

You **stool on** somebody when you inform on them: *I had a copy of the exam in advance, but somebody stooled on me to the teacher.*

stop /stɒp/: **stops, stopping, stopped**

○ **stop around** *or* **stop round**

You **stop around**, or **stop round**, when you visit someone for a while: *Mary asked me to stop around after work.* ▫ *Stop round when you can!*

○ **stop by**

You **stop by** when you visit a place briefly: *At 11.30, I reminded myself to stop by at Frasers.* [*same as* **drop by, drop in**]

○ **stop off**

You **stop off** somewhere when you spend a short time there before continuing your journey to another place: *I* *stopped off at Jim Groeling's place to discuss some architectural drawings.* □ *They stopped off in Wolverhampton to change trains.*

○ **stop up**

1 You **stop up** a hole or passage when you fill or cover it so that nothing can get in or out: *Don't stop up that vent. It keeps damp out of the chimney.* [*same as* **block up**] **2** (*BrE*) You **stop up** when you don't go to bed until after your usual time: *Patrick stopped up to watch the American football.* [*same as* **stay up**]

storm /stɔːm/: **storms, storming, stormed**

○ **storm off**

Someone who **storms off** rushes away in an angry mood: *He hurled a chair across the set and then stormed off to his dressing-room.*

straighten /'streɪtən/: **straightens, straightening, straightened**

○ **straighten out** *or* **straighten up**

1 You **straighten out** something that is bent, twisted or otherwise forced out of shape when you make it straight again or put it back into its normal shape: *He tried to straighten out the brim, but it had been curled and folded so often it was beyond repair.* **2** You **straighten out** or **straighten up** a confused or troublesome situation when you put things right or solve problems: *When is someone going to straighten out this mess?* [*same as* **straighten up**, **put right**, **sort out**] **3** You **straighten out** someone who is confused or worried, or who misunderstands something, when you help them to think clearly or calmly, or explain things to them: *Alan had got the wrong end of the stick, so we had to straighten him out and reassure him that we hadn't intended to criticize his work.* [*same as* **put straight**, **put right**] **4** You **straighten out** someone who is behaving badly or foolishly when you persuade them to behave in a sensible or acceptable way: *It'll take more than a prison sentence to straighten him out.* [*same as* **put right**]

strike /straɪk/: **strikes, striking, struck** /strʌk/

○ **strike back**

You **strike back** when you attack in turn someone who has attacked you: *Karpov struck back in the very next game.* [*same as* **hit back**]

○ **strike out**

1 Someone who **strikes out** involves themselves in new activities or new business, especially independently of groups or organizations they belonged to before: *His sisters struck out for themselves.* **2** You **strike out** somewhere when you begin to walk or travel in that direction, perhaps with energy or determination: *Swimming against the current, he struck out as smoothly as a seal.* **3** You **strike out** something written or printed when you cancel it by drawing a line through it; to **strike out** anything is to cancel it: *Strike out any references to the USSR and substitute the Russian Federation.* □ *Any foods you suspect are causing problems must be struck out of your diet.* [*same as* **cross out**, **delete**; *compare* **x out**] **4** (*informal*) You **strike out** when you fail to achieve or obtain something: *Arnie couldn't get anyone to go to the prom with him. He'd struck out again.* **5** (*AmE*) In baseball, you **strike** a batter **out** when you throw three good pitches and he does not hit any of them; you **strike out** when you do not hit any of three good pitches: *Morrison struck Smith out.* □ *When Ruth struck out, the game was lost.*

○ **strike up**

1 You **strike up** a friendship or a conversation with someone, especially one that is unplanned and develops naturally and pleasantly, when you begin it: *We met on the cross-Channel ferry and struck up a conversation.* **2** Musicians **strike up** when they begin to play; you can also say that their music **strikes up** when it begins, or that they **strike up** a particular tune when they begin to play it: *A small group of musicians struck up the opening bars of the first hymn.*

string /strɪŋ/: **strings, stringing, strung** /strʌŋ/

○ **string along** (*informal*)

1 Someone **strings** you **along** when they deceive you into doing or believing something: *Try to string her along for a while longer. We've almost got everything we want.* [*same as* **lead on**] **2** You **string along** with someone when, for a short while, you travel with them or spend time with them: *He'd strung along with a group of settlers heading west.* [*same as* **go along, tag along**]

stumble /'stʌmbəl/: **stumbles, stumbling, stumbled**

○ **stumble across** *or* **stumble on**

You **stumble across** someone or something, or **stumble on** them, when you meet someone, or discover something, unexpectedly and by chance: *Exploring the caves, he stumbled across a quantity of guns and ammunition.* ❑ *They found the track and, on the second night, stumbled on the signal light.* [*same as* **come across, come upon, chance on** (*formal*)]

suit /suːt/: **suits, suiting, suited**

○ **suit up** (*AmE*)

Someone, such as an athlete or astronaut, **suits up** when they put on their uniform or space suit: *The game was cancelled even before the team had suited up.* ❑ *The astronauts suited up hours before the shuttle blasted off.*

sum /sʌm/: **sums, summing, summed**

○ **sum up**

1 You **sum** something **up** when you state its main features or characteristics: *I would sum it up by saying that cars are for work, not for worship.* ❑ *A happy holiday course in a sublime setting sums up Ufford Park nicely.* [*same as* **summarize**] **2** You **sum up** someone or something when you quickly form an accurate opinion of what they are like: *A good thing is the ability to sum up your close colleagues.* [*same as* **size up**] **3** Something **sums up** a situation when it represents it accurately because it is typical of it: *The word 'disastrous' would pretty accurately sum up the whole sorry escapade.* [*same as* **epitomize, typify, symbolize**] **4** At the end of something such as a formal discussion, you **sum up** when you state the main points that were discussed or the agreements that were

reached; a court judge **sums up** when he or she reminds the jury what the main evidence and arguments are, before the jury considers its verdict: *When summing up, the trial judge said the counsel's comment was improper.*

swallow /'swɒloʊ/: **swallows, swallowing, swallowed**

○ **swallow up**

1 Something that **is swallowed up** becomes part of something larger and loses its separate identity: *Brown Mills was eventually swallowed up by the expanding city.* ❑ *Tory ideology was about to be swallowed up by the centrist Christian Democrats.* [*same as* **absorb**] **2** To **swallow** something **up** is to use large amounts of it, or all of it, very quickly: *The National Curriculum swallowed up most teaching time.* ❑ *France's nuclear weapons swallow up almost a third of defence spending.* **3** One thing **is swallowed up** by another when the other hides it so that it seems to disappear: *When the sun finally appeared, the reds and golds were swallowed up in daylight.*

sweat /swɛt/: **sweats, sweating, sweated**

○ **sweat out** (*informal*)

Someone who **sweats out** a difficult or unpleasant experience or period of time suffers or endures it until the very end, waiting for it to finish: *They left us to sweat it out for the next three days.*

sweep /swiːp/: **sweeps, sweeping, swept** /swɛpt/

○ **sweep away**

1 To **sweep** something **away** is to destroy it or remove it completely: *He joined the Kennedy administration and began sweeping away waste wherever he could find it.* ❑ *We would expect a Labour government to sweep away all these laws.* **2** Natural forces such as winds and waves **sweep** objects **away** when they destroy them or carry them away: *The storm raged on, sweeping away huts and trees.* ❑ *They believe the volcano will erupt and sweep away the new Christian retreat being built on its slopes.* **3** You **are swept away** by emotions or feelings when they control your behaviour, especially causing you to behave foolishly: *A flow of desire swept her away at the thought of being together with Lucy.* [*same as* **carry away**]

switch /swɪtʃ/: **switches, switching, switched**

○ **switch off**
1 You **switch off** televisions and other electrical appliances when you stop them working by pressing the switch that cuts the supply of electricity: *Don't forget to switch it off after leaving the office.* ▫ *Switching the recorder on and off without being seen proved more difficult than he'd expected.* ▫ *They were watching television and didn't even switch off when he came in.* **2** You can say that you **switch off** when you stop listening or giving attention to someone or something: *As soon as you mention politics, they just switch off.* **3** You can say that someone **switches off** behaviour of a certain kind when they suddenly stop behaving that way, perhaps so suddenly that it makes you think their behaviour wasn't genuine: *She can switch the charm off and on like a light.* [*same as* **turn off**]

○ **switch on**
1 You **switch on** televisions and other electrical appliances when you make them begin working by pressing the switch that lets electricity flow to them: *She filled the kettle and switched it on.* ▫ *He climbed into the car and switched on the radio and the heater.* **2** You can say that someone **switches on** behaviour of a certain kind when they suddenly begin behaving that way, perhaps so suddenly that it makes you think their behaviour is not genuine: *You can tell she's bored rigid. She's never been able to switch on an expression of interest or enthusiasm like some can.* [*same as* **turn on**]

○ **switch round** *or* **switch around**
You **switch** things **round** when you put each in a position that one of the others was in before: *Someone must have switched the bottles round.* [*same as* **swap round**]

tag /tag/: **tags, tagging, tagged**
○ **tag along**
Someone who **tags along** with you joins you or goes with you, especially when you have not asked them: *His little brother always tagged along when we went anywhere.*

○ **tag on**
Something that **is tagged on** is added, perhaps as an afterthought, or to something that is already complete: *The comment about costs was tagged on at the end of his letter.* [*same as* **tack on, add on**]

tail /teɪl/: **tails, tailing, tailed**
○ **tail off** *or* **tail away**
Something **tails off** when it gradually decreases in strength, intensity or value, especially before disappearing completely: *Acceleration only begins to tail off above 120mph.* ▫ *His voice tailed off and he sat down heavily.* ▫ *Initial enthusiasm tails off as the new aid becomes a routine element of lessons.* [*same as* **drop off, fade away, peter out**]

take /teɪk/: **takes, taking, took** /tʊk/, **taken**
○ **take aback**
Something that **takes** you **aback** surprises you greatly or shocks you: *She was clearly taken aback at this suggestion.* ▫ *They were taken aback as the huge hangar doors blew open.*

○ **take after**
You **take after** an older member of your family when you are similar to them in the way you look or behave: *My family say I take after my mother in that she could make do and be happy.* ▫ *She had a trace of dark hair on her pate, just to show she took after her parents.*

○ **take away**

1 You **take** something **away** when you remove it from where it was and take or put it somewhere else: *She took her hand away from Anna's mouth.* ▫ *The contractors take it away and dilute it before spreading it thinly on the soil.* ▫ *When the roof was taken away, ruin took over and spread throughout.* **2** To **take** something **away** is also permanently to remove it or make it disappear: *Work has taken away the identity we had before.* ▫ *They kill; they take away another's life.* ▫ *The guards at the airport took it away and ate it.* ▫ *Removal men came to take away the sets.* **3** Someone who **is taken away** is forced to leave with others, especially police officers: *'What is the charge? You have taken away innocent men.'* ▫ *They were taken away for questioning.* ▫ *The police would come and take me away.* ▫ *His father came and took him away to Hambury.* **4** You **take** something **away** when you ignore it or disregard it: *When you take away all the sociological claptrap, policing is all about dealing with folk.* **5** What you **take away** from an experience is what you learn from it, or what memories or impressions of it stay in your mind when it is over: *The abiding impression I'll take away from Namibia is the vastness and emptiness of the country.* **6** You **take** one number or amount **away** from another when you find the difference between them by subtracting one from the other: *Taking 55 away from 102 leaves 47.*

○ **take back**
1 You **take** something **back** when you take it to where it was earlier: *You'll have to take that chair back into the house if it starts to rain.* **2** You **take back** something you have borrowed when you return it to the person who lent it to you: *'Oh no! I've forgotten to take my library books back!'* **3** You **take back** something you have bought when you return it to the shop and ask for a replacement, or for your money to be returned, because it is faulty or no longer suitable; the shop **takes** it **back** when they agree to give you a replacement or return your money: *If it isn't working properly you should take it back.* ▫ *You've*

obviously used it, so we can't take it back.* **4** You **take back** something you used to own or possess when you take possession of it again, perhaps using force: *Our mission was to take back from the Boche those few miles of battered ground.* [*same as* **regain** (*formal*)] **5** You **take** someone or something **back** when you take them with you when you leave: *She could not take him back to America with her.* ▫ *They took the duck back to the cabin.* **6** Something **takes** you **back** when it causes what happened or existed earlier to happen or exist again: *This week's rise takes many pensioners back to where they were 18 months ago.* ▫ *This took gold prices back to where they were the day before Iraqi tanks rolled into Kuwait.* **7** After ending your friendship or relationship with someone, you **take** them **back** when you agree to start up your friendship or relationship again: *Aunt Lucy would not have taken her back.* [*same as* **have back**] **8** You **take back** something you have said when you admit that you should not have said it and that it is not right or true: *'If you don't take that back, I'll smash your face!'* [*same as* **retract** (*formal*)] **9** You can say that something **takes** you **back** when it makes your remember or think about a past time or period: *Hearing that old recording again really takes me back.*

○ **take down**
1 You **take** something **down** when you move it from a higher position to a lower one: *He reached up and took it down.* **2** You **take down** something that is fixed to a wall or other vertical surface when you remove it: *The vines were taken down from their wires and their ends tied.* ▫ *Alan had decided to take down all the posters in his bedroom.* **3** You **take down** something that has been built when you separate it into the parts it has been built from: *The exhibition's being taken down today.* ▫ *It's time we took down the Christmas decorations.* [*same as* **dismantle** (*formal*); *opposite* **put up**] **4** You **take** something **down** when you make a written note of it: *The vehicle's details were taken down*

and reported back to Holbaek. ◻ *She took down his words in her swift hand.* [*same as* **note down**, **set down**, **write down**] **5** You can use **take down** when talking about taking something or someone to any place at some distance from where you are: *He's setting up a golf course in Cornwall and he's taken Margaret and Suzie down there with him.* ◻ *Take this down to desk number twenty-three.* ◻ *We'll take you down to the town centre in the minibus.*

○ **take in**
1 You **take** something or someone **in** when you take them with you when you enter a place: *He went into the study taking the case in with him.* **2** An establishment or organization **takes** someone **in** when it accepts or admits them as a guest or a member: *It's one of the few organizations that will take in homeless families and help them get back on their feet.* ◻ *She supplements her pension by taking in lodgers.* **3** You **take** something **in** when you understand, notice, observe or judge it: *I haven't had time to take everything in.* ◻ *You need to be highly intelligent to take in the situation instantaneously.* ◻ *They strolled around the gardens taking in the various delights on offer.* [*compare* **pick up**] **4** To **take in** something is to include it as a part of something larger: *This enlarged area now takes in much land amenable for agricultural purposes.* ◻ *Their area of responsibility takes in some of the city's most deprived estates.* **5** You **are taken in** by someone when you are fooled or deceived by them: *We were completely taken in by his appearance of friendly concern.* **6** You **take** something **in** when you visit it or go to see it, while staying in or touring a place: *Not surprisingly, they'll be taking in all the usual touristy sites, like the Parthenon.* **7** You **take** something **in** when you take it into your house from outside: *They make ideal houseplants if you take them in for the winter.* **8** Someone who **takes in** work such as washing earns money by doing other people's washing in their own home: *The inhabitants made a precarious living by taking in each other's washing.* **9** You use **take in** when talking about substances such as food, water and air that enter your body: *Plants take in carbon dioxide and give out oxygen.* [*compare* **take up**] **10** To **take in** a piece of clothing is to make it narrower by repositioning the joins at the edges: *The dress'll have to be shortened and taken in at the waist.* [*compare* **take up**, **turn up**; *opposite* **let out**]

○ **take off**
1 You **take off** a piece of clothing you are wearing when you remove it from your body: *The man had taken his shoes off and hung his feet over a chair.* ◻ *He knelt to take off the laced boots.* [*opposite* **put on**] **2** You can use **take off** in any of numerous ways which have the idea of removing something or making something disappear as part of their meaning: *Put the cloth on for the winter and take it off in summer.* ◻ *We can take the top off and feel the wind in our hair.* ◻ *That should take the strain off your back.* ◻ *That takes a load of pressure off me.* ◻ *Just take these other duties off my shoulders.* ◻ *Take off eye make-up gently with a cotton bud.* ◻ *The Captain had been either dismissed or taken off the case.* ◻ *They're taking Test cricket off TV in order to boost the radio audience.* [*opposite* **put on**] **3** An aeroplane or a bird **takes off** when it leaves the ground and begins flying: *It's not unusual to see pilots take off towards a heavy rain shower.* ◻ *We were supposed to take off for Malta twelve hours ago.* **4** Something that **takes off** suddenly or immediately becomes very successful or very popular: *The enterprise which had begun to take off in Napoleonic Paris had made enormous progress.* **5** You can also say that something **takes off** when it suddenly rises sharply to a very high level: *This is the unemployment rate which stops inflation taking off.* **6** You **take** your mind, eyes or attention **off** something when you think, look, or give your attention to, something else: *He just couldn't take his eyes off her.* ◻ *The accounts may take my mind off being cross with you.* ◻ *The Holbein case had taken the focus off the Canaletto and Zoffany.* **7** You **take** time **off** when

you have a period not doing what you normally do, especially not working: *These jobs enable women to take time off to have children.* ❑ *He has elected to take 24 hours off.* [*compare* **take out**] **8** You **take off** when you begin a journey, or begin an activity of any kind: *They plan to take off in a camper van.* ❑ *Before you take off on your campaign, make sure you know you can meet voters' needs.* **9** (*informal*) You also **take off** when you leave: *He took off as soon as he saw the policeman heading towards him.* **10** You **take** someone **off** somewhere when you take them with you when you go there, perhaps suddenly or unexpectedly: *She had taken Maggie off to the sunshine.* **11** You **take** something **off** someone who owns or possesses it when you use force to take possession of it: *Peter came running to his Mum saying the bigger boys had taken his ball off him.* [*same as* **get off**] **12** (*informal*) You **take** someone **off** when you imitate the way they look or behave, especially in order to amuse others: *She's brilliant at taking off the boss; has us all in fits of laughter.* [*same as* **mimic**; *compare* **send up**] **13** You **take off** an amount when you reduce a total by that amount: *It's slightly damaged so we'll take 10% off the price.* [*same as* **subtract**, **deduct**; *opposite* **put on**, **add on**]

○ **take on**
1 You **take** something **on** when you accept it as a job or responsibility: *He will perhaps set up home with someone else and take on a new job* ❑ *There is the reluctance of central government to take on new expenditure.* ❑ *They will find it harder to take on large loans.* **2** Someone who **is taken on** is accepted as an employee or member: *The university was willing to take on an inspector.* ❑ *Clubs tended to take on large numbers of hopefuls at low rates.* **3** (*informal*) To **take** someone **on** is to challenge or fight them: *He had the courage to stand up to Dublin and take Dublin on.* ❑ *They voted to take on the powers of the Yugoslav assembly.* **4** Something that **takes on** a new or different quality begins to have that quality: *Any liberal democracy will eventually take on an expansionist*

line. ❑ *The search for beauty seems to take on a different aspect.* ❑ *Faces took on a different expression.* ❑ *Free-market economics took on a different meaning last week.* **5** A vehicle **takes on** passengers or cargo when passengers join it or cargo is loaded on: *They stopped at Tarbert to take on water and fuel.*

○ **take out**
1 You **take** something **out** when you remove it from the place it was in, or from its container: *I take a handful out every day.* ❑ *Don't take everything out of the freezer yet.* ❑ *It will look better if we take out those awful shoulder pads.* ❑ *At this request, passengers would take small change out of pocket or handbag.* ❑ *He had taken out a little yellow fiddle and was warming up.* ❑ *Goldberg took out his polka-dotted handkerchief.* **2** You can use **take out** in any of numerous ways in which the idea of removing something or making it disappear is part of the meaning: *These gases have to be taken out before bottling.* ❑ *Prune when you see long growths taking the goodness out of the tree.* ❑ *Money would be taken out of the economy.* [*opposite* **put in**] **3** You **take** someone **out**, *eg* to a restaurant or cinema, when you take them there with you and pay for their entertainment, often as a way of forming a romantic relationship with them: *She had been willing to take her and her friends out for meals.* ❑ *He took her out; they fell in love and started to live together.* ❑ *Perhaps he would take the nurse out after he was home from hospital.* [*compare* **go out with**] **4** You often use **take out** when talking about formal or legal agreements in which money is paid: *Four million people are estimated to have taken out the new savings scheme.* ❑ *We will take out insurance against the repatriation of profits.* ❑ *Take out a subscription today and we'll enter you in our fabulous prize draw.* ❑ *Do you take out a new loan before the old one is paid off?* **5** You **take** time **out** when you spend time doing something different from what you normally do: *Ned was able to take a year out from his university course.* [*compare* **take off**] **6 a** (*slang*)

To **take** someone **out** is to kill them: *There are rogue cops out there taking out IRA terrorists.* [*same as* **knock off.** (*informal*), **bump off** (*informal*)] **b** Soldiers **take out** an enemy's vehicle, building or other location when they destroy it: *It'll be a night mission so we can take out the enemy positions under cover of darkness.*

○ **take over**

1 You **take over**, or **take** something **over**, when you gain control of something, or responsibility for something, in place of someone else, either by using force or authority, or when invited after someone else has finished: *The management committee will take over and run the whole operation.* □ *These are the contenders to take over leadership of the mainstream computer industry from IBM.* □ *I think Mary and Janice had better take over junior Biology.* □ *They called on Nu to take over as Prime Minister.* □ *They would take over some of the tasks now carried out by management.* □ *Whitehall has the power to take over the duties of local authorities.* □ *I gather you're taking over this case as well.* □ *They allowed the military to take over the railways to get supplies.* **2** You **take** someone **over** to a place when you take them with you when you go there: *We'll take him over to the embassy for a J-1 visa.* **3** Something that **takes over** becomes more important, powerful, influential or popular: *What happens to the diet when stress and temptation take over?* □ *She told herself not to let negative thoughts take over.* □ *This is the time for jazz to take over from calypso.* **4** You **take over** a place when you begin living or working there after someone else has left: *His son'll take over the farm when he retires.* **5** Something that **takes** you **over** occupies all your attention, energy or thoughts, perhaps making you behave strangely or unreasonably: *It started as a hobby, but now it's an obsession that's taken him over completely.* **6** You **take** time or trouble **over** something when you are careful to do it properly or well: *Look at all the trouble she's taken over dinner.*

○ **take to**

1 You **take to** someone or something when you begin to like them or decide you like them: *My mother never really took to her.* □ *I wondered how they would take to steak and kidney pud.* □ *No-one could have been better suited for the role, nor taken to it with more enthusiasm.* [*opposite* **take against**] **2** You **take to** something, or **take to** doing it, when you begin to do it as a regular habit or activity: *Henry had taken to aeronautics recently.* □ *A number of competitors have taken to slinging innuendo around.* **3** Take to is sometimes used to refer to the action of someone who, suddenly or and with a definite purpose, goes to a particular place, often in order to escape from something or someone: *Her own son had taken to the hills.* □ *Severe flooding had forced the villagers to take to higher ground, salvaging what they could as they fled.*

○ **take up**

1 You **take** something or someone **up** when you take them with you when you go or move to a place or position that is, or is thought to be, higher than where you start from: *A new rail service was introduced that would take them up twice a week to Irvine.* □ *A van stood by to take the bottles up to the municipal bottle bank.* □ *The therapist supports the leg and takes it up gently.* □ *She took him up the front steps.* □ *The administrator took us up in a lift.* **2** (*formal*) You **take** something **up** when you lift it and begin to hold or carry it: *He had paused before taking up his pen.* □ *Disgust filled me whenever I took up a brush and shovel.* □ *He took the poker up and turned a log over.* [*same as* **pick up**] **3** You **take** something **up** when you start doing it as a regular activity, hobby or job: *You decided to take up floristry because you saw an advertisement.* □ *None of them had taken up smoking.* **4** You can also use **take up** when talking about states or conditions that are beginning to exist: *They have to complete such courses before taking up employment.* □ *It would be necessary for her to take up more permanent residence at the Lodge.* **5** Something **takes up**

time, space or effort when it uses it or occupies it: *Sorting out the clothes took up literally half the visit.* ❑ *A great deal of time is taken up with swopping spies.* ❑ *Routine maintenance will continue to take up time.* ❑ *In a public place it will not take up any space.* ❑ *The greater part of the first volume is taken up with a narrative of past events.* **6** You **take up** a particular position or attitude when you adopt or assume it: *The group would dismount and take up their preliminary positions.* ❑ *Your opponent takes up a left fighting stance.* **7** You **take** something **up** when you discuss it or deal with it: *The honourable member for Stafford will take that up with his Conservative colleagues.* ❑ *I should indeed take the matter up with the Senate.* ❑ *The number of cases taken up by Amnesty now stands at over 42,000.* **8** You **take up** something that is offered or is available when you accept it: *Theological colleges were eager to take up the new opportunities.* ❑ *'Do let's take up the offer.'* ❑ *Not every woman takes up that challenge.* ❑ *Twenty percent of pensioners do not take up benefits they are entitled to.* **9** You **take up** something that has stopped, or that someone else has finished, when you continue it: *Peter Dew takes up the story.* **10** You **take up** something that is fixed to the floor or the ground when you detach it and lift it: *All the floorboards will have be be taken up, and the timbers treated.* ❑ *Leave the onions to dry off before taking them up and storing them.* **11** To **take up** a substance is to absorb it, especially from the ground or from a lower place: *With this system the tomato plants will take up essential minerals more readily.* [*compare* **take in**] **12** To **take up** something such as a dress or coat is to make it shorter by folding the bottom edge up and stitching it: *We'll have to take the curtains up about six inches.* [*opposite* **let down**; *compare* **take in**, **turn up**]

talk /tɔːk/: talks, talking, talked

○ **talk back**

Someone **talks back** to a person in authority when they answer them in a rude or disrespectful way: *Many of them now stand up and talk back to the managing director.* [*same as* **answer**

back]

○ **talk down to**

Someone **talks down to** you when they speak to you in a way that shows they think they are more important, experienced or intelligent than you: *They are fed up of being talked down to and dictated to.* [*same as* **patronize**]

○ **talk into**

You **talk** someone **into** something, or **talk** them **into** doing something, when you persuade them to do it: *They had to be talked into even showing up at all.* ❑ *I'm definitely not going, so don't try to talk me into it.* [*opposite* **talk out of**]

○ **talk out of**

You **talk** someone **out of** something, or **talk** them **out of** doing it, when you persuade them not to do it: *He threatened to stop eating but I talked him out of it.* [*opposite* **talk into**]

○ **talk over**

Two or more people **talk** something **over** when they discuss it: *I'll talk it all over with Alan.* ❑ *They'll be talking over old times in Santander this week.*

○ **talk to**

1 You **talk to** someone when you have a conversation with them or address spoken words to them: *John is the only person I could talk to about it.* ❑ *She's better to talk to than write to.* ❑ *Cats like to be talked to.* ❑ *'How dare you talk to me like that!'* **2** You **talk to** someone who has done something wrong when you speak angrily to them: *The headmaster will have to talk to you if your behaviour doesn't improve.*

○ **talk up** (*AmE*)

You **talk up** something, or **talk** it **up**, when you praise or promote it: *The travel agent was talking up holidays in Austria.* ❑ *Everyone was trained to talk the company up.*

○ **talk with** (*usually AmE*)

You **talk with** someone when you have a conversation with them: *The field-worker was talking with two plain-clothes men.* ❑ *Daggy comes over and talks with me and Marie a bit.*

tally /ˈtali/: tallies, tallying, tallied

○ **tally up** (*AmE*)

You **tally up** something, or **tally** it **up**, when you add it up: *Tally up the bill so* *we can leave.* □ *Tally the damage up and send me an invoice.* [*same as* **total up**]

tap /tap/: **taps, tapping, tapped**

○ **tap into**

To **tap into** a store or supply of something is to gain access to it: *The smaller machines tap into the central database.* □ *You're tapping into a person's past.*

tee /tiː/: **tees, teeing, teed**

○ **tee off** (*AmE; informal*)

You **tee** someone **off** when you make them angry: *That comment about French houses really teed Annette off.* □ *Your mood teed off everyone at the party.*

tell /tɛl/: **tells, telling, told** /toʊld/

○ **tell apart**

You can **tell** similar people or things **apart** when you can identify which is which, not mistaking one for the other: *The different works are not always easy to tell apart.*

○ **tell off**

Someone who **tells** you **off** speaks to you angrily because you have done something wrong: *His mum told him off for being such a cheat.* □ *He is, in effect, told off by Maeve Binchy.*

○ **tell on**

You **tell on** someone who has done something wrong when you tell someone in authority about it: *Please don't tell on me; I'll do anything you say.* [*same as* **grass on** (*informal*), **split on** (*informal*)]

think /θɪŋk/: **thinks, thinking, thought** /θɔːt/

○ **think ahead**

You **think ahead** when you consider what will happen in the future and usually make plans for dealing successfully with it: *This is caused by poor basic training and not thinking ahead.* □ *You should try to think ahead to your financial future.*

○ **think back**

You **think back** when you make an effort to remember something in the past: *I look at the glass and think back to the work and the mistakes I've made.* □ *She thought for a few seconds, thinking back to the Thursday of the fire.* [compare **look back**]

○ **think over**

You **think** something **over** when you consider it carefully in order to reach an opinion or decision: *Can you give me a couple of days to think it over?* □ *Once he'd thought it over, he decided it wasn't such a good idea after all.*

○ **think up**

You **think** something **up** when you invent or create it in your mind: *It's time to start thinking up new ideas.* □ *Thinking up suitable costumes kept the ladies occupied for weeks beforehand.*

throw /θroʊ/: **throws, throwing, threw** /θruː/, **thrown**

○ **throw away**

1 You **throw away** something you no longer want or need when you get rid of it, *eg* by putting in a bin: *The American family was throwing away an average of 750 cans a year.* □ *Throw that old anorak away immediately.* **2** You **throw away** something such as a chance you are given, or an ability you have, when you fail to make proper use of it and waste it: *They didn't expect their rivals to throw their lead away so foolishly.*

○ **throw up**

1 To **throw up** something such as dust or dirt is to cause it to rise into the air: *Blood mingled with the dust thrown up by the battle.* **2** (*informal*) Someone **throws up** when they force the contents of their stomach out through their mouth: *Not unless they think a client's about to throw up over the upholstery.* [*same as* **be sick, vomit**] **3** You **throw** something **up**, especially your job, when you stop doing it or you give it up: *You can't just throw up your job and go off without telling anyone where you're going.* **4** To **throw up** things such as problems or ideas is to create them or produce them: *No amount of lonely pacing could throw up any alternative in his mind.* □ *They deal as effectively as possible with whatever problems these casual encounters throw up.* **5** (*AmE*) If you **throw up** their fault or past mistake to someone, you mention it, usually often: *My boss will always throw up that bungled deal to me.*

tick /tɪk/: ticks, ticking, ticked

○ **tick off** (*especially BrE*)

1 You **tick off** an item on a list when you write a mark next to it, to show that it has been dealt with: *She should have ticked off Miss Vine's name on her list.* **2** (*informal*) Someone **ticks** you **off** when they speak angrily to you because you have done something wrong: *His aunt ticked him off for being rude to Sophia.*

○ **tick over** (*BrE*)

1 A vehicle's engine **ticks over** when it runs at its steady minimum rate while the vehicle is not moving: *I'm worried about a scraping noise I can hear when the engine is ticking over.* [*same as* **turn over**] **2** You can say that work, or a business, **is ticking over** when progress is slow but steady or regular: *The Christmas period kept stores ticking over.*

tide /taɪd/: tides, tiding, tided

○ **tide over**

Something that **tides** someone **over** allows them to survive a brief or temporary period of difficulty: *She gave us enough money to tide us over until I got paid.* [*same as* **see through**, **get through**]

tidy /ˈtaɪdɪ/: tidies, tidying, tidied

○ **tidy up**

1 You **tidy** something **up** when you arrange the things in it in a neat and tidy order; you can also say that you **tidy up**: *We tidied up and I gave her a hug.* **2** You **tidy** yourself **up** when you make yourself look neat and smart: *They tidied him up to his satisfaction.* □ *I had my hair cut, to tidy it up.* **3** You also **tidy** something **up** when you satisfactorily complete what was left unfinished or undone: *The budget plan will tidy up your current financial position.* □ *We used the editing features to tidy it up.*

tie /taɪ/: ties, tying, tied

○ **tie down**

1 You can use **tie down** to talk about limits or restrictions: *It's not easy to get away for a holiday. I feel more tied down than ever before.* □ *They originate from a broadly defined area but cannot be tied down to a specific village or town.* **2** You **tie** someone or something **down** when

you fasten them to the floor or a surface with ropes or straps: *The patient was tied down so that he couldn't struggle during the treatment.* [*same as* **lash down**] **3** Soldiers are **tied down** when their enemy prevents them from making progress and forces them to stay in one place: *Their brigade was tied down by Serb artillery.*

○ **tie into** (*AmE*; *informal*)

1 You **tie into** someone when you criticize or physically attack them: *His mother caught him smoking and tied into him.* □ *I ran for help when I saw the gang tie into the new boy.* **2** You **tie into** something when you attack it or do it with great energy or enthusiasm: *Dad put down his glass and tied into his steak.*

○ **tie up**

1 You **tie** something **up** when you wrap string round it to fasten it or make it secure: *Tie it up as close to the fingers as you can.* **2** An animal that **is tied up** is fastened by rope to a post or other fixture to prevent it from moving or escaping; a person who **is tied up** has had their arms or legs, or both, tied together to prevent them from moving or escaping: *The four youths had tied up a fourteen-year-old boy.* **3** (*informal*) Something that **is tied up** is being used or occupied, and is therefore not available for any other purpose or for anyone else to use: *Parent companies have their capital tied up in idle stocks.* □ *You have to be prepared to tie up £1000 for at least two years.* **4** (*informal*) You can say that you **are tied up** when you are busy with something and not available to do something else: *Mr Saunders is tied up until late afternoon, but he could probably fit you in tomorrow sometime.* **5** (*informal*) To **tie** something **up** is to settle or finish it, *eg* by making decisions or completing what was previously left undone: *We still have to tie up a few minor details, but the contract will almost certainly go ahead.* [*compare* **wind up**, **wrap up**] (*informal*) **6** You **tie up** your shoelaces when you tie them in a bow in order to fasten your shoes. **7** A boat that **is tied up** is tied to a post or other fixture, *eg* in a harbour. **8** (*BrE*) One thing **is tied up** with another when it is closely connected or related to it: *The crisis in Asia would become tied up with the course of events in Europe.* **9** (*AmE*) Traffic is **tied up** when the vehicles cannot move because of an accident or congestion: *That wreck tied up traffic for an hour.*

tip /tɪp/: tips, tipping, tipped

○ **tip off** (*informal*)
You **tip** someone **off** when you warn them that something secret is going to happen, or tell them that it has happened: *The press had been tipped off that the Health Secretary was going to make an announcement.*

tire /taɪə(r)/: tires, tiring, tired

○ **tire out**
Something that **tires** you **out** exhausts you or makes you very tired: *Now that she's getting on in years, a couple of hours with the grandchildren tires her out.* [*same as* **wear out**]

tone /toʊn/: tones, toning, toned

○ **tone down**
To **tone** something **down** is to make it less intense, severe or extreme: *Attempts to tone down Dixons' garish image have yet to bear fruit.*

○ **tone up**
Someone **tones up** their body or their muscles when they make their muscles stronger with physical exercise: *A sensible diet with regular exercise to tone up the muscles should be enough to keep you fit and healthy.*

top /tɒp/: tops, topping, topped

○ **top up** (*BrE*)
You **top up** a container of liquid when you add more liquid to make it full or make a complete measure; you can also say that you **top up** the liquid, especially when it is an alcoholic drink: *Keeping the pots topped up with water raises humidity.*

toss /tɒs/: tosses, tossing, tossed

○ **toss off** (*AmE*)
You **toss** something **off**, or **toss** it **off**, when you make or do something quickly and easily: *As soon as I mentioned cartoons, Eric tossed off a few.*

total /'təʊtəl/: totals, totalling (*AmE* totaling), totalled (*AmE* totaled)

○ **total up** (*AmE*)
You **total up** something, or **total** it **up**, when you add it up: *The authorities totalled up the number of deaths.* ⊐ *Please total the bill up.* [*same as* **tally up**]

touch /tʌtʃ/: touches, touching, touched

○ **touch down**
An aircraft **touches down** when it lands: *A lone plane touched down and took him off.* [*opposite* **take off**]

○ **touch up**
1 To **touch** something **up** is to make slight changes to alter or improve it: *Someone suggested she touch up her lipstick.* **2** (*BrE; informal*) To **touch** someone **up** is to get sexual pleasure from touching their body, usually without being invited to: *He's one of those creeps who thinks it's amusing to touch up the waitresses.* [*same as* **feel up** (*informal*)]

tower /'taʊə(r)/: towers, towering, towered

○ **tower above** *or* **tower over**
1 One person or thing **towers above** another, or **towers over** them, when they are, or it is, much taller than they are: *The tall bulky building towered above him.* ⊐ *The dog jumped on me, towering over me with his paws on my shoulder.* **2** You can also say that one person or thing **towers above** another, or **towers over** them, when they are far better than them or far more impressive: *He towered above all the other poets of his generation.*

toy /tɔɪ/: toys, toying, toyed

○ **toy with**
1 You **toy with** a possible course of action when you try to decide whether or not to take it: *We toyed with the idea of bringing her down from the gallery onto the stage.* **2** Someone **toys with** you when they enjoy keeping you in a state of uncertainty, *eg* by not giving you a direct answer or by delaying a decision: *Roy was only toying with me, eventually agreeing to participate in good spirit.* **3** You **toy with** an object when you handle it with small movements, casually or while concentrating on

something else: *He looked abstractedly into the distance, toying with his silver cufflink.* [*same as* **play with**]

track /trak/: **tracks, tracking, tracked**

○ **track down**

You **track** someone or something **down** when you find them after a long search: *The prisoner will be tracked down and caught.* □ *He would track her down mercilessly.* □ *Have you managed to track down that missing file yet?*

trade /treɪd/: **trades, trading, traded**

○ **trade in**

You **trade in** something you own when you give it as part payment for a newer, more expensive replacement: *Some retailers will allow you to trade in your old PC for a more up-to-date model.*

trip /trɪp/: **trips, tripping, tripped**

○ **trip up**

1 You **trip up** when you catch your foot or leg against something, causing you to stumble or fall over; someone **trips** you **up** when they deliberately create an obstacle, often their own foot or leg, for you to catch your foot or leg against in this way: *He tripped up as he approached the queen and fell in an undignified heap at her feet.* □ *Every time I ran past he hit me again or tripped me up.* **2** You **trip** someone **up** when, with clever arguments, you cause them to say something wrong, make a mistake or reveal a secret: *You had better have your story straight because their lawyer will do everything he can to trip you up and rubbish your evidence.*

trot /trɒt/: **trots, trotting, trotted**

○ **trot out** (*informal*)

You can use **trot out** to emphasize how boringly familiar, or casually expressed, are the ideas, excuses or explanations that someone offers: *These easy phrases are trotted out in the course of gossip.*

try /traɪ/: **tries, trying, tried**

○ **try for**

You **try for** something when you attempt to achieve or obtain it: *I don't know whether to try for a place in the front row or work towards qualifying for the back row.* □ *This encouraged him to try for promotion.*

○ **try out**

1 You **try** something **out** when you do or use it for a first time in order to find out if you like it or if it is useful or effective: *It was too windy to try it out.* □ *I took these two guitars into the studio to try them out.* **2** You **try** someone **out** when you give them a short task as a test of their ability: *He's trying out new skating partners.* **3** (*AmE*) You **try out** for a competitive position when your skills are tested, especially as an athlete or actor: *The team needs a quarterback, so I think I'll try out.* □ *Gregg tried out for the part of King Lear.*

▶*noun* **tryout: tryouts:** A **tryout** is a test of your skills for a competitive position, especially as an athlete or actor: *I was so disappointed when I was sick and missed the tryouts.*

tune /tjuːn/: **tunes, tuning, tuned**

○ **tune in** *or* **tune into**

You **tune in** when you listen to a particular radio programme or watch a particular television programme; you can also say that you **tune into** a programme: *Listeners who tune in next week will hear the result of our competition.* □ *You should have tuned into '40 minutes' on the subject of geriatric romance.* [*compare* **listen in**]

turn /tɜːn/: **turns, turning, turned**

○ **turn against**

Someone, especially someone you usually rely on for support, **turns against** you when they change their alliance and begin to oppose you; someone who **turns** them **against** you persuades them to do this: *The Maronites and other Christian groups turned against the French.* □ *Muslims have missed a great opportunity to turn public opinion against Rushdie.*

○ **turn around** *or* **turn round**

To **turn around** something that is failing, or **turn** it **round**, is to reverse its poor progress so that it begins to become successful: *The Herald hopes that her financial aplomb will turn around its ailing circulation.*

○ **turn away**

1 You **turn away** from someone or something when you turn your body into a position of no longer facing them: *I turned away so that Jeff wouldn't be able to see my tears.* **2** You **turn** something **away** from someone or something when you turn it into a position of no longer facing them: *Marie turned her face away.* ◻ *Do not turn your hips away from your opponent.* **3** Someone who **is turned away** is dismissed or rejected, or not allowed to enter: *It has refused to turn refugees away from its embassy.*

○ **turn down**

1 To **turn** someone **down** is to refuse what they are asking or offering; to **turn** something **down** is to refuse to accept it: *He turned down the role.* [*same as* **decline**, **reject**] **2** You **turn down** an appliance when you adjust its controls to reduce the flow of power to it, which reduces the sound, heat, *etc* that it produces; you can also say that you **turn down** the sound, heat, *etc*: *Turn the heating down; it's far too hot in here.* ◻ *Turn that TV down. I can hear it at the other end of the house.* [*opposite* **turn up**] **3** When you leave a main road you are driving on and enter a minor one that it connects with, you can say that you **turn down** that minor road: *From there, turn down Follyhouse Lane.*

○ **turn in**

1 You **turn in** something you have borrowed, or something in your possession, when you give it to someone in authority: *They could turn their guns and knives in without fear of prosecution.* [*same as* **hand in**] **2** You **turn in** written work you have finished when you give it to the person or authority who has asked for it or who will judge it: *Those who haven't turned in their essays by the end of the week won't have them marked.* [*same as* **submit**] **3** (*informal*) You **turn in** when you go to bed: *After you've gorged yourself on all the fun and nightlife that Benitses has to offer, you can turn in for the night and leave it all behind.* **4** To **turn** someone **in** is to tell the police or other authority that they have committed a crime or other wrongdoing, or perhaps take them to the police: *It would be better for everyone if he turned himself in.*

○ **turn off**

1 You **turn off** an appliance when you adjust its controls to stop power flowing to it, so that it stops working; you can also say that you **turn** the power **off**: *Drain the tank and turn the electricity off.* ◻ *The last one out turns off the lights.* **2** You **turn off** a road you are travelling on when you leave it: *I turned off by the stop signal.* ◻ *I turned off the road when I drew alongside the Brigadier.* **3** Something that **turns** you **off** causes you to lose interest or enthusiasm: *Her rather high-pitched speaking voice was thought by her image-makers to turn voters off.* [*same as* **put off**; *opposite* **turn on**] **4** You can also say that something **turns** you **off** if it causes you to lose sexual interest, or prevents you from developing any: *All his attempts to arouse her seemed only to turn her off.* [*opposite* **turn on**]

○ **turn on**

1 You **turn on** an appliance when you adjust its controls to allow power to flow into it, causing it to start working: *I turn on the light above my seat.* [*opposite* **turn off**, **turn out**] **2** You can say that someone **turns on** a particular kind of behaviour when they suddenly begin to display it, suggesting it is not genuine or sincere: *When he feels like it, he can turn on the charm like turning on a tap.* **3** A person or animal **turns on** you when they suddenly or unexpectedly attack you, violently or with angry words: *You will upset them and they may turn on each other.* **4** To **turn** something such as a gun or light **on** someone or something is to move it into a position of aiming or pointing at them: *She doesn't like it when the spotlight is turned on her.* **5** When one thing **turns on** another it depends on that other thing happening: *Liability was seen to turn on the question of whether the victim was likely to respond.* ◻ *The outcome turns on the block votes of union delegates.* [*same as* **hang on**, **hinge on**] **6** Something that **turns** you **on** makes you sexually excited: *The sight of all that naked flesh doesn't turn me on in the slightest.* [*same as* **arouse**] **7** You can also say that something **turns** you **on** when it causes you to become interested or excited: *He says that he gets turned on by the danger.* [*opposite* **turn off**]

○ **turn out**

1 People often use **turn out** when talking about what finally or eventually happens or what is finally or eventually discovered to be true: *Two of the men turned out to have family problems.* ❑ *It might simply turn out to be a consequence of bad taste.* ❑ *The photos didn't turn out too well.* ❑ *It turns out Lewis had checked with the college.* ❑ *Thankfully it has turned out all right for baby and mother.* ❑ *It turned out that East German security wanted to take their identity away.* **2** You **turn out** an appliance, especially a light, when you adjust the controls to stop the flow of power to it, causing it to stop working: *Be sure to turn out the lights when you leave.* [*opposite* **turn on**] **3** (*BrE*) Someone who **is turned out** of a place is forced to leave it: *She turned everyone else out of her room.* ❑ *They were turned out of their cottages and forced off the land.* [*same as* **put out**, **throw out**, **evict**] **4** You **turn out** a container when you empty it of its contents, especially by lifting it up and pouring the contents out: *Her small son had opened the biscuit box and turned out the contents on the kitchen floor.* **5** To **turn** things **out** is to produce them, especially in large quantities: *Some of the stuff they turn out is absolute rubbish.* ❑ *The purpose of 'English' was to turn out critics.* **6** People who **turn out** for an event go there to take part or watch: *Large crowds would turn out to support the Fair.* **7** You can say that someone **is** well **turned out** when they have a neat or smart appearance: *She's always neatly turned out in a smart skirt and jacket.*

○ **turn over**

1 You **turn** something **over** when you turn it in such a way that the top or upper side becomes the bottom or lower side: *He turned her hands over and examined the backs.* ❑ *He takes up the poker and turns over another log.* **2** You **turn** something **over** to someone when you formally give them posses-

sion of it or responsibility for it: *They turned their country over to Syria.* **3** You **turn** something **over** to a different use when you change its use: *Millend had left the cloth trade and been turned over to corn and saw milling.* **4** You **turn over** someone who has committed a crime or other wrongdoing when you take them to the police or other authority: *They'll be turned over to the French police once the extradiction formalities are completed.* **5** When you are watching television or listening to the radio, you **turn over** when you begin to watch or listen to a different programme; you can also say that you **turn** the television or radio **over**: *Boy had turned it over to a boxing match.* **6** (*BrE*; *informal*) To **turn** a room or other place **over** is to cause great damage by carrying out a thorough search: *They returned to find the office had been turned over by the police.* **7** An engine **turns over** when it works steadily at its minimum rate of power: *Keep the engine turning over, engage first gear, and draw away slowly.* [*same as* **tick over**] **8** You **turn** something **over** in your mind when you think about it carefully: *When he'd had a quiet moment to turn it all over in his mind, he realised that he had probably made a grave mistake.* **9** (*AmE*) In American football and basketball, a player or team **turns over** the ball when they lose possession of it to an opposing player or the opposing team; the ball is **turned over** when possession changes: *Marlow was hit hard and turned the ball over to White.* ❑ *Dallas turned the ball over six times in the game.* ❑ *There was a scramble on the floor, and the ball was turned over.*

▶ *noun* **turnover**: **turnovers**: In American football and basketball, a **turnover** occurs when a player or team loses possession of the ball to an opposing player or the opposing team: *Smith committed the turnover.* ❑ *Washington suffered two turnovers in the first half.*

○ **turn round** *see* **turn around**.

○ **turn to**

You **turn to** someone when you ask them to give you help or advice: *There is a* *wealth of support to turn to when you need help.* □ *The couple must now turn to the Investors' Compensation Scheme.* □ *There are voices you turn to as a friend.*

○ **turn up**

1 To **turn up** is to arrive or appear: *The classroom teacher may be concerned with the parents that don't turn up.* □ *Surely Dennis wouldn't turn up late?* □ *Everton supporters turn up in their thousands week after week.* □ *He had turned up for work as usual.* **2** Something that is **turned up** is discovered by chance: *They'd been nosing about and had turned up some pretty unsavoury details about his private life.* **3** You **turn up** an appliance, especially one that produces sound or heat, when you adjust its controls to increase the power supplied to it, causing it to work more intensively; you can also say that you **turn up** the power, or **turn up** the energy the appliance produces: *The pop music had been turned up quite loud now.* □ *We turn up the volume.* □ *It was like the mantle of a gas lamp turned up very slowly.* [*opposite* **turn down**] **4** To **turn up** a piece of clothing such as a dress or pair of trousers is to shorten it by folding the bottom edge or edges and sewing the fold: *These jeans will have to be turned up by at least two inches.* [*compare* **take up**, **take in**]

urge /ɜːdʒ/: **urges, urging, urged**
○ **urge on** *or* **urge upon**

1 You **urge** a person or animal **on** when you do or say something to encourage them to continue with something or go faster: *The horse was faced with a frightening object that he didn't want to go past, and yet was being urged on by his rider.* □ *The Prime Minister, urged on by her newest economic advisor, forced*

through the most anti-Keynesian budget of modern times. **2** You **urge** something **on** or **upon** someone when you try to persuade them to accept it: *Klein was urging equipment that we couldn't afford on us, all the time insisting that we couldn't do without it.* □ *We were afraid to refuse the food that they urged upon us.*

use /juːz/: **uses, using, used**
○ **use up**

1 You **use** a supply of something **up** when you consume it bit by bit, and leave none: *We've used up all the spare light bulbs.* □ *The rockets flew in a straight line until their fuel was used up.* □ *Sprinters often collapse when they cross the line because they've used up the reserves of oxygen in their blood.* **2** You **use** something **up** when you make sure that none of it is wasted or has been thrown away: *Karen made a stir-fry to use up the remains of the turkey.*

verge /vɜːdʒ/: **verges, verging, verged**
○ **verge on** *or* **verge upon**

One thing **verges on** or **upon** another when it is very close to being or becoming that thing: *Then they would break into convulsions of laughter, verging on hysteria.* [*same as* **border on**]

visit /ˈvɪzɪt/: **visits, visiting, visited**
○ **visit with** (*AmE*)

Someone **visits with** you when they pay you a visit, especially at your home: *You can take it with you when you're visiting with your aunt in the fall.*

vote /vəʊt/: **votes, voting, voted**
○ **vote on**

You **vote on** something when you take a vote to decide whether it will be done: *When they come to vote on it, it's likely to* *be very close-run thing.*

○ **vote through**

Something **is voted through** when a majority of people vote for it and it can be put into effect: *These changes were voted through at the last council meeting.*

wade /weɪd/: **wades, wading, waded**

○ **wade through** (*informal*)

You **wade through** things such as a great many boring or difficult books or other written material when you read or deal with them slowly and with a great deal of effort: *Then he's got to wade through the red boxes before going to bed.* [*same as* **plough through**]

wait /weɪt/: **waits, waiting, waited**

○ **wait on** *or* **wait upon**

1 The people who **wait on** you in a restaurant are the people employed to serve you with the food and drink that you have ordered. **2** You **wait on** or **upon** someone else when you do everything for them and get them everything they need or want: *You got fed regularly and women waited on you and asked you how you felt.* ❑ *'You do not think or care, lying here day after day, waited upon and given in to, without worries or anxiety.'* **3** (*informal*) You **wait on** someone when you wait for them, staying where you are for a time until they arrive: *Kevin was waiting on me at the bus-stop.* **4** (*BrE*; *informal*) If someone says **'wait on'** to you they are asking you to wait for them until they are ready to come with you, or they are asking you to stop what you are doing: *'Wait on, I think I may have found what we were looking for.'* [*same as* **hang on** (*informal*)] **5** You **wait on** somewhere when you stay there for

longer than you had originally planned to allow more time for someone to arrive or something to happen: *Jack waited on in her dressing-room until after eleven.* [*same as* **stay on**] **6** (*formal*) You **wait on** or **upon** an event when you wait until it happens before acting or making a decision: *'What are you waiting on?'* ❑ *Parliament had to wait upon the king's response.*

wake /weɪk/: **wakes, waking, woke** /wəʊk/, **woken** /'wəʊkən/

Note that in American English **waked** is often used as the past tense and past participle of **wake**.

○ **wake up**

1 You **wake up**, or you **waken up**, when you stop sleeping and become conscious; someone or something **wakes** you **up** when they do something to make you stop sleeping, such as shaking you or making a loud noise: *Margaret woke up cold. What had woken her up? A noise? A bad dream?* ❑ *a thin, piercing sound, like the wail of a child that has just wakened up and found himself alone.* **2** Something **wakes** you **up** from an inactive state resulting from laziness or boredom, or it **wakens** you **up**, when it causes you to be more active or feel more energetic: *A word from you might wake him up a bit and make him start working.* ❑ *The by-election defeat had the effect of wakening up the Conservatives who'd been pretty complacent about winning until then.* **3** If someone tells you to **wake up** or **waken up** they are telling you rather rudely to be pay more attention to what is going on around you: *Wake up, you lot. That was a dismal performance.* ❑ *You'd better waken up if you don't want to end up at the bottom of the league.*

waken /'weɪkən/: **wakens, wakening, wakened** *see* **wake**.

walk /wɔːk/: **walks, walking, walked**

○ **walk away**

Someone who **walks away**, or **walks away** from a situation leaves or abandons it because they no longer want to be involved in it or it is too difficult or complicated to deal with: *Do what Jahsaxa wants and get out. You've walked away from worse situations than this before.*

○ **walk away with** (*informal*)

You **walk away with** a prize when you win it easily: *There doesn't seem to be anyone who can stop him walking away with the World Driver's Championship.* [*same as* **walk off with** (*informal*)]

○ **walk in**

1 If someone **walks in** they come into the room where you are: *They were talking about Edith and the money when Henry walked in.* ◻ *He has this annoying habit of walking in without knocking.* **2** If people are able to **walk in** somewhere they can get in very easily because the doors are not kept locked or there is no proper security system: *There's no security guard and just about anyone could walk in.*

○ **walk into**

1 You **walk into** trouble or a dangerous situation when you get into it through your own carelessness or lack of good judgement: *He turned the corner and walked straight into a rioting mob of football hooligans.* ◻ *You can't just walk into a war zone and expect to be protected from the carnage.* **2** You can say that someone **walks into** a job when they get the job without much apparent effort: *It seems to me that people from his sort of background can just walk into any job they like.*

○ **walk off with**

1 You **walk off with** the honours or the prize in a competition when you win them easily: *It seems as if the top ten firms are walking off with all the prizes these days.* [*same as* **walk away with**] **2** (*informal*) Someone who **walks off with** something steals it or takes it without the owner's permission: *It seems that he calmly walked off with ten thousand pounds worth of jewels.*

○ **walk out**

1 Employees **walk out** when they stop working and leave their workplace in a group as a protest against their employer: *The men in the machine shop are threatening to walk out if they don't get a pay rise this year.* **2** You **walk out** of a meeting or a performance in the theatre when you leave it abruptly before it has ended to show your anger or disapproval: *He walked out of the Cabinet, and resigned.* ◻ *There were boos and cat-calls, and some of the audience walked out.*

warm /wɔːm/: **warms, warming, warmed**

○ **warm to** *or* **warm towards** *or* **warm toward**

1 You **warm to** a task or an idea when you become more enthusiastic about it or interested in it: *After initial nervousness, he found himself warming to the task.* **2** You **warm to** or **towards** a person when you begin to like or approve of them more: *I think Mother's warming to you at last.* ◻ *Almost despite herself, Candice found herself warming towards this strange little man.*

○ **warm up**

1 You **warm up** cold food when you heat it gently until it is warm enough to eat: *She served us some warmed-up leftovers.* **2** The weather **warms up** when the temperature rises; a place that has been cool or cold **warms up** when it gradually gets warmer: *The high pressure will be forced northwards and it will warm up considerably in the next few days.* ◻ *The kitchen had warmed up enough for them to shed their outdoor clothes.* **3** You **warm up** when your body gradually gets warmer after been cool or cold; something **warms** you **up** when it makes you feel less cold or gives you a feeling of warmth: *He put his hands inside his jacket to warm them up.* ◻ *A nice bowl of hot soup will warm you up.* [*opposite* **cool down**] **4** An event or activity **warms up**, or the pace of something **warms up**, when it gets more lively or more intense: *Now the competition really warming up, with three throwers battling for the lead.* [*same as* **hot up**] **5** An engine or other machine **warms up** when it reaches a condition where its parts are warm and it is running smoothly a short time after you have switched it on or started it: *Let the engine warm up before you disengage the choke.* **6** A performer or comedian **warms up** an audience when they make them relax and begin to enjoy themselves by telling them jokes or amusing them before the main show: *He used to warm up the 'Have I Got News For You' audience before stardom beckoned.* **7** An athlete or sportsman **warms up** when he or she does a series of relatively gentle exercises or they practice their shots to prepare themselves for an event: *The substitute goalkeeper's warming up on the sidelines. It looks as if Mark Bosnich is coming off.* [*same as* **limber up**]

wash /wɒʃ/: **washes, washing, washed**

○ **wash over**

1 A feeling **washes over** you when it seems to flow suddenly through your whole body: *Relief washed over her.* **2** If something that others are or would be affected by **washes over** you, you don't notice it or are unaffected by it: *Heidi let the whole thing wash over her as if she had no personal involvement in it at all.*

○ **wash up**

1 (*BrE*) You **wash up** when you wash the dirty dishes and cutlery that have been used to prepare and serve a meal: *I'll wash up if you dry.* **2** (*AmE*) You **wash up** when you wash yourself with soap and water to remove any dirt from your body, especially from your face and hands: *You boys go and wash up before dinner.* **3** Something **is washed up** by the sea or a river when it is carried to and left on the shore by the force of the waves or current: *He collected pieces of driftwood washed up along the shore.* ❑ *After a couple of days the bodies are usually washed up further downstream.*

waste /weɪst/: **wastes, wasting, wasted**

○ **waste away**

Someone **wastes away** when they gradually become thinner and weaker, usually because of illness or disease: *We had to watch helplessly as he wasted away before our eyes.*

watch /wɒtʃ/: **watches, watching, watched**

○ **watch out**

If someone tells you to **watch out** they are telling you to be careful so that you avoid danger or trouble: *Watch out! There's a lorry pulling out of that side street.* [*same as* **look out**]

○ **watch over**

You **watch over** someone or something when you guard them or look after them: *shepherds watching over their flocks.*

water /ˈwɔːtə(r)/: **waters, watering, watered**

○ **water down**

1 You **water down** a liquid such as wine or beer when you make it thinner or weaker by adding water to it: *Sometimes the children were given wine; watered down, of course.* [*same as* **dilute**] **2** You **water down** things such as comments, criticisms or proposals when you alter them to make them less controversial or extreme, so that they are easier to accept: *After sustained pressure from wealthy landowners, the legislation was heavily watered down.* [*same as* **tone down**]

wave /weɪv/: **waves, waving, waved**

○ **wave aside**

You **wave aside** an idea, objection or criticism, or you **wave** it **aside**, when you show that you are not willing to consider it because you think it is unimportant or irrelevant: *Our protests were waved aside; they carried on regardless.*

○ **wave off**

You **wave** someone **off** when you wave goodbye to them as they leave: *Our entire class came to wave us off at the airport.*

○ **wave through**

You **wave** something **through** when you give permission for it happen or be used without investigating or checking it properly or thoroughly: *They hope to convince the regulators in the US that the drug is safe (most other countries having already waved it through).*

wear /weə(r)/: **wears, wearing, wore** /wɔː(r)/, **worn** /wɔːn/

○ **wear away**

1 A material **wears away**, or it **is worn away**, when it gradually becomes thinner or disappears completely because of repeated pressure or rubbing: *The stone was gradually worn away by the drip drip of water over the centuries.*

□ *The leather was wearing away at the top of the boots near the ankle.* **2** A period of time **wears away** when it passes slowly: *The afternoon wore away and still the sun beat down.* [*same as* **wear on**]

○ **wear down**

1 Something **wears down,** or **is worn down,** when it gradually gets shorter or thinner because of repeated pressure or rubbing: *Eventually, the action of the sea will wear down the rocks until sand is formed.* □ *His clothes were clean but shabby, and the heels of his boots were worn down.* **2** Something **wears** you **down** when it is repeated so often or goes on for so long that it weakens you or makes you less and less able to resist it: *Charlie was trying to wear her down; writing, phoning, calling unexpectedly in the middle of the afternoon.* **3** (*AmE*) If you **wear** a sports opponent **down,** your strength or persistence weakens them: *The teenager had worn the defending champion down by the third set.*

○ **wear off**

A feeling or the effect of a drug **wears off** when it becomes less and less and finally disappears: *Hopefully, by that time the effects will have worn off.* □ *After the first awkwardness wore off, the party went with a swing.*

○ **wear out**

1 If something that has been used a lot **wears out,** or **is worn out,** it gets so weakened or rubbed through that it can no longer be used: *We disturb wildlife, pollute air, drop litter and literally wear out the footpaths.* **2** Someone or something **wears** you **out,** or you **wear** yourself **out** doing something, when they make you, or you become, physically or mentally exhausted: *Their longer than usual visit had obviously worn her out.* □ *Chris wore herself out trying to get the harvest in single-handed.* [*same as* **tire out**]

weigh /weɪ/: **weighs, weighing, weighed**

○ **weigh up**

1 You **weigh** a situation **up** when you study it carefully so that you know all about it and are therefore able to make a judgement about it: *I was sorry I hadn't weighed it up more thoroughly beforehand.* **2** You **weigh up** two or more alternatives when you consider each carefully before deciding on one of them: *We have to weigh up the benefits of medical assistance and of letting Nature take its course.* **3** You **weigh** someone **up** when you make a careful study of their behaviour or reactions so that you know what they are like: *He thought he'd got me weighed up and eating out of his hand.* [*same as* **size up**]

whale /weɪl/: **whales, whaling, whaled**

○ **whale away** (*AmE; informal*)

You **whale away** at someone or something when you criticize or physically attack them with great energy: *The candidates whaled away at each other during the debate.* □ *Dad's face became red as he whaled away at the tree.*

while /waɪl/: **whiles, whiling, whiled**

○ **while away**

You **while away** the time doing something if you spend it in that way: *Meg and Harry while away the hours until dinner doing jigsaws.*

whomp /wɒmp/: **whomps, whomping, whomped**

○ **whomp up** (*AmE; informal*)

You **whomp up** something such as a meal when you prepare it, often in a hurry: *Grandmother said she would whomp up breakfast while we dressed.*

wig /wɪg/: **wigs, wigging, wigged**

○ **wig out** (*AmE; informal*)

Someone **wigs out** when they react to something with extreme behaviour, usually either becoming very excited or very worried and frightened: *Lela knew that Walt would wig out if she told him she was leaving.* □ *Dad wigged out when he heard my exam results.*

win /wɪn/: **wins, winning, won** /wʌn/

○ **win over** *or* (*BrE*) **win round**

You **win** someone **over,** or you **win** them **round,** when you succeed in persuading them to agree with you or give you their support: *an attempt by Labour to win over Middle England* □ *It took some persuasion, but we won him round in the end.*

wind /waɪnd/: **winds, winding, wound** /waʊnd/

○ **wind down**

1 A clock, clockwork device, or machine **winds down** when it is about to stop and works more and more slowly: *The toy wound down and came to a halt under the kitchen table.* **2** You **wind down** some activity when you gradually bring it to an end: *You've arrived a bit late; the conference is winding down.*

○ **wind up**

1 You **wind up** a mechanical clock or watch when you turn a key to tighten the spring mechanism that makes it work. **2** A business company **is wound up** when it is closed or ceases trading: *He's thinking of winding up the company unless he can find a suitable buyer soon.* **3** You **wind up** an activity when you bring it to a conclusion or end: *They wound up the conference by singing 'The Red Flag'.* [*compare* **tie up**, **wrap up**] **4** (*BrE*) You **wind up** the window of a vehicle when you close it by turning a handle inside. **5** (*BrE*; *informal*) You **wind** somebody **up** when you amuse yourself by pretending that something is true or has happened so that you can enjoy their reaction: *'That's not true; you're winding me up, aren't you?'* **6** (*BrE*; *informal*) You also **wind** somebody **up** when you do or say something to them that makes them very annoyed or upset: *She sometimes winds him up so much, it takes all his self-control not to strangle her.* **7** (*informal*) You **wind up** somewhere when you find yourself in that place or position, often when you didn't set out to get there: *He's one of those kids that generally winds up in a young offender's institution* [*same as* **end up**, **land up** (*informal*)]

wipe /waɪp/: **wipes, wiping, wiped**

○ **wipe off**

A large proportion of the value of something **is wiped off** when it is lost: *Millions will be wiped off our share value.*

○ **wipe out**

1 Things **are wiped out** when they are destroyed or got rid of completely: *The snow has virtually wiped out today's racing programme.* [*same as* **eradicate**] **2** A debt **is wiped out** when it is repaid in full.

wire /waɪə(r)/: **wires, wiring, wired**

○ **wire up**

You **wire up** an electrical or electronic apparatus when you fit it with electrical wires so that it can be connected to the power supply: *The bomb had been wired up to the heating system.*

work /wɜːk/: **works, working, worked**

○ **work off**

1 You **work off** a feeling such as anger or frustration when you do some energetic activity to get rid of it; you **work off** excess weight when you take exercise to get rid of it; you **work off** the effects of a large meal when you take exercise to make yourself feel better: *Going to the gym is a great way of working off stress.* **2** If you owe someone money and you **work off** the debt you do work for them as a way of repaying them. **3** (*especially BrE*) A machine **works off** electricity or some other source of power when it uses that power source in order to operate: *Will this machine work off the mains?* [*compare* **work on**]

○ **work on**

1 You **are working on** something when you putting effort or thought into finishing it or improving it: *'Have you finished that report yet?' 'I'm working on it.'* **2** When you **work on** someone you use various means of persuasion to try to make them to agree to something: *June said she was working on the boss to give her an extra week's holiday.* **3** Something **works on** batteries when it takes the power it needs to operate from them: *She bought me a radio, of the kind that worked on batteries.*

○ **work out**

1 You **work out** a mathematical problem when you find the answer by calculation; you **work out** a problem when you solve it by thinking about it carefully and logically: *Let me show you how to work out percentages on your calculator.* ❑ *This is the figure that will be used to work out their roof tax.*

[*same as* **figure out**] **2** You **work out** the details of a plan when you finalize them by thinking about them, discussing them with others or making calculations: *We are working out ways of using new course structures, perhaps with part-time study.* **3** You **work** problems or difficulties **out** when you manage to solve them successfully: *They'll have to work out a solution that suits both partners.* **4** You say you can't **work** someone **out** when their behaviour is too strange or difficult for you to understand: *He's not like anyone I've ever met before. I can't work him out.* [*same as* **figure out**, **make out**] **5** You can say that things **have worked out** when they have come to a satisfactory or successful conclusion. **6** Something **works out** well or badly when it has a good or bad result or ending: *We had a few minor panics, but it all worked out okay in the end.* [*same as* **turn out**] **7** You **work out** when you do a series of exercises regularly in order to keep fit and healthy: *'He works out, you know, and plays a lot of handball and tennis.'*

○ **work out at**

Something **works out at** a certain amount if it is calculated to be that amount: *The bill worked out at more that twenty pounds a head.* [*same as* **come out at**]

○ **work under**

You **work under** someone when you do a job under their direction or with them as your boss: *You'll be working under Miss Hopeton in Accounts.*

○ **work up**

1 You **work** yourself or others **up** into a state of *eg* anger or excitement, when you make yourself or them get into that state: *By then, he'd worked himself up into a frenzy.* **2** You **work up** an appetite when you do some sort of activity that makes you hungry; you **work up** the courage or enthusiasm to do something when you gradually develop it: *By the time I'd worked up the courage to ask him, he'd left for the evening.* **3** (*AmE*) You **work up** something, or you **work** it **up**, when you develop it;

something is **worked up** when it is developed: *We took a week to work up the plan.* ▫ *The comedy act was worked up by Walter.*

wrap /rap/: **wraps, wrapping, wrapped**

○ **wrap up**

1 You **wrap up** something, or you **wrap** it **up**, when you enclose it in paper or cloth to form a package or parcel: *You'd better wrap up those Christmas presents before anyone sees them.* ▫ *The sleeping child was wrapped up in his coat.* **2** People **wrap up** when they put on warm clothes to protect them from the cold: *The skaters on the frozen loch were all wrapped up warmly.* **3** (*informal*) You **wrap up** a deal or task when you bring it to a satisfactory or successful conclusion: *I'm pretty confident we can wrap this up before the close of business tonight.* [*compare* **wind up**, **tie up**]

write /raɪt/: **writes, writing, wrote** /rəʊt/

○ **write down**

You **write** something **down** when you record it by writing it on paper with a pen or pencil: *I know I wrote his telephone number down somewhere, but I can't remember where.* [*same as* **note down**, **set down**, **take down**]

○ **write off**

1 You **write off** money that someone owes you, or that you have lost, when you accept that you will not get it back: *The high-street banks have had to write off millions of pounds in bad debts.* **2** You **write** something **off** when you decide that it is not going to succeed and that you will not spend any more time, effort or money on it: *He said he wasn't going to waste any more time on it; he'd written it off as a bad experience.* **3** You **write** someone **off** when you lose all hope that they will return, recover from a serious illness, or begin to behave reasonably: *You shouldn't write him off just because he made one mistake.* ▫ *I must admit we'd written him off, but then he seemed to make a miraculous recovery.* **4** (*BrE*) You **write** your car **off** when you crash it and damage it so badly that it is not worth the cost of repairs.

○ **write out**

1 You **write** something **out** when you write it on paper in full: *I wrote out my name and address on the back of the cheque.* **2** You **write out** something such as a cheque when you fill in all the necessary details and sign it: *He said he would write me out a cheque but I insisted on cash.* ◻ *The doctor said he would write out a presciption and I could collect it the next morning.*

x /ɛks/: **x's, x-ing, x-ed**

○ **x out** (*AmE*)

You **x** something written **out**, or **x** it **out**, when you delete it, especially by marking x's through it: *I'll x out 'butter' on the grocery list.* ◻ *We had to x several lines out to shorten the play.* [*compare* **strike out**]

Language Study Panels

LANGUAGE *study*

Native speakers of English intuitively create new phrasal verbs and understand those created by fellow native speakers. This is naturally something that learners cannot do with anything like the same instinctive ease.

The following panels on adverbial particles will help you with this aspect of language use. These panels give the broad range of meanings that each particle has, and show which of the particles are used by native speakers to form new phrasal verbs.

These panels will help you to develop your knowledge of how phrasal verbs are formed and how they function in English. By showing the range of meanings that each particle has, and identifying those particles and meanings that are used in modern English to form phrasal verbs, you will begin to understand phrasal verbs more easily, and feel more confident in your own use of them.

aback /əˈbak/ *adverb*

In the past, **aback** was used in many of the ways that **back** is now used. In modern English, the adverb **aback** is found only in the phrasal verb *take aback*.

about /əˈbaʊt/ *adverb* or *preposition*

About is frequently found in phrasal verbs and is used quite often in the production of new phrasal verbs. It is commonly used simply to link the verb to its object, as in *talk about, hear about, see about* and *worry about*. However, **about** can also have various distinct meanings, and shades of meaning, when used in phrasal verbs. Note that **around** and **round** are often substituted for **about** without changing the meaning of the phrasal verb.

movement in different directions

In this sense, **about** is usually used to show that the movement referred to by the verb does not have any particular pattern, being somewhat random and often playful. Phrasal verbs with this sense include *jump about, run about* and *look about*.

action in different places

This sense is closely related to the first, in that it also suggests a lack of pattern or plan. Here, however, the meaning of **about** refers more specifically to action that takes place first in one place and then in another. The action is also sometimes rough or violent. Phrasal verbs with this sense include *ask about, throw about, bang about*, and *scatter about*.

lack of activity, purpose or pattern

Used in this sense in phrasal verbs, **about** implies lack of activity or purpose, often with the added suggestion of laziness or foolishness. Examples include the phrasal verbs *hang about, stand about, loaf about, wander about, play about* and *mess about*. Many phrasal verbs with this sense are informal or vulgar.

happening

In a small group of phrasal verbs, which includes *bring about, come about* and *set about*, **about** refers to something happening or being caused.

turning, surrounding and enclosing

In phrasal verbs with this sense, such as *turn about, gather about* and *fence about*, **about** is used as a slightly more formal or literary alternative to **around** or **round**.

above /əˈbʌv/ *preposition* or *adverb*

Although **above** is a very common word in English, it is only found in a small number of phrasal verbs. These combinations have one of two senses, the first a literal sense and the second figurative.

higher position or level

The literal sense of **above** refers to actual movement or position in relation to other people or things. Examples of phrasal verbs with this sense are *fly above*, *tower above*, and *soar above*.

better or more important

This sense extends the first sense in that the higher position or level being referred to is figurative rather than literal. Thus, when you *get above* yourself, you think you are more important than other people, when you *rise above* something petty or unpleasant, you don't allow yourself to be upset by it, and when a performer is said to *tower above* all others they are considered by everyone to be the best by far.

across /əˈkrɒs/ *preposition* and *adverb*

When **across** combines with verbs to form phrasal verbs, its meanings relate to movement from one side of something to the other, to discovering something, and to the communication of information from one person to another.

movement from one side to the other

Across is used in its literal sense with many verbs of movement, for example *walk across*, *jump across* and *push across*. In phrasal verbs that have this literal sense, **over** can often be substituted for **across** without much change of meaning, for example *go across /over* and *jump across /over*.

discovering

Across is also used to refer to the action of discovering or encountering a person or thing, unexpectedly or by chance, as in senses of the phrasal verbs *run across*, *come across*, and *stumble across*. Note that **over** cannot be substituted for **across** in those senses of phrasal verbs in which **across** has this meaning.

communicating or telling

In non-literal senses of the phrasal verbs *get across*, *put across* and *come across*, the meaning of **across** relates to the communication of information between people, especially the way in which information is communicated, or the impression made by the communicator on his or her audience.

after /ˈɑːftə(r)/ *preposition*

After has three main meanings when used in phrasal verbs.

following

The general and literal sense of **after** is used to show that one thing happens later than, or follows, another. This sense of following, when it is used in phrasal verbs, often relates to people being followed, chased or hunted, as in *go after*, *come after*, *run after* and *chase after*. Sometimes this broad sense of following is extended to include the idea of making oneself available to attend to someone's needs, as in *look after*.

wanting, desiring

After is also used to refer to the feeling of wanting something or the action of trying to get it, as in *ask after*. This sense is often a development of the idea of chasing or hunting, as in *go after*, *run after* and *chase after*. In other combinations with this sense, the feeling suggested is a strong desire, as in *hunger after*, *hanker after* and *lust after*.

imitating or copying

The last main sense of **after** is in phrasal verbs that refer to the action of imitating or copying, as in *call after*, *name after* and *take after*.

against /əˈɡeɪnst/ or /əˈɡɛnst/ *preposition*

Against is quite a common word in English and it combines quite readily with verbs to form phrasal verbs. Its basic sense relates to relationships between two things, especially relationships that involve difference, opposition or conflict, and in phrasal verbs it has four main senses that are an extension of this basic sense.

opposing

Against combines with verbs that refer to the actions of one person or thing that opposes another as in *go against, turn against, plot against, protest against, fight against, battle against*, and many more.

protecting

In this sense, **against** refers to the person or thing that might cause harm to the person or thing being protected, as in the combinations *guard against, protect against* and *insure against*.

comparing

In this sense, **against** is used in phrasal verbs that refer to the action of comparing one thing with another, or with others. Examples include the phrasal verbs *check against, match against* and *weigh against*.

being a disadvantage

The final sense of **against** found in phrasal verb combinations relates to a fact or circumstance that will prevent things advancing or improving, as in *count against, work against* and *hold against*.

Against is also sometimes used as the third element in phrasal verbs, e.g. *be up against* and *come up against*.

---

ahead /əˈhɛd/ *adverb*

Ahead occurs in only a few phrasal verbs, with two main senses:

the future

Some phrasal verbs with **ahead** refer to the future. Thus, you *look ahead* or *think ahead* when you consider what might happen in the future, and something *lies ahead* if it will happen in the future.

making progress

Ahead can refer to the idea of making progress, as in *go ahead*. The progress may be faster than that of others, as in *get ahead* and *pull ahead*, or the progress may be made very rapidly or forcefully, as in *push ahead* or *press ahead*.

along /əˈlɒŋ / *adverb* and *preposition*

Along readily combines with verbs to form new phrasal verbs. The combinations with **along** have three main meanings.

moving

Along is used in its literal sense, and as a preposition, in combinations such as *go along*, *stroll along* and *move along*. This literal sense is of movement in a certain direction, for example following the direction of a road or path. In some informal phrasal verbs where **along** is used as an adverb, this idea of movement is modified to suggest leaving or departing, as when people say they must *get along* or *push along*.

progressing

The first literal sense of moving is extended to the action of making progress in *help along*, *coast along*, *go along* and *come along*. This meaning is extended further in combinations that include the idea of manipulating people or situations in order to make some progress towards a goal, as in *play along* and *string along*.

accepting and agreeing

Used as an adverb, **along** combines with some verbs to indicate acceptance of or agreement with other people. Thus, when you and another person don't *get along*, your different opinions or ways of doing things make it difficult for you to be friendly with each other, and when you *go along with* something, you agree to it.

going together

Phrasal verbs such as *bring along*, *come along* and *tag along* refer to the action of accompanying someone, or of people or things going somewhere together.

among /əˈmʌŋ/ *preposition*

Among (with its slightly formal British English alternative **amongst**) is not a very common word in English, nor is it used very often to form phrasal verbs. The small number of phrasal verbs in which it appears have two main meanings.

being surrounded

This sense refers to a position in which someone is literally surrounded by numerous people or things, as in *stand among*, *sit among* and *scatter among*. **Among** combines readily with verbs of movement to form new phrasal verbs with this sense. Sometimes the meaning of being surrounded is extended to suggest a close association or interaction with the surrounding people, as in the phrasal verbs *go among* and *walk among*.

being part of a group

In phrasal verbs with this sense, **among** is used when the person or thing being referred to is part of a larger group, because that person or thing is considered to have something in common with other members of the group. Examples include the phrasal verbs *count among*, *number among*, *class among*, and *rank among*.

apart /əˈpɑːt/ adverb

Apart is a fairly common word in English. Its basic meaning is the opposite of **together**, and relates to the state of things that are some distance from each other and are not, or are no longer, joined or touching.

In phrasal verbs, **apart** occurs with two main meanings.

breaking or detaching

Phrasal verbs with this sense may refer to actual breaking or detaching. Thus, *fall apart* can be used to refer to something from which parts that used to be attached firmly have now fallen off; and *tear apart* refers to the action of destroying something by tearing pieces off it. Sometimes, this literal breaking or detaching sense is extended to refer to emotional or physical pain or collapse. Thus, when a person is said to *fall apart*, what is meant is they have lost control of their emotions or their ability to do normal things; and when something is said to *tear* someone *apart*, it causes them deep and lasting emotional pain.

separating

Apart is also used in a group of phrasal verbs whose meanings relate to the action of separating people and things. Most commonly, it is used in this sense to refer to the separation of two people who formerly had some sort of close bond; so that former partners or lovers may *drift apart* or *grow apart*. When you can't *tell* two individuals *apart*, you can't identify any differences that would enable you to distinguish one from the other.

around /əˈraʊnd/ *preposition* and *adverb*

Around is a fairly common word in English and has six main senses when used in phrasal verbs. Note that **about** and **round** can often be substituted for **around** with very little change of meaning, and this is especially done in British English.

moving

This first, literal meaning of **around** relates broadly to movement in different directions, often without a definite aim or purpose, as in *run around*, *dance around*, and *glance around*. In closely related meanings, **around** can refer to movement or action in different places, as in *ask around* and *shop around*, or to action that results in something being put in different places, as in *scatter around* and *spread around*.

lack of activity or purpose

Another common use of **around** is in phrasal verbs that suggest a lack of activity or purpose, for example *hang around*, *lie around* and *stand around*. In a number of phrasal verbs this meaning is extended to suggest foolish or irresponsible behaviour, as in *fool around* and *mess around*.

surrounding

The third most common meaning of **around** is with verbs that suggest the act of surrounding by people or things, as in *gather around* and *cluster around*.

centred on

A further related sense is found in phrasal verbs that refer to something that all other things relate to or are linked to, or to something that everyone concentrates their attention on, as in *centre around* and *revolve around*.

turning

A small number of phrasal verbs with **around** have to do with the action of turning, as in *look around*, *spin around* and *swivel around*.

avoiding

This is the meaning of around in combinations such as *skirt around* and *talk around*.

as /az/ or /əz/ *preposition*

As is one of the commonest prepositions in English, but occurs in only a small number of phrasal verbs. These all refer to the nature or function of something, as in *know as* and *mark as*. Sometimes, the nature or function is false, or different from what was originally intended, as in *pass as*, *do as* and *serve as*.

aside /əˈsaɪd / *adverb*

Aside is not a very common word in English, nor is it used very frequently to form phrasal verbs. It has three main senses when it is used in combination with verbs, and for all these senses new phrasal verbs can be created, usually with verbs of movement.

movement towards the side

The basic and literal sense of **aside** relates to movement towards the side, as in the phrasal verbs *move aside*, *look aside* and *step aside*. This sense is extended in some phrasal verbs, such as *stand aside* and *step aside*, where it is used to refer to the act of giving your place or position to someone by moving aside to make the place available for that person to occupy.

dismissing or rejecting

Senses of certain verbs of movement combined with **aside**, such as *wave aside* and *sweep aside*, have this second non-literal meaning of dismissing or rejecting something, or getting rid of it.

keeping separate or saving for the future

Some phrasal verbs with **aside** refer to the action of separating or keeping things separate, as in *lay aside* and *set aside*. Both *lay aside* and *set aside* also have extended meanings that suggest that what is being kept separate is saved for use in the future.

at /at/ *preposition*

At is a very common word in English and its basic sense relates to identifying the position of something in space and time. **At** is used quite often to create new phrasal verbs with both the meanings shown below.

aiming or directing

By linking verbs to their object, **at** is used to create the sense of aiming or directing. Examples of phrasal verbs where **at** is used in this way include *aim at*, *look at*, *throw at*, *laugh at*, *point at*, and many more.

attacking or striking

At also links to their object verbs that refer to some sort of physical attack, or the action of hitting something. Examples include *grab at*, *strike at* and *fly at*.

away /əˈweɪ/ adverb

Away is a very common word in English. In phrasal verb combinations, it is used in seven main senses, all but the last of which are commonly used to create new phrasal verbs.

moving to a distant place

The literal and commonest sense of **away**, referring to movement to a further or distant place, is found in the combinations *go away, move away* and *send away*.

not getting involved

The second meaning of **away** found in phrasal verbs refers to the action of not coming or not getting involved, as in *stay away, keep away* and *back away*.

taking or removing

The sense of taking or removing someone or something is found in *break away, pull away, tear away* and *snatch away*. The action referred to by the verb is often rough, abrupt or sudden.

disappearing and destroying

Away is used with verbs that refer to the action of disappearing or the act of destroying which causes something to disappear, such as *die away, fade away, melt away, drop away* and *waste away*. Note that most combinations with this sense suggest that the act or process of disappearing is slow or gradual.

continuing

Phrasal verbs such as *plug away, work away* and *slog away* are used when referring to something that continues for a period of time. These combinations also often contain the suggestion of difficult or rapid activity.

getting rid of things

A less common use of **away** is in phrasal verbs that refer to getting rid of things, and sometimes people. Examples include *drive away, frighten away, throw away* and *wash away*.

storing and hiding

Lastly, **away** is used in phrasal verbs that relate to actions of storing, hoarding or hiding. These include *file away, put away* and *tidy away*.

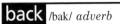 /bak/ *adverb*

Back is a common word in English and occurs in many phrasal verbs in this dictionary. **Back** has five meanings when used in phrasal verbs.

moving and positioning

The commonest sense of **back** relates to the act of moving away from, or of positioning something away from, a front or central point, as in the phrasal verbs *drop back, fall back* and *hang back*. Sometimes, in an extension of this sense, the movement relates to lack of progress, as in *hold back* and *set back*.

returning and repeating

Phrasal verbs such as *double back* and *go back* contain the notion of returning to the place or position you were in before. In *give back, hand back* and *send back* the action is one of returning to someone something you have borrowed or that you owe to them. In *answer back, fight back* and *strike back*, someone responds to an attack by in turn attacking their attacker, either physically or verbally. The sense of repeating an action is found in the phrasal verbs *play back, read back* and *go back over*.

regaining possession

The third sense is related to the second in that it includes the notion of something being returned. In phrasal verbs with this sense, however, the focus is on the fact that something is being returned from someone rather than to someone. Examples include *get back, take back* and *win back*.

past time

Phrasal verbs that refer to past time include *date back, think back* and *look back*.

controlling and limiting

There is a group of verbs combined with **back** whose meanings relate to the act of controlling or limiting something, be it one's emotions, money or forward progress. Examples include *cut back, pare back, hold back, fight back* and *scale back*.

before /bɪˈfɔː(r)/ *preposition* and *adverb*

Before is a very common word in English. Though there are no phrasal verb entries with **before** in this dictionary, it does occur in a small group of phrasal verbs, with two main meanings.

time

Phrasal verbs with **before** can refer to a time earlier than the present (*come before* and *go before*), or to a time in the future (*lie before*).

presenting

Before also occurs in phrasal verbs that refer to the action of presenting something to someone so that they can consider it or make judgements about it. Examples include *come before*, *put before* and *lay before*.

behind /bɪˈhaɪnd/ *adverb* and *preposition*

Behind is a fairly common word in English, though it appears in only a small number of entries in this dictionary. Its basic meaning relates to position in space and time, and the senses below are extensions of this basic sense.

leaving or staying

This literal sense of **behind** is found in a few phrasal verbs that refer to the action of leaving, or staying somewhere when others have gone. Examples include *leave behind*, *stay behind* and *stop behind*.

progress

In other phrasal verbs, **behind** relates to the notion of making poor progress compared to others. Examples include *fall behind*, *lag behind* and *get behind*.

below /bɪˈloʊ/ *preposition* and *adverb*

Below is not a very common word in English and its broad meaning relates to a lower position. While there are no phrasal verbs with **below** in this dictionary, it is usually found in combinations that refer to movement in or on boats and ships. Thus, you *go below* when you go down from the deck to the inside of a boat or ship.

beneath /bɪˈniːθ/ *preposition* and *adverb*

Beneath is not a very common word in English being a slightly more formal variant of **under**. Although there are no entries in this dictionary for phrasal verbs with **beneath**, it does combine with a small number of verbs, an example of which is *marry beneath* meaning to marry a person of a lower class or position in society.

between /bɪˈtwiːn/ *preposition*

Between is a fairly common word in English and broadly refers to something in a middle position in relation to two or more people or things, or a barrier or gap separating two people or things. Phrasal verbs with **between** include *come between* and *stand between*, both of which are used to refer to what prevents someone from having or achieving something they want; *pass between* is used to refer to something that is communicated from one person to another.

beyond /bɪˈjɒnd/ *preposition* and *adverb*

Beyond is not a very common word in everyday English, and only occurs in a very few phrasal verbs, none of which have entries in this dictionary. Its basic meaning relates to a position further from something or someone: for example, the phrasal verbs *get beyond* and *go beyond* both refer to making greater progress or further advances than someone or something else.

/baɪ/ *adverb* and *preposition*

By is a very common word in English and occurs in several phrasal verbs in this dictionary. Though it has numerous and varied meanings, four main senses of **by** can be identified when it is used in combination with verbs.

passing

The most common use of **by** is found in phrasal verbs that refer to the action of passing. The meaning of the phrasal verb may be of literal movement past something, as in *go by, push by* and *brush by*. However, there can also be a more general reference to movement or progress of any kind: for example, time can *pass by, slip by* or *tick by*; and you *scrape by* if you do or achieve only just enough to make progress.

visiting

When combined with certain verbs, **by** is used to refer to visiting a person or place briefly. Phrasal verbs with this sense include *call by, come by* and *stop by*. Note that phrasal verbs with this sense are usually used in fairly informal contexts.

obeying or remaining loyal

By is used in a few phrasal verbs that relate to the idea of obeying something or someone, or remaining loyal to them. Thus, you *abide by* a law or *live by* a principle, and you *stick by* or *stand by* someone.

storing or keeping

The last main sense of **by** is found in the phrasal verbs *lay by* and *put by*. These both refer to the action of keeping something for later or future use.

 **down** /daʊn/ *adverb* and *preposition*

Down is a very common word in English and also occurs in many phrasal verbs in this dictionary. Its literal sense refers to movement from above to a lower place or position, as in the phrasal verbs *fall down*, *sit down* and *throw down*. It combines with many verbs of movement in this sense, and because the meanings of these phrasal verbs is usually obvious, they have not been given an entry in this dictionary (unless they have a further non-literal sense). **Down** is also used in several non-literal senses, explained below.

making or becoming smaller or lower

In the phrasal verbs *come down*, *slow down*, *calm down* and *turn down*, **down** refers to reducing or lowering the rate or level of something. Many new and informal phrasal verbs are formed using **down** in this sense: for example *dumb down*, meaning to reduce a high standard to a lower one in order to be suitable for less educated people.

fastening, securing and fixing

Down is used in phrasal verbs such as *nail down*, *pin down* and *strap down* to suggest that the fastening, securing or fixing action is made by hitting, pressing or pushing downwards from above.

destroying and breaking

In this sense, **down** is used to suggest that the action is one of ending something or its complete destruction, disintegration or failure, as in *burn down*, *break down* and *bring down*. New phrasal verbs are quite readily created with this sense of **down**.

defeating

This sense is broadly related to the last, but with **down** suggesting the notion of defeating someone or something, as in *face down*, *grind down*, *knock down* and *vote down*.

recording and writing

Down is also quite commonly used to show that something is recorded or written on paper, as in the combinations *copy down*, *mark down*, *note down*, *set down*, *take down* and *write down*.

eating and drinking

In this sense, **down** is used with verbs that have to do with eating or swallowing actions, where it is often used to show that the action is quick or abrupt. Examples of phrasal verbs with this sense include *gobble down* and *gulp down.* An extension of this sense is found in the phrasal verbs *hold down, keep down* and *stay down,* which are used to talk about food and drink remaining in the stomach of someone who feels that they might vomit.

force, firmness and authority

Down can also be used to suggest that the action referred to is forceful or firm, as in *clamp down, crack down, slam down* and *come down on.*

passing from one generation to the next

In combinations such as *pass down* and *hand down,* **down** refers to the transfer of something from the older generation to a younger one.

cleaning, polishing, smoothing and flattening

In the final sense, **down** is used with verbs relating to cleaning, polishing, smoothing and flattening as in *wash down, sand down, clean down, rinse down* and *press down.*

In English, there are some phrasal verbs with **down** that are entirely idiomatic and in which **down** has no identifiable sense when separated from the verb. A good example is the informal phrasal verb *go down* meaning 'to happen', as in: *He wanted to find out what was going down.*

for /fɔː(r)/ or /fə(r)/ *preposition*

For is one of the most common words in English, and it is widely used in combination with verbs. It often has very little meaning at all, being used simply as a way of linking a verb to its object. For example, you *ask for* something when you ask someone to give it to you, and you can *account for* something if you are able to explain where it is or why it has happened. **For** can also occur as the third element in phrasal verbs, as in *make up for, cut out for* and *stick up for*. It also appears in some phrasal verbs that have very idiomatic meanings, for example: to *spoil for* a fight means to be eager to fight someone or have an argument with them; to *fall for* someone is to fall deeply in love with them; and to *live for* something is to consider it the only thing that makes your life worthwhile.

For has two common meanings when used in phrasal verbs.

aims and purposes

For is often used to refer to an aim or purpose, as in the phrasal verbs *apply for, make for* and *head for*. It sometimes suggests that the aim or purpose is a result of a decision or choice, as in *press for, push for* and *opt for*.

actions and states relating to other people

For can also refer to actions or states that relate to other people, and in this sense it is often replaced by the phrase *on behalf of*, especially in more formal contexts. Thus, to *fear for* someone is to be afraid that something bad will happen to them; to *root for* someone is to support them enthusiastically; and to *feel for* someone who is sad or in trouble is to feel sympathy for them.

forth /fɔːθ/ *adverb*

Forth is a rather literary and formal word and is now most commonly found as the second element in a phrasal verb. In its basic sense it refers to going out or coming out, and phrasal verbs with **forth** have one of three main senses related to this basic sense.

movement forward

Forth refers to energetic movement forward, away or out of a place. The person or thing that is moving usually also has some firm intention or purpose, as in *venture forth*.

appearing or being produced

In the second sense, **forth** refers to something appearing or being produced. It sometimes suggests that what appears has a powerful effect, or comes or goes forcefully, like a rushing flow of water, as in *pour forth* and *send forth*.

presenting

Forth is also used to suggest the idea of presenting, declaring or describing something such as an opinion or plan, usually energetically and forcefully, as in the previous two senses. Examples of phrasal verbs with this sense include *hold forth* and *set forth*.

forward /ˈfɔːwəd/ *adverb*

Forward is one of the commoner adverbs in English, and is frequently used to form phrasal verbs in its literal sense of movement in a direction ahead or in front. Phrasal verbs with this basic sense include *lean forward*, *leap forward*, *press forward*, *sit forward* and *surge forward*, and there are many more verbs of movement that can be used with **forward** in this sense. There are three further senses of **forward** that extend the meaning of this basic sense.

movement in time

Forward can refer to movement in time, either to an earlier or later time, as in *bring forward*, *take forward*, *carry forward*, *put forward* and *look forward to*.

presenting or offering

Forward can also relate to the presenting or offering of something, often of yourself, as in *come forward* and *step forward*.

developing or making progress

Lastly, **forward** refers to something developing or making progress, as in *move forward*. It sometimes suggests the idea of concentrating on the future, and forgetting the past, as in *go forward*.

from /frɒm/ *preposition*

From is a very common word in English, but occurs in only a small number of phrasal verbs. Phrasal verbs with **from** have two broad meanings.

source or origin

From can indicate the source or origin of something, as in the phrasal verbs *come from*, *date from* and *hail from*. Sometimes the meaning is more specific to the gathering of information with **from** indicating how or where this information is obtained, as in *hear from* and *derive from*.

hiding, excluding and separating

The second broad sense of **from** used in phrasal verbs suggests that something is hidden or someone prevents it from being seen or becoming known. Examples with this sense include *keep from* and *conceal from*. A slight extension of this sense contains the idea of stopping or resisting, as in *withhold from* and *shield from*.

From is also found as the third element in phrasal verbs, as in *get away from*, *break away from* and *set apart from*.

/ɪn/ *adverb* and *preposition*

In is one of the most common words in English, and its broad sense relates to movement from the outside of something to the inside. This sense is present in many of the more specific meanings shown below.

entering and arriving

There are many phrasal verbs in which **in** has this literal sense, and their meanings are often very clear, as with *come in*, *go in* and *invite in*. More numerous are combinations that basically mean the same but whose meanings are less clear, often because the verb is not used in its literal sense. Thus you *check in*, *book in* and *sign in* when you formally register your arrival; and people *flood in*, *crowd in*, *pour in* and *pile in* when large numbers of them enter.

gathering and collecting

In can also refer to the gathering or collecting of things. Combinations with this sense include *bring in*, *get in*, *fetch in* and *take in*. The phrasal verbs *cash in* and *trade in* combine the sense of collecting with the sense of exchanging.

adding and including

There are many phrasal verbs in which **in** relates to the adding or including of things. Thus you can *add in*, *build in*, *include in*, *fit in* and *put in* things that will form a new part of something. Some phrasal verbs include the idea of things being mixed together, as in *merge in*, *mix in* and *stir in*, and this sense of mixing can be extended further to suggest that the things that are mixed match each other well, as in *blend in* and *tone in*.

interrupting and involving

In can also relate to the action of interrupting or involving, as in *barge in*, *break in*, *cut in* and *want in*. Often these phrasal verbs refer to the actions of people who interrupt by involving themselves where they are not wanted, as in *butt in* and *muscle in*.

preventing and limiting

In is also used with verbs to refer to the actions of people and things that prevent or limit something, as in *lock in*, *block in* and *snow in*. Often the sense refers not to a physical state, but to the way people feel, as in *hem in* and *pen in*.

breaking

The group of phrasal verbs with this sense contain the suggestion of breaking, of broken parts falling or being forced towards the inside of something, as in *cave in*, *break in*, *kick in* and *smash in*.

remaining

Phrasal verbs with **in** can also refer to the fact of remaining somewhere, often at home, instead of going away. Included in this group are *stay in*, *stop in* and *eat in*.

sleeping

A small number of phrasal verbs with **in** refer to the act of going to or staying in bed. You *turn in* when you go to bed, and you *sleep in* or *lie in* when you remain in bed longer than you normally would.

Some phrasal verbs with **in** have very idiomatic meanings that can't be grouped with any of the senses shown above. These are often used in informal contexts, for example *pack in*, meaning to give up or stop doing something, and *stand in* meaning to act as a substitute or replacement for another person. [*see also* **into**]

---

into   /ˈɪntuː/ *preposition*

Into, like **in**, has a broad sense relating to movement from the outside of something to the inside. This sense is also present in the more specific meanings of phrasal verbs with **into**.

entering and arriving

Most phrasal verbs with **in** with this sense can also be formed using **into**. Thus, *come into*, *go into*, *invite into*, *check into*, *book into*, *sign into*, *flood into*, *crowd into*, *pour into* and *pile into* all have the same meanings as the combinations with **in**. The only difference is that **into** is used instead of **in** when there is an object, i.e. when the phrasal verb is transitive rather than intransitive.

putting or placing

A large group of phrasal verbs with **into** have meanings that relate to the putting or placing of things somewhere, for example *fit into*, *set into* and *slot into*. This sense of putting can also be combined with the sense of entering, as in *drum into*, *sink into* and *tap into*.

hitting or striking

Some phrasal verbs refer to the action of one thing hitting or striking another: *bump into*, *crash into* and *plough into*.

changing nature or substance

A fairly large group of phrasal verbs have meanings that relate to the process by which the nature or substance of something changes or is changed, for example *turn into*, *grow into*, *lapse into* and *make into*. This change can be the result of different things being combined or mixed, as in *blend into* and *merge into*.

forcing and persuading

Finally, there is a small group of phrasal verbs in which **into** is used to refer to something that someone is forced to do. Examples include *press into*, *push into* and *talk into*.

[*see also* **in**]

of 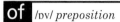 /ɒv/ *preposition*

Of is a very common word in English and indicates relationships between things. When combined with verbs it often has very little meaning and functions as a linking word between the verb and its object. In several groups of phrasal verbs, however, **of** can indicate a specific relationship between the verb and its object.

cause or origin

Phrasal verbs in which **of** is used to show that the thing referred to is the cause or origin of the action of the verb include *die of*, and the fairly formal *born of*, as in: *An alliance born of necessity.*

communication and interpretation

A group of phrasal verbs with **of** have to do with the communication and interpretation of information and knowledge. These combinations include *say of* and *make of*.

quality and characteristic

Other phrasal verbs with **of** refer to a stated quality or characteristic that someone or something has, as in *reek of* and *smack of*. The verb is usually used in a non-literal way in these combinations.

removal

Phrasal verbs in which **of** is used to show that the thing referred to is being removed, taken away or kept from the person concerned include *strip of*, *starve of* and *rob of*.

off /ɒf/ *adverb* and *preposition*

Off is found in many phrasal verbs with a wide variety of senses. Its basic meaning, of which all the others are extensions, is of movement away or departure, as in *move off* and *set off*. **Away** is sometimes used instead of **off** in phrasal verbs with this basic sense.

movement from a higher to a lower position

This is a slightly more specific sense of the basic sense of movement away, in that it refers to movement from a higher position to reach a lower position. Combinations with this sense include *jump off*, *get off*, *fall off* and *step off*.

decreasing, lessening or declining

Off is also combined with verbs to show that the intensity or volume of something goes down or declines, as in *cool off* and *slacken off*. In a non-literal sense, it is also used to show that something's quality has declined, as in *go off* in the meaning relating to food that has become unfit to eat.

separating or blocking

Off can also be used with verbs that refer to actions or states in which things are separated from others by putting up a barrier or creating a division or blockage of some sort, as in *block off*, *fence off* and *partition off*.

stopping or preventing

In an extension of the previous sense, verbs that combine with **off** can relate to the preventing of an attack of some sort, as in *fight off*, *stave off*, *hold off* and *head off*.

removing, eliminating or disposing

Off is used in another group of phrasal verbs to emphasize that someone or something is completely removed, often using some degree of force. Examples include *chop off*, *cross off* and *wash off*. The general meaning of removing or getting rid of something is also found in a small subgroup of more idiomatic phrasal verbs, such as *bump off*, meaning to kill, and *cart off*, meaning to take someone or something away against their will or by force.

beginning or starting

Phrasal verbs with **off** that relate to something beginning or something being caused to happen include *lead off*, *trigger off*, *spark off* and *kick off*.

ending, stopping, disconnecting or cancelling

New, and informal, phrasal verbs are often formed with this sense, which indicates or implies that something is ended or cancelled, as in *leave off*, *turn off, call off* and *switch off*. Many phrasal verbs with this sense have the opposite meaning when **on** is substituted for **off**.

finality or completeness

Off is used as an intensifier in phrasal verbs such as *kill off, finish off, pay off* and *sell off*, suggesting that the actions have finality and completeness.

rejecting, dismissing or ignoring

Off can also imply that the action of the verb is one of rejecting, dismissing or ignoring, as in *brush off, shrug off, write off* and *laugh off*.

public display or attention-seeking

In this group of mainly derogatory phrasal verbs, **off** is used to suggest that the main aim of the action is to get other people's attention. The best known example of a phrasal verb with this sense is *show off*.

absence from work or school

A group of mostly informal phrasal verbs with **off** is used when referring to absence from work or school, especially when the absence is unauthorized or without good reason. The group includes *stay off*, *skive off* and *bunk off*.

avoiding heavy punishment

A further group of phrasal verbs with **off** refer to the fact of avoiding heavy punishment, when this form of punishment would be appropriate to the seriousness of the crime. Examples include *get off* and *let off*.

using or consuming

Phrasal verbs such as *dine off* and *live off* are part of a group indicating that someone or something is used as a source of food, energy or power, or as a means of existence or survival. Note that **on** can often be substituted for **off** in combinations with this sense.

getting rid of or taking, using deception or dishonesty

Off combines with a group of verbs used in non-literal senses to suggest that deception or dishonesty is used to get rid of a person or thing, or to take something from someone. Examples of phrasal verbs with this sense include *rip off*, *palm off* and *fob off*.

exploding or firing

Off is also used with verbs that relate to actions concerned with the discharge of firearms or other explosive devices, as in *set off*, *blast off* and *go off*.

on /ɒn/ adverb and preposition

On is used in a great many phrasal verbs, both in its literal sense and in non-literal senses. Its literal meaning has to do with place or position. It is also found in combination with many rather formal verbs, such as *enlarge on*, *impinge on* and *touch on*, where its function is mainly to connect the verb to its object, and where **upon** is quite often used as a variant. In its basic literal meaning **on** is combined with many verbs that refer to a particular place or position. It often indicates that direct contact is made with something, usually from above. Some examples of phrasal verbs using **on** in its basic sense are *rest on*, *place on*, *lie on*, *land on* and *step on*, though there are many more.

movement in the direction of

On is commonly found in combination with verbs that indicate that the action referred to is directed towards a particular thing or place, as in *focus on*, *fire on*, *look on* and *shine on*. Some combinations with this literal sense also have non-literal senses.

in or into a vehicle, ship, or aircraft

Some phrasal verbs with **on** refer specifically to movement to a position inside or on top of a vehicle. These include *get on*, *hop on*, *pile on* and *take on*.

continuing

On is also used with verbs to suggest that the action continues beyond a certain point or for an extended period of time. New phrasal verbs are often created with this sense, both in British and American English. Some of the most familiar phrasal verbs with this sense are *work on*, *follow on* and *get on*, and there are also many that are more idiomatic in meaning, such as *rave on*, *carry on* and the informal *witter on*. Some phrasal verbs suggest that the process of continuing or progressing is very slow or difficult, as in *drag on*, *plod on*, *struggle on*, *battle on* and *soldier on*.

encouraging to continue or go forward

The next group of phrasal verbs with **on** includes the idea of encouraging someone to go forward or continue with some course of action. These include *come on*, *cheer on* and *lead on*.

dressing

Phrasal verbs with **on** that refer to the act of dressing include *put on*, *pull on* and *slip on*.

attaching, fastening or adding

A further group of phrasal verbs with **on** indicate or suggest that something is attached or fastened securely to something else. The meaning may be literal or figurative. Examples of combinations with this sense include *stick on*, *peg on*, *pin on* and *latch on*. In more formal or literary English **upon** is sometimes used instead of **on** for phrasal verbs with this sense.

beginning, connecting or causing to work

The next group of phrasal verbs with **on** includes the idea that something has begun, or is connected to the thing that provides it with the power to operate. Examples include *turn on* and *switch on*.

using as a basis or source

Verbs combined with **on** can show that the person or thing referred to is what is used as the source or basis for the action, or is the cause of the condition of the subject. Combinations with this sense include *act on*, *draw on* and *thrive on*.

consuming

Related to the previous sense, this sense refers to eating, or using something as fuel. Examples include *lunch on*, *dine on* and *run on*. **Off** can be substituted for **on** in all these phrasal verbs, and **upon** can also be used as a variant with the verbs referring to eating.

attacking

Turn on and *round on* are two examples of a group of phrasal verbs that suggest a sudden attack or violent action directed against a particular person or target.

arranging to happen

A small group of phrasal verbs combined with **on** suggest that something is arranged or made available at a particular place or time. Thus, if people *put on* a show of some sort, they make all the arrangements required for its performance. Similarly, when someone *lays on* food or transport, they provide it for others, free of charge.

discovering

Chance on and *stumble on* are two examples of phrasal verbs that show that something is discovered or comes into view suddenly or unexpectedly. **Upon** is sometimes used instead of **on** for phrasal verbs with this sense.

transferring

Hand on and *pass on* are examples of another group of phrasal verbs whose meanings all have to do with the transfer of something from one person to another, or from one generation to the next.

Some phrasal verbs with **on** are so idiomatic in meaning that they cannot be included in any category. For example, you *have* someone *on*, or you *kid* them *on*, when you playfully make them think that something is true when it isn't.

On sometimes occurs as the third element in phrasal verbs, as in *cash in on*, *crack down on*, *home in on* and *take out on*.

onto /'ɒntuː/ *preposition*

Onto refers to movements in or on a stated place or position, as in *jump onto, throw onto, fall onto, load onto* and *scramble onto*. It may also refer to the action of attaching, fastening or transferring something to something else, as in *build onto, cling onto* and *hang onto*.

out /aʊt/ *adverb*

Out is a very common word in English and is very frequently used in combination with verbs. Its basic meaning is of movement from the inside to the outside.

leaving

Phrasal verbs with **out** used in this first literal sense indicate that someone or something leaves a place or moves outside or away from it. Some examples of phrasal verbs with this sense are *go out, get out, drive out, walk out, fly out* and *sail out*.

removing and deleting

Some examples of phrasal verbs with **out** that have this sense are *cross out, score out, take out, squeeze out, scoop out* and *x out*. New and informal combinations with this sense are quite common.

excluding and omitting

This sense indicates that someone or something is excluded, omitted, rejected or forced from a place or group. Examples include *rule out, leave out, miss out, cast out* and *blot out*.

searching, obtaining, discovering, solving

Find out, seek out, work out and *check out* are all examples of phrasal verbs that include the sense of discovering information that is not previously known or is difficult to obtain, or of solving a problem. Some phrasal verbs in this group are more idiomatic, for example *ferret out, root out* and *dig out*.

emerging, appearing, or beginning

Out is also used in some phrasal verbs that refer to something appearing or emerging, often from a place where it has been hidden or concealed. Examples include *hatch out, break out, pop out* and *come out*.

projecting

Jut out, poke out and *stick out* are all examples of phrasal verbs relating to the idea of projecting outwards and away from a surface or object.

outside, outdoors or away from home

A group of phrasal verbs with **out** refer to events or activities that go on outside, beyond or away from your normal surroundings at home or at work. These include *camp out, cook out, eat out, ask out, invite out, send out, lease out*, the more idiomatic *farm out*, and figurative *branch out*.

choosing or selecting

Single out and *pick out* are two examples of phrasal verbs with this sense. The selection made may be from a group or from a number of possible alternatives.

making a sudden loud noise

There is quite a large group of verbs with **out** that suggest that a noise is made suddenly or loudly, often causing the listener to be startled by its suddenness or volume, such as *cry out, shout out, blare out, scream out* and *bawl out*.

producing

Out also combines with verbs to create the sense of something being produced rapidly and in large quantities, as in *churn out, crank out, trot out* and *rattle out*.

finishing, extinguishing or disappearing completely

This sense is found in the phrasal verbs *go out, run out, peter out* and *conk out*. The sense is extended to refer to actions that result in a person becoming unconscious, as in *black out, knock out, pass out* and *crash out*.

distributing

Give out, hand out, dole out, divide out and *pay out* are all examples of phrasal verbs with this broad sense.

extending and stretching

Stretch out, reach out, hold out and *eke out* are some of the group of phrasal verbs that contain the idea of extending or stretching in at least one of their meanings.

expanding and increasing

Let out, flesh out and *balloon out* are three examples from the group of phrasal verbs that relate to something being expanded, or increasing in size or extent.

completeness

This important sense produces a great many new phrasal verbs with **out**, which is used as an intensifier to show that the action referred to has an element of thoroughness or completeness. Commoner phrasal verbs with this sense include *work out*, *clear out* and *iron out*.

continuing until something is complete

This sense implies that the action of the verb is continued for some time until the situation referred to is over or can be brought to an end. Examples of phrasal verbs with this sense are *hold out*, *last out* and *stick out*.

recording, demonstrating or putting down on paper

Map out, *sketch out* and *rough out* are three of the phrasal verbs whose meanings indicate that a particular method of demonstrating, recording or planning is being used.

attacking

Some combinations with **out** show that the action is one of attacking someone or something with blows or verbal insults. Examples include *hit out* and *lash out*.

Note that **out** is also used in quite a number of very idiomatic phrasal verbs: for example, you *fall out* with someone when you stop being friendly with them, usually because you have argued; you *strike out* when you fail; and you *carry* something *out* when you put it into practice.

over / oʊˈvə(r)/ *preposition* and *adverb*

Over is a very common word in English, and is frequently used as a particle in phrasal verbs. Its basic meaning is similar to **above**. As a preposition, it is often used simply to link the verb with its object. However, other phrasal verbs can be grouped according to their shared senses.

above or directly above

Over is used in its literal sense in the phrasal verbs in this group. The action happens in a place or position above something else, as in *fly over, tower over* and *live over*. In an extension to this literal sense, **over** can also imply that the movement is from a higher to a lower position, as in *bend over* and *lean over*. In a further extension to the basic sense, the reference is to the act of supervising or being in charge of others, as in *rule over, preside over* and *watch over*.

movement across from one side to the other

Phrasal verbs made up of verbs of movement with **over** can also have the literal sense that indicates that the movement is across and above something from one side to the other. Examples include *clamber over, climb over, crawl over, cross over, hop over, leap over* and *walk over*. Sometimes the sense is of something being placed so that it goes over the top of something and down on either side, as in *drape over, hang over* and *sling over*.

covering or hiding

This sense is exemplified by the combinations *paint over, concrete over, freeze over, ice over, cover over, spread over* and *gloss over*.

movement to the side

A small group of phrasal verbs with **over** indicate that the movement is from one side or sideways. Thus, a car *pulls over* when it moves to the side of the road and stops; and you *move over* when you move your whole body sideways.

overflowing

Boil over, brim over and *spill over* are examples of phrasal verbs that indicate that something, especially a liquid, flows out of and escapes from a container.

communicating a feeling or impression

Over is also used in a small number of phrasal verbs to indicate that something is communicated to others, as in *put over, get over* and *come over*. **Across** is often used instead of **over** for phrasal verbs with this sense.

ending, finishing or completing

Over is also used in a group of phrasal verbs that imply that a temporary situation has ended or finished, and things have returned to normal, as in *blow over*.

doing something again

A small group of phrasal verbs, used especially in American English, use **over** to show that something is done again. These include *do over* and *start over*. The British English equivalents are *do again* and *start again*.

looking, examining or considering

Combinations with this sense include *go over*, *check over*, *talk over* and *think over*. There is usually the added implication that the examination is careful and methodical.

falling

Fall over, *knock over*, *tip over* and *trip over* all contain the sense of falling or being pushed from an upright position to a horizontal one, on the ground.

transferring or changing position

Over also combines with verbs to give the broad sense that something is being transferred from one person to the other, or changed from one position to another. Examples include *switch over* and *hand over*.

remaining

In the final sense, **over** can suggest that something stays in the same place or in the same state for a certain period of time. Thus, to *hold* something *over* is to not do it until a later time and to *sleep over* with someone is to visit them and spend the night in their house.

overboard /ˈoʊvəbɔːd/ *adverb*

Overboard is used with verbs of movement to show that movement referred to is being made from a position on or in a ship or boat into the water, as in *fall overboard* and *jump overboard*. Certain phrasal verbs with **overboard** have additional non-literal senses. For example, people sometimes say that someone *is going overboard* when that person is behaving in an extreme or excessive way. *Throw overboard* also has both literal and non-literal senses, the non-literal one meaning to abandon something or get rid of it completely.

past /pɑːst/ *preposition* and *adverb*

Past occurs in a number of phrasal verbs that include verbs of movement, though there are no phrasal verb entries with **past** in this dictionary. Its basic sense shows that the movement referred to involves coming up to or alongside someone or something, and then continuing beyond the point where that person or thing is located. Examples of phrasal verbs with **past** where the verb is used in its literal sense include *drive past, float past, flow past, hurry past* and *walk past*. Another group of phrasal verbs with **past** refer to movements in time: for example, time is often said to *fly past* when it goes by quickly; and days, weeks or years may be said to *drag past* when time passes slowly.

The only idiomatic phrasal verb with **past** is *put past*, which is normally used with a negative in the form of a fixed phrase. Thus, when someone says that they wouldn't *put* something *past* someone, they mean that they wouldn't be surprised if that person did it or had done it.

round /raʊnd/ *adverb* and *preposition*

Round is a very common word in British English and has many different senses. In phrasal verbs, it has nine identifiable senses. For most phrasal verbs, **around** or **about** can replace **round** in at least some of the senses of the phrasal verb with no change of meaning. Note that in American English the form **around** is usually used.

moving

The literal meaning of **round** relates broadly to movement in different directions or to action in different places, as in *move round*, *chase round* and *pass round*. **Round** combines quite freely with the literal senses of verbs of movement to form phrasal verbs.

turning

The second most common occurrence of **round** is in phrasal verbs that refer to the action of turning, usually of turning to face in the opposite direction, as in *look round*, *swing round* and *wheel round*. *Spin round*, *swivel round* and *turn round* can refer to the action of turning repeatedly in a circular motion. This repeated motion can be emphasized by repeating the particle, as in *spin round and round*.

persuading

The idea of turning to face in the opposite direction is extended in a small number of phrasal verbs that relate to the act of persuading someone to change their opinion or decision, such as *bring round*, *talk round* and *win round*.

surrounding

Another group of phrasal verbs has the idea of surrounding as part of their meaning. This group includes *wrap round* and *gather round*.

focusing

A small group of phrasal verbs with **round**, for example *centre round* and *revolve round*, are used to refer to something that all other things relate to or are linked to, or to something that everyone concentrates their attention on.

avoiding

In some phrasal verbs with **round**, the idea of moving past something on a circular course is extended to refer to the act of avoiding something. Phrasal verbs with this sense of avoiding include *talk round*, *skirt round* and *get round*.

visiting

Included in the group of phrasal verbs with this sense are *call round*, *drop round* and *go round*.

making or becoming conscious again

Phrasal verbs that have a sense that refers to regaining consciousness after fainting, being knocked out or being under anaesthetic, include *bring round*, *pull round* and *come round*.

lack of activity or purpose

Examples of phrasal verbs with **round** that include the idea of lack of purpose or activity are *stand round* and *hang round*.

through /θruː/ *adverb* and *preposition*

Through has various meanings when used in combination with verbs. The basic and literal meaning refers to movement that goes from one side of something and out the other side, as in the phrasal verbs *pass through*, *slide through* and *jump through*.

passing from one side to the other of a solid barrier

This sense is an extended meaning of **through** in its basic sense and refers to movement from one side to the other of a solid object or some other sort of barrier. Examples include *cut through*, *slice through*, *break through* and *see through*.

doing something thoroughly or properly

Examples of phrasal verbs with this sense are *think through*, meaning to think very carefully and logically about something, and *heat through*, meaning to heat something, especially cold food, until it becomes thoroughly warm or hot.

looking at or reading

In an extension of the previous sense, **through** as a preposition is often combined with verbs to indicate that something is looked at, examined or read from beginning to end, as in *glance through* and *leaf through*.

accomplishing and completing

This group of phrasal verbs contains the idea of completing or ending something, often after a struggle or some degree of difficulty. Examples of phrasal verbs with this sense are *sail through*, *put through* and *get through*.

to /tuː/ or /tə/ *preposition* and *adverb*

To is a very common word in English. It often has very little meaning, and its main function is as a linking word to show the relationship between things. As a preposition, **to** is used with many verbs to show that the movement or action is directed towards a particular person, place or end, as in *go to*, *admit to* and *look to*. It is also used as an adverb in a small number of phrasal verbs that have to do with moving something, such as a door or window, so that it closes, for example *push to*. Other combinations in which **to** is used as an adverb are *come to*, meaning to recover consciousness, and *set to*, meaning to begin doing something, usually in an energetic way.

To often occurs as the third element in phrasal verbs, as in *feel up to*, *get up to*, *hang on to* and *lead up to*.

together /təˈgɛðə(r)/ *adverb*

Together occurs in a fairly small number of English phrasal verbs. Its basic sense has to do with joining or combining two or more people or things, and the three main senses described below are all connected with this basic sense.

closeness or close contact

Together is combined with verbs to indicate that two or more people or things are in a position close to each other, as in *gather together* and *glue together*, or that they share some sort of relationship with each other, as in *live together* and *sleep together*.

forming a whole or unit

Another small group of phrasal verbs with **together** refers to people or things that fit or combine with each other to form a whole or unit, as in *piece together* and *hang together*.

cooperating

The final group of phrasal verbs with **together** refers to a number of people who form a group in order to do something that they wouldn't be able to do as individuals, as in *band together*, *club together* and *get together*.

towards /təˈwɔːdz/ *preposition*

Note that in American English the form **toward** is often used. Four broad senses are created when **towards** is combined with verbs.

movement in the direction of

Phrasal verbs that include **towards** in its commonest, literal meaning concern movement in the direction of someone or something and include such combinations as *advance towards*, *glance towards*, *head towards*, *march towards*, *point towards* and *run towards*. Sometimes, this basic meaning is used to show that the movement in a particular direction is figurative rather than literal: for example, to *lean towards* or *incline towards* a particular view or opinion is to have a tendency or inclination to favour that view or opinion.

in or to a facing position

The second literal meaning of verbs combined with **towards** refers to being in a position facing someone or something, as in *face towards*, *turn towards* and *look towards*.

attitude or feelings

A further sense is found in a group of phrasal verbs with more idiomatic meanings. Here **towards** is used to indicate how the action relates to the person or thing concerned, as in *feel towards*.

purpose

The idea of doing or using something for a particular purpose is found in the last group of phrasal verbs. Thus, you *put* money *towards* something when you contribute some money to meet part of its cost, and you *work towards* something when you work over a period of time with a particular goal in mind.

under /'ʌndə(r)/*preposition* and *adverb*

Under is a fairly common word in English but occurs in a relatively small number of phrasal verbs, of which there are three groups, distinguishable by their broad senses.

movement and position

Under occurs in phrasal verbs whose meaning relates to the movement of one thing to a position below another, or below a surface, as in *pull under.*

hierarchy

The sense of being below something is extended in the second group of phrasal verbs that refer to the position of someone who is given orders by a person in authority. Examples include *come under, work under* and the more idiomatic *buckle under.*

defeat or destruction

Under also features in a few phrasal verbs that have defeat or destruction as part of their meaning, such as *go under.*

up /ʌp/ adverb and preposition

Up is one of the commonest words in English and is the particle that occurs most frequently in phrasal verbs. The basic sense of **up** relates to the movement of something from a lower to a higher level or position, and this sense in found in many phrasal verbs including *look up, move up, reach up, jump up, sit up, dig up* and *pick up.*

increasing

Another very common use of **up** is in phrasal verbs that have the idea of increasing as part of their meaning, such as *cheer up, grow up, hurry up, save up* and *speed up.*

improving

Related to the notion of increasing is the idea of improving, and there are numerous examples of phrasal verbs with **up** that have this broad meaning, such as *brush up, smarten up, spice up* and *tone up.*

finishing and completing

Another common occurrence of **up** in phrasal verbs relates to something finishing or being finished, as in *drink up, eat up, swallow up* and *wind up.* Linked to the idea of finishing is the idea of something coming or being brought into a final state or condition, as in *heal up, fill up, tidy up, wash up* and *wrap up.* The idea of completeness is extended to refer to the complete destruction of something, or the breaking of it into pieces, as in *burn up, grind up, mash up* and *tear up.*

fastening, and forming a barrier

Up also occurs in a good many phrasal verbs whose meanings relate in some way to the idea of fastening, such as *button up, lace up, stitch up, tie up* and *zip up.* A related sense suggests the idea of a gap or space being filled to form a barrier, as in *board up, clog up, dam up, jam up, plug up* and *stop up.*

spoiling and damaging

This next group of phrasal verbs convey the idea of something being spoiled or damaged as in *break up, mess up, mix up,* and the informal *foul up* and *muck up.*

preparing

Phrasal verbs that include the sense of preparing something – especially a meal – as part of their meaning include *brew up, cook up, heat up, start up* and *warm up.*

gathering

Other phrasal verbs with **up** contain the idea of gathering things, as in *heap up*, *pile up*, *round up* and *stack up*. Some refer to the idea of people coming together in a group, or as a pair, as in *gang up*, *join up*, *meet up* and *team up*.

approaching, reaching and touching

There are also many phrasal verbs that have the idea of approaching as part of their meaning, such as *close up*, *creep up* and *steal up*. The idea of two people or things coming so close to each other that they touch or stay in contact is found in *cuddle up* and *snuggle up*.

giving

A small number of combinations with **up** have the idea of giving as part of their meaning, as in *cough up*, *pay up*, *settle up* and *stump up*. Most phrasal verbs with this sense suggest that the giving is done reluctantly.

inventing and producing

A few phrasal verbs with **up** include the notion of inventing or producing, such as *come up with*, *cook up*, *make up* and *think up*.

dividing

Another small group of phrasal verbs with **up** relate to the action of dividing things, or cutting them into portions, as in *cut up*, *carve up*, *divide up* and *slice up*.

crushing and squeezing

Certain phrasal verbs, such as *screw up* and *scrunch up*, have to do with the actions of pushing, crushing or squeezing something so that it becomes compressed.

upon   /əˈpɒn/ *preposition*

Upon is not a very common word in English. However, because it is a more formal variant of **on**, it can occur in a large number of phrasal verbs, though **on** is far more common. **Upon** isn't used as a variant for the more informal, slang or vulgar phrasal verbs with **on**, though the main senses listed at the panel for **on** also apply to **upon**. However, there are a very small number of phrasal verbs that occur only with **upon**, including *put upon* and *loose upon*.

with   /wɪð/ *preposition*

With is one of the commonest words in English and it occurs in a fairly large number of phrasal verbs with five main senses.

connections relating to people

Phrasal verbs with **with** that contain the idea of some sort of connection between people include *live with*, *meet with*, *sleep with* and *visit with*. Sometimes the connection is an argument or confrontation, as is suggested in the idiomatic phrasal verbs *mess with*, *tangle with* and *trifle with*. Elsewhere, the connection between the people has been broken or is being broken, a sense found in the phrasal verbs *break with* and *finish with*.

connections relating to things

Included in this group of phrasal verbs are the frequently used phrasal verbs *deal with*, *do with* and *lie with*, used to refer to the subject, nature or cause of something.

taking action

Amongst the group of phrasal verbs that have the idea of taking action as part of their meaning are *grapple with*, *juggle with* and *wrestle with*. Some phrasal verbs of this group show that the action is also unwanted and unwelcome, as in *interfere with*, *meddle with* and *tamper with*.

giving and providing

In a few phrasal verbs with **with**, often used in the passive, the idea of giving or providing is present in their meanings. These include *endow with*, *land with* and *saddle with*.

giving support

Agree with and *side with* contain the idea of giving support to another person. The idea of continuing support is found in the phrasal verbs *hold with*, *stick with* and *stay with*.

With frequently occurs as the third element in phrasal verbs, as in *come up with*, *get away with*, *keep in with* and *take up with*.

---

without /wɪˈðaʊt/ *preposition*

Without is a fairly common word in English but only occurs in a very few phrasal verbs, all of which have the idea of lack or absence of something as part of their meanings. Examples include *do without* and *go without*.